Welcome to the EVERYTHING® series!

These handy, accessible books give you all you need to tackle a difficult project, gain a new hobby, comprehend a fascinating topic, prepare for an exam, or even brush up on something you learned back in school but have since forgotten.

You can read an *EVERYTHING*® book from cover-to-cover or just pick out the information you want from our four useful boxes: e-facts, e-ssentials, e-alerts, and e-questions. We literally give you everything you need to know on the subject, but throw in a lot of fun stuff along the way, too.

We now have well over 100 *EVERYTHING*® books in print, spanning such wide-ranging topics as weddings, pregnancy, wine, learning guitar, one-pot cooking, managing people, and so much more. When you're done reading them all, you can finally say you know *EVERYTHING*®!

FACTS
Important sound bytes of information

ESSENTIALS
Quick handy tips

ALERT
Urgent warnings

QUESTIONS?
Solutions to common problems

THE
EVERYTHING
Series

Dear Reader,

Once, when I was telling stories to some colleagues about the antics of my three horses, one of them said, "I had no idea horses had so much personality." That comment made me realize how little non-horse people know about the true nature of the horse.

Horses can be mischievous—they can trick you into thinking that they are not paying any attention to that unlatched gate but the minute you turn your back to fill the water tub, they are out the door! They beg—for food, for scratches, for more attention than you are giving some other horse. And, although I hate to attribute human emotions to animals, I think horses can get a bit jealous—when I come back from my riding lesson that I take on school horses, my mare sniffs every inch of my body with a look on her face that seems to be disbelief that I have actually been with another horse.

Once you become a caretaker for a horse, your world will change forever. It is at once a rewarding and ominous task. You will become obsessed with learning as much about horses as you can. In the true form of the *Everything*® series, this book will give you information on every aspect of horse care that you could imagine, and some you probably didn't even think of, whether you're new to horses or an old pro.

Above all, enjoy your horse. And when you can't be in the barn, enjoy this book.

Sincerely,

Cheryl Kimball

THE EVERYTHING® HORSE BOOK

Buying, riding, and caring for
your equine companion . . .
so complete you'll think a
horse wrote it

Cheryl Kimball

Adams Media Corporation
Avon, Massachusetts

EDITORIAL
Publishing Director: Gary M. Krebs
Managing Editor: Kate McBride
Copy Chief: Laura MacLaughlin
Acquisitions Editor: Bethany Brown
Development Editor: Lesley Bolton

PRODUCTION
Production Director: Susan Beale
Production Manager: Michelle Roy Kelly
Series Designer: Daria Perreault
Layout and Graphics: Arlene Apone,
Paul Beatrice, Brooke Camfield,
Colleen Cunningham, Daria Perreault,
Frank Rivera

An Everything® Series Book.
Everything® is a registered trademark of Adams Media Corporation.

Published by Adams Media Corporation
57 Littlefield Street, Avon, MA 02322 U.S.A.
www.adamsmedia.com

ISBN: 1-58062-564-9
Printed in the United States of America.

J I H G F E D C B

Library of Congress Cataloging-in-Publication Data

Kimball, Cheryl.
The everything horse book / by Cheryl Kimball.
p.   cm.
Includes bibliographical references (p. 275)
ISBN 1-58062-564-9
1. Horses I. Title
SF285 .K49 2001
636.1—dc21   2001046306

This publication is designed to provide accurate and authoritative information with regard to the subject matter covered. It is sold with the understanding that the publisher is not engaged in rendering legal, accounting, or other professional advice. If legal advice or other expert assistance is required, the services of a competent professional person should be sought.
—From a *Declaration of Principles* jointly adopted by a Committee of the American Bar Association and a Committee of Publishers and Associations

Illustrations by Barry Littmann

This book is available at quantity discounts for bulk purchases.
For information, call 1-800-872-5627.

Visit the entire Everything® series at everything.com

DEDICATION

To Pat and Breezy, Karen and Alana, who started it all;

To everyone involved with Piper Ridge Farm in Limerick, Maine,
including a world-class lineup of clinicians, who keep me on
track as best they can, given my ability;

To my parents, who, though they may not have given in
to my pleas for a horse, definitely taught me to love
and respect animals;

To Jack, who seems to think it is natural that I consider the
animals under my care to be my friends;

And, although it is part of their charm that they will never
read this book, to my horse friends, past, present, and future.
If this book helps even one human to treat even one horse
with the respect and care horses deserve, it will have been
worth all of the hours it took to write it.

Permissions for the Color Photographs

Photo 1: Courtesy of the Appaloosa Horse Club, 2720 West Pullman Road, Moscow, Indiana 83843.

Photo 2: Courtesy of the American Paint Horse Association, 2800 Meacham Boulevard, Fort Worth, Texas 76137.

Photo 3: Courtesy of the American Quarter Horse Association, 1600 Quarter Horse Drive, Amarillo, Texas 79102.

Photo 4: Courtesy of the Tennessee Walking Horse Breeders' and Exhibitors' Association, P.O. Box 286, Lewisburg, Tennessee 37091.

Photo 5: Courtesy of the American Connemara Pony Society, 2360 Hunting Ridge Road, Winchester, Virginia 22603.

Photo 6: Courtesy of the Kentucky Horse Park, 4089 Iron Works Pike, Lexington, Kentucky 40511.

Photo 7: Courtesy of the Kentucky Horse Park.

Photo 8: Courtesy of the Kentucky Horse Park.

Photo 9: Courtesy of the American Shire Horse Association, P.O. Box 739, New Castle, Colorado, 81647-0739.

Photo 10: Courtesy of the Kentucky Horse Park.

Photo 11: Courtesy of the Kentucky Horse Park.

Photo 12: Courtesy of the Foundation Quarter Horse Registry, Box 230, Sterling, Colorado 80751.

Photo 13: Courtesy of the American Morgan Horse Association, 122 Bostwick Road, P.O. Box 960, Shelburne, Vermont 05482-0960.

Photo 14: Courtesy of the Kentucky Horse Park.

Photo 15: Courtesy of the Wilkinson Pony Farm, 2590 South Engleman Road, Alda, Nebraska 68810.

Photo 16: Courtesy of the American Saddlebred Horse Association, 4093 Iron Works Parkway, Lexington, Kentucky 40511.

Contents

Acknowledgments

Thanks to:

Sue Ducharme, riding pal, expert wordsmith, and crafter of Chapter 10, Beyond Conventional Health Care;

Lesley Bolton, who as I write this section is in the process of making the rest of the book into something better than it was when she received it;

Everyone at Adams Media who touches this project—I know how hard they work to make good books;

Pam Liflander, who is, of course, my favorite editor;

And anyone else I pestered with questions—whether or not they knew I was writing a book. These people and many others helped make this book the best it could be; any factual errors in this book are all mine and will gratefully be corrected if brought to my attention.

Introduction

When I was a kid, I was drawn to horses like a magnet to metal. When Helene—the only girl in my neighborhood to own a horse—and her chestnut gelding, Rowdy, raced by our house, I didn't hide my envy. My friends and I "played horses" on the elementary school playground; the fire escape supports, where we returned to rest and nicker at each other after a good gallop around the school building, served as stalls. My family always indulged my obsession with gifts of horse statues, horse pins, horse books, and occasionally the dreaded horse needlepoint pillow—but alas, never an actual horse.

It wasn't until I was well into my teens that real horses became a big part of my life. My friend Karen and I would hop in my blue Volkswagen beetle on beautiful sunny days after high school, crank open the sunroof, and race off to our friend Pat's to ride her horses. We were lucky to live near ocean and woods, and we could ride for miles across sandy beaches and along forest trails; indoor arenas were simply not a part of our horse world back then.

In my senior yearbook, Karen prophesized: "I know you'll have a horse of your own someday." Finally, at age twenty, I did get a horse, a young buckskin Quarter Horse mare. But after two years of fun as well as frustration, a job and a boyfriend began to take up what time I had. Horses were relegated to a less important position; I sold my little mare and didn't really think much about horses for over a decade.

At around age thirty-four, I had become settled in a career and a long-term relationship. I took a couple of riding lessons late one winter, just for chuckles and grins. Then, on a whim, I went to visit my horse friend Pat, whom I hadn't seen in years, and horses suddenly became of interest to me again. She had a young gelding for sale—"Cheap," she announced the minute I walked through the door. I bought him, and the rest, as they say, is history.

Through a series of events instigated by the fact that I had this two-year-old horse to start under saddle and no idea how to do it, I became involved in a philosophy of horsemanship, sometimes referred to as "natural horsemanship" (discussed in Chapter 12, "Types of

Horsemanship") that fulfills me both intellectually and physically: I think about horses all of the time, and I haven't seen the inside of a fitness center since I bought that young gelding. I have come to thoroughly enjoy working with young horses and cannot imagine ever again being without the company of a horse.

The key to having fun with horses, I think, is to remember that they are horses. They are not puppies and cannot be treated like puppies without seriously endangering your life. They are not kids, despite various attempts to approach them with psychological profiles more suited to children. That all said, I'm not suggesting that you don't pamper your horses—give them treats (in their buckets, though, not out of your hand—see Chapter 11 for my opinion on that!), coo at them, go downright crazy and put holiday decorations on their stall doors (out of reach of the horse, please!)—but never underestimate their strength and their self-preservation instinct. Grant them their horse qualities.

Respect your horses as living, breathing, decision-making animals, and treat them in a manner that will encourage their respect for you (rather than their fear of you!) in return. From this approach, you will have a partnership beyond imagination with a half-ton animal that could crush you like a bug but wouldn't even dream of it because you have proven that you are 100 percent reliable in a world full of horse-eating monsters. When your horse prefers to be with you more than anything else on the planet, it is both an honor and a privilege beyond your wildest dreams. When I go into the pasture and my mare leaves her horse pals to come visit with me, get a little scratch, and blow her silky breath on my neck, Ed McMahon could be knocking at the door with that oversized check in his hands and I wouldn't move to go get it.

I hope this book serves as enough of an introduction to horses that you may also take one more step along the path to being unfulfilled without the company of horses. There's an endless amount to be learned—both through books and mostly from the horses themselves—and I can practically guarantee that you will never be bored again in your life with a horse or two around the house.

I wish you the best in all your equine endeavors. Above all, stay safe, and may your trails and those of your equine companions be lined with good footing and capped with cloudless blue skies.

CHAPTER 1

History of the Horse

The evolution of the horse is a well-studied topic; in fact, archaeologists have discovered the fossils of a complete horse skeleton. Nonetheless, research shows some contradictions in the details of when and where horses were domesticated and ridden. New information continues to unfold. And who knows? Another significant discovery could be made any minute! One thing is certain though: Humans and horses have had an interrelated history.

This chapter offers a chronological look at some of the highlights of the current facts known about the early evolution of the horse. It also includes information about periods in which the use of the horse was significant, such as in times of war and during the settling of the American West.

The Ancient Horse

75 Million Years Ago

The earliest ancestor to all hoofed animals is *Condylarthra,* which lived over 75 million years ago. Condylarthra had five toes on each limb, was the size of a fox, and was a herbivore that lived in the swamplands of the Northern Hemisphere.

QUESTIONS?

What is a herbivore?
A **herbivore** is an animal that subsists totally on plant life. Horses are herbivores. This distinction makes the horse a prey animal (with those that hunt them considered predators), a category that contributes greatly to the overall behavior of the species.

55 Million Years Ago

Hyracotherium was a family of leaf browsers that descended from the Condylarthra. Most *Hyracotherium* had four toes on each limb, with the exception of one variety, which had only three working toes on its hind feet. This unique variety is the first "horse"; it appeared on Earth approximately 55 million years ago, at the beginning of the Eocene Epoch. Fossils of *Eohippus,* as the first horses have been called, showed the mammal to be smaller than a dog. *Eohippus* lived primarily in North America.

25 Million Years Ago

As the Eocene Epoch gave way to the Miocene Epoch around 25 million years ago, the *Eohippus* evolved into the three-toed *Mesohippus,* then into the *Mercyhippus,* which still had three toes but with a single toe more prominent. The toe of the horse wasn't the only thing to evolve. The tooth structure began to develop to accommodate the changing food source as the Miocene Period brought open grasslands. In turn, the skull became larger to accommodate larger teeth. As the skull became larger, the rest of the animal needed to adapt to support the changing weight distribution.

FACTS

Partway up the horse's leg, past the knee on the inside, is what seems to be a calloused piece of skin usually around the size of two quarters. Called the chestnut, this is said to be what remains of the first of three toes the horse lost during its evolution. The two other toe vestiges can be found as a hard nodule behind the fetlock.

6 Million Years Ago

Changing habitat from swamplands to dry savannahs caused the horse to evolve from a creature with multiple toes to one with a single toe, which is better adapted to roaming dry ground. We can thank the Pliocene Epoch for *Pliohippus,* the first single-toed horse; *Pliohippus* serves as a prototype for our own *Equus.* According to *The Kingdom of the Horse,* by Elwyn Hartley Edwards (Crescent, 1991), *Pliohippus* had a ligament-sprung hoof and longer legs with flexing ligaments, which gave way to a running action similar to that of the modern horse.

1 Million Years Ago

The evolution from *Pliohippus* to *Equus* took place over 5 million years. Due to changes in climate and land mass during this time, *Equus* found its way from North America to South America and spread across Asia, Europe, and Africa. The following table summarizes the evolution of the horse.

EVOLUTION OF THE HORSE

Eohippus	Four toes	50 million years ago	Paleocene Epoch
Mesohippus	Three toes	40 million years ago	Paleocene/Oligocene Epochs
Mercyhippus	Three toes	30 million years ago	Oligocene Epoch
Pliohippus	One toe	10 million years ago	Between Misocene and Pliocene Epochs
Equus	One toe	Present	Pliocene Epoch

30,000 Years Ago

An ivory horse carved from a mammoth tusk was found in a cave in Germany; it was dated at around 30,000 years old. The very worn carving, measuring 2.5 inches long, was believed to have been carried for good luck during hunts for horse meat.

12,000 Years Ago

A cave drawing from this period was found in Puerte Viesgo. The drawing showed a horse wearing what appears to be a primitive sort of bridle, but no other significant evidence has been found to verify humans riding horses in this early age—the same age as the domestication of the dog—although some scant evidence has emerged that horses were in fact ridden as many as 3,000 years earlier than this.

According to Xenophon (430–355 B.C.): "If one induces the horse to assume that carriage which it would adopt of its own accord when displaying its beauty, then, one directs the horse to appear joyous and magnificent, proud and remarkable for having been ridden."

8,000 Years Ago

The equid disappeared from the North American continent during this period, and to this day, no definitive explanation for this disappearance has been determined. Horses did not return to North America until the fifteenth century A.D. (See "Horses in North America," in this chapter, for more information.) The following table lists the six equids in existence today.

4000–3000 B.C.

This is considered the true age of the domestication of the horse. Up until this point, horses were merely a source of food and, therefore, an object of prey. The domestication of the horse has been thought to have first taken place on the steppes north of the Black Sea. Evidence found in China of mounted warriors supports the theory that horses were extensively ridden for the first time around 4000 B.C.

SIX EQUIDS IN EXISTENCE TODAY	
Equus burchelli	The plains zebra of Africa
Equus zebra	The mountain zebra of South Africa
Equus grevyi	The most horse-like zebra
Equus caballus	The domestic horse
Equus hemonius	The ass of Asia and of the Mideast
Equus asinus	The ass and the donkey of northern Africa

2000 B.C.

The horse was thought to be first harnessed in the Near East around this time. Evidence of man's early interactions with the horse comes mostly in the form of tapestries, relief pottery, and other works of art depicting battle scenes and exemplifying the human reverence for the horse's beauty.

FACTS

In 1994, Dr. David Anthony and Dorcas Brown founded the Institute for Ancient Equestrian Studies in the Department of Anthropology at Hartwick College in Oneonta, New York. The institute, which is dedicated to archaeological research concerning the origins of horseback riding and the impact of riding on human society, is affiliated with the Institute for the History and Archaeology of the Volga in Samara, Russia. Both institutes can be found online at *http://users.hartwick.edu/~iaes.*

1500 B.C.

Until this period, horses were typically too revered to do lowly agricultural work. Initially, they were hitched up with oxen yokes, but the design cut off the horse's wind. So a padded collar was designed to better suit the horse. Metal snaffle bits were perfected to take the place of nose rings, which were used to control the animal. Horses were also heavily domesticated in China at this time and used to pull chariots.

1350 B.C.

The first records of systematic training, conditioning, and caretaking of horses were found from this time period; they were written by a man named Kikkuli. Kikkuli was a Mittani, an Aryan group with cultural ties to India. Tablets were found that showed Kikkuli's instructions to the Hittite rulers prescribing care of harness racing horses. The Hittites, although clearly gaining their equestrian knowledge from other peoples, were credited with the development of the Arabian horse and were noted for their highly mobile equestrian troops.

500 B.C.

Well into the last centuries B.C., horseback riding had been not only mastered but also common. Scythian warriors, who had the first recorded geldings and whose wealth was measured in horses, were skilled in the art of battle on horseback. Since they believed that their wealth followed them to the afterworld, many artifacts were found in their burial grounds. Sometimes hundreds of horses were found buried with them.

Significant Recent Equine Discoveries

1879

Marcelino de Sautuola, a Spanish engineer who was also a serious amateur archaeologist, was exploring a cave with his five-year-old daughter in the mountains of France when she noticed on the cave ceiling drawings that included horses. Studies of these drawings in the now-famous Altamira cave have determined that they are from a period between 30,000 and 10,000 years ago.

1881

In 1881, a wild herd of *Equus Przewalskii,* considered to be the forebear of all domestic horses, was found in Mongolia.

1920

Parts of a horse skull were discovered in Kent, England, by Sir Richard Owen. Originally classified as *Hyracotherium*, after further discoveries around the world, the skull was eventually reclassified as *Eohippus*.

FACTS

Przewalskii's horse was discovered in the remote regions of Mongolia around 1881 by the Russian explorer Nikolai Mikhailovich Przewalskii. It is believed to be the closest ancestor to the ancient horse in existence. Described as being around twelve hands with a stocky body and short legs, it currently is believed to be extinct in the wild and to exist only in captivity, although it has never been thoroughly domesticated.

1940

Four teenagers discovered the Lascaux Caves in southern France. The walls of different rooms in the cave are heavily illustrated, including drawings of many horses that resemble the present-day Przewalskii's horse. According to research, the paintings date back 17,000 years, to the Magdalenian Age. Many Web sites offer views of the cave, which has been closed to the public since 1963. Check out the official Web site at *www.culture.fr.*

1950

In 1950, scientists began using carbon isotopes (carbon dating) to determine the age of ancient objects. This allowed for much more accurate classification and identification of archaeological findings.

Horses in North America

The Great Disappearing Act

One of the great mysteries of the horse is its disappearance 8,000 years ago from the North American continent, this despite the fact that *Eohippus* evolved here over a period of millions of years. The horse migrated south to South America and west across the land bridge of what is now the Bering Strait into Asia. Further climate and geographical changes during the Ice Age pushed them farther into the Mideast and Africa. It is believed that those that remained in North America succumbed to a fatal disease.

Many Thanks, Spanish Conquistadors!

The horse was being ridden and domesticated and becoming a crucial member of civilization in other parts of the world, long before it reappeared in North America. In fact, it didn't reappear until the fifteenth century A.D. Christopher Columbus is credited with this reappearance, when he brought them to the West Indies. And Ponce de Leon is thought to be responsible for bringing Andalusian-bred stock into what is now Florida.

By the seventeenth century, Native American tribes along the Mexican border began to use horses, as did American settlers in the West. In addition, the Native Americans used horses to barter with other tribes, which allowed the horse to move across the rest of the western United States. Some of these horses escaped captivity, thus marking the beginning of the wild (or, more accurately, feral) horse bands in the American West.

ALERT

Mustangs have been wild all their lives. Their first interaction with humans is often when they are rounded up, branded, and vaccinated—making their impressions of humans rather unfavorable. It's probably better that they be adopted by people who are experienced at handling difficult horses or who have access to experienced help.

Today, the Bureau of Land Management (BLM) is the U.S. government institution responsible for the care and management of the wild equine herds still in existence in the United States. In the 1950s, Velma B. Johnston became concerned about the manner in which wild horses were being harvested for commercial reasons. Her campaign was loud and her audience receptive, leading to the passing in 1959 of Public Law 86-234, which controlled the way wild horses and burros were hunted. But it wasn't until 1971 that Public Law 92-195, the Wild Free-Roaming Horse and Burro Act, was passed, which provided for the management, protection, and control of the wild horse and the burro populations. Numerous amendments have passed since. Management of the wild horses, referred to as mustangs, has included regular removal and dispersement (a portion through private adoption).

For information about adopting a mustang, contact the Bureau of Land Management, National Wild Horse and Burro Program, P.O. Box 12000, Reno, Nevada 89520; 800-417-9647; or check out their Web site at *www.wildhorseandburro.blm.gov.*

Horses in Modern Battle

Ancient civilizations utilized the horse in battle to carry soldiers and pull chariots, making armies mobile in some of the harshest climates in the world. The horse has been heavily used in modern warfare as well:

- The Boer War in South Africa (1899–1902) produced a huge demand for horses, mules, and donkeys. Thousands of wild horses in America were captured and shipped overseas, with over 500,000 said to have died over the course of the war.
- Horses were also in great demand during World War I. Records show that hundreds of thousands were abandoned in the deserts.
- In 1939, the Polish army is noted to have had 86,000 horses, the Germans, almost 1.2 million.

Cowboys, Horses, and the Settling of the American West

A cowboy without a horse in the old west was really just another guy. Luckily, there were plenty of horses back then. As a result, we have the legend of the American Cowboy and his horse.

Horses were everywhere. They were used for mounted transportation; to haul carriages and stagecoaches; to move and round up cattle; and inevitably as entertainment in the form of racing and rodeos. Still today, the heritage of the American West is well celebrated in the United States.

The Pony Express

The Pony Express was a short-lived and much romanticized part of American history. St. Joseph, Missouri, was the site of the eastern edge of the Pony Express route, with Sacramento, California, the western destination. The intent was to shorten the time for mail to cross the country until the railroad was complete—up until that point, most mail would go by steamship around South America to California, which would take a month. William Russell, William Waddell, and Alexander Majors thought of the idea of offering ten-day delivery via a horse-and-rider relay of seventy-five to 100 miles each rider and less than fifteen miles each horse. The Pony Express company bought 400 horses to stock the route through Kansas, Nebraska, Colorado, Wyoming, Utah, Nevada, and on into California.

ESSENTIALS

Check out the following Web sites for fascinating stories about the "old west":

www.americanwest.com   www.nationalcowboymuseum.org
www.oldwestmuseum.org   www.autry-museum.org

As an innovative idea, the Pony Express was a great success. However, as a business, it was a failure; it lasted only nineteen months, and its owners were said to have lost $500,000. If you want to learn more about this fascinating venture, check out the Pony Express Museum, 914 Penn Street, P.O. Box 244, St. Joseph, Missouri 64502; 800-530-5930; *www.ponyexpress.org.*

Recent History of Horses in the United States

The equine population in the United States crested around 1920. In 2000, *Equus* magazine estimated registrations for the American Quarter Horse at 145,000, followed by the paint horse at approximately 71,000; the Thoroughbred at 37,000; the Tennessee Walker at 14,000; the Standardbred, Arabian, and Appaloosa close together at approximately 11,000 each; and Anglo-Arabs, Half-Arabs, Morgans, and Saddlebreds bringing up the rear.

Solving Mysteries of the Past

Many books have been written about the evolution of the horse. Although you will find differing opinions and even small contradictions in factual details from one book to the next, what is consistent throughout is a well-deserved reverence and fascination by humans for an animal that has made an undeniable contribution to the advancement and civilization of humankind.

Discoveries are still being made about the horse. And even small discoveries can change some major assumptions. For instance, it was thought that early domestication of the horse did not include any significant riding by humans. However, later excavations of horse skulls with teeth worn presumably by bits show that riding actually occurred much earlier than archaeologists had first believed, in fact, 3,000 years earlier. It's hard to keep up with the horse!

CHAPTER 2
Horse Breeds

All horses are fundamentally the same—they exhibit basically the same herd behavior, possess a strong sense of self-preservation, and have four legs and a tail. However, there are dozens of breeds, and each one has different physical and, to some degree, behavioral characteristics.

Horse lovers typically favor a particular breed or two, usually due to the breed's physical appearance or the kind of horse-related activity or sport the person wants to undertake. Which breed is right for you? I'll help you answer that question in this chapter as we take a look at the differences and similarities among breeds.

Finding Your Favorite Breed

I have two Quarter Horses, and while there is something about the physical sturdiness of this breed that I like a lot, I find myself also attracted to the Arabian breed—and finally bought a yearling Arabian to add to my growing collection. Despite the opinions of a few people I spoke with when I was looking for an Arabian to purchase, I have found that I can handle and educate my Arab in the same way that I did my Quarter Horse youngsters and with the same level of success. However, even with all the similarities among my horses, there are differences. For one thing, my Arab has taken a lot longer to develop physically than the Quarter Horses did. I didn't start her under saddle until she was three because she seemed too scrawny and undeveloped, whereas my quarter horses were well developed enough to start under saddle and ride (at least lightly) as two- and three-year-olds. As for behavior, my Arab's personality is very different from that of my two Quarter Horses, but each of the quarter horses are significantly different from each other as well. So I remain convinced that Arabs can be handled in the same manner as Quarter Horses.

If you find a breed that attracts you, the next step is to hang around a barn that raises that breed and see what you think. Talk with the breeder about his or her attraction to the breed and why he or she picked it to concentrate in. What does the breeder do with his or her horses? What do the people who buy this breed tend to do with them? Watch the horses interact with each other; watch them being ridden, driven, or handled. Handle and ride one yourself if possible. When it comes to horses, hands-on research is always the best way to find out the most.

Maybe you'll ultimately decide that a horse is a horse is a horse and that breed matters little when it comes time to buy one of your own. But you have to narrow your search down somehow, and breed is certainly a reasonable place to start!

The following is an overview of the breeds that are common in the United States. Perhaps you will start to see which one or two of the breeds attracts you the most and is best for the kind of horse activity you find yourself leaning toward.

The Most Common Breeds

The breeds that are used mostly for riding under saddle are known in the horse world as "light" horses, as opposed to heavy work horses, which are also known as "draft" horses. The next few sections highlight the most common light horse breeds you will run across in your search.

QUESTIONS?

What is a hand?
In tack room terms, a **hand** is the unit used to measure horse height. One hand equals four inches; thus, a horse that stands 15 hands tall is 60 inches, or 5 feet, tall at the wither.

Thoroughbred

This is the breed that the nonhorse world is most familiar with because of its predominance on the racetrack. The Thoroughbred horse tends to stand in excess of 16 hands and its ancestry, as well as that of many other breeds, can be traced back to the Arabian horse. The Thoroughbred's tall, lean conformation makes it a perfect candidate for racing. In fact, this breed capable of a single stride of over 20 feet and speeds of up to 40 miles per hour. The Thoroughbred came to be considered a great horse to mix with the pedigrees of other breeds.

Characteristics of the Thoroughbred include a tall, slender frame, good for racing like the wind for long distances; a great lung capacity; and a strong competitive spirit. Thoroughbreds start their race training very young, typically working mounted in their yearling year and then on to professional racing as two-year-olds.

Many Thoroughbreds are retired from racing by the time they are five years old—an age when most saddle horses are just starting their riding careers in earnest! The best of the best of these retired Thoroughbreds are used for breeding, and the rest are often sold at reasonable prices to equestrians looking for dressage, three-day event, or jumping prospects. One needs to be very careful and very knowledgeable in purchasing a retired racehorse. Although lameness is perhaps the most pervasive issue, it usually does not significantly affect the Thoroughbred's performance as a pleasure mount.

American Quarter Horse

The American Quarter Horse is the first breed native to the United States; the colonists bred them to fulfill their passion for short-distance racing. The American Quarter Horse has become by far the most popular breed in terms of the annual number of registrations in America today.

The Quarter Horse has developed into two very distinct lines:

- One is a taller, leaner horse as the result of considerable mixing of Thoroughbred lineage with the Quarter Horse breed. In fact there is an appendix to the American Quarter Horse registry that is specifically for registering horses who are half Quarter Horse and half Thoroughbred. Of these horses, the one with the more Thoroughbred-type build is often found in the English riding disciplines such as eventing, dressage, and jumping.
- The other line consists of a stockier, shorter horse, usually referred to as the "foundation type," noted for muscular, powerful hindquarters useful in ranch work tasks as well as barrel racing, cutting, reining, and other events where sharp turns, quick bursts of speed, and sitting back on their haunches are important abilities.

FACTS

Many celebrities have "secret" horse lives. Actor Patrick Swayze rides and raises Arabian horses with his wife on their farm outside Los Angeles. Ballplayer Nolan Ryan, golfer Hal Sutton, newscaster Tom Brokaw, actor William Shatner, former second lady Marilyn Quayle, and actresses Andie MacDowell and Bo Derek, among many others, also ride.

Before the Quarter Horse breed became heavily influenced by Thoroughbred mixing, their form was more short and stocky—referred to as "bull dog"–type conformation—than that of the Quarter Horses popular today. There has been great interest over the last ten years or so to preserve this original foundation type in the breed. Two organizations have developed that are devoted to the foundation Quarter

Horse. They are the Foundation Quarter Horse Registry, P.O. Box 230, Sterling, Colorado 80751; 970-522-7822; *www.fqhrregistry.com;* the other is the National Foundation Quarter Horse Association, P.O. Box P, Joseph, OR 97846; 541-426-4403; *www.nfqha.com.* These registries have specific requirements. For instance, to be registered in the NFQHA, a horse's pedigree must have no more than 20 percent Thoroughbred blood (the association will research this information for you for a fee). The NFQHA believes that by removing this Thoroughbred mix, the original founding Quarter Horse mix of mostly Barb, Mustang, Arab, and draft horse will return.

The Quarter Horse also has a well-established racing circuit. Their propensity as sprinters (the "quarter" in their name allegedly coming from their quarter-mile racing prowess) is tested at tracks around the country.

Quarter Horses have developed a reputation for being easy going, smart, and mostly agreeable to work with. But keep in mind that although they are all that, they are also horses like all others. While they do seem to have a more innately gentle way of going, they can be as high strung and fearful as any breed of horse if handled and treated in a manner conducive to those traits.

Arabian

The Arabian is perhaps the breed most often visualized when horses are imagined. With flowing manes, flaring nostrils, and fancy tails, the breed originated in the desert regions of Arabia, giving them a well-deserved reputation for endurance. Arabian, or some cross of Arabian, is the horse of choice for the long-distance riding circuit.

General Ulysses S. Grant was responsible for the Arabian horse coming to the shores of the United States. In 1873, he was given two stallions as a gift by the Sulton Abdul Hamid II of Turkey while on a trip to the Mideast. Grant gave one of the stallions to Randolph Huntington, who imported two mares and two stallions from England in 1888, thereby creating the first Arabian breeding program in the United States. In 1906, an expedition to Arabia took place, specifically to import Arabian horses; twenty-seven were shipped to Boston. From there the Arabian breed took off in the United States and has remained popular ever since.

Arabians are truly unique in that their spines have one fewer vertebrae than other horses. Thus they have specific saddling requirements, if only to accommodate a shorter back. They are known to be late developers and are said to not be fully grown until they are around seven or eight years old.

The Arabian horse comes in a few basic types, including:

- The Egyptian-style Arab tends toward a slender frame with a predominantly "dished" face.
- The Polish type, which is a stockier horse.

Morgan

As the tale goes, a Vermont gentleman named Justin Morgan brought us this compact breed of horse; in fact, his stud shared his name. Justin Morgan the horse was known to be extraordinarily strong and fast. When he was used at stud, he threw his physical characteristics to all of his offspring. The demand for his stud service and the resulting offspring was so great that the army ultimately bought him. It is said that the Standardbred can thank the Morgan for its development.

Morgan horses have more pronounced gaits, which is characteristic of a "carriage" breed; thus, they are quite often taught to pull a wagon or cart of some kind. They are very sturdy horses with a tendency to have very sturdy feet.

Standardbred

The Standardbred horse is another racing breed, but Standardbreds are raced not by a jockey under saddle but in harness with a sulky and driver. One of their unique gaits is the "pace," in which the front and back leg on the same side move in unison rather than the typical trot movement of diagonal pairs.

Standardbreds have an average height of 15 hands, which usually places them shorter than their racing counterparts, the Thoroughbred. Their coloring is most often bay (see "Horse Colors" later in this chapter).

Saddlebred

Although the American Saddlebred is not the most popular horse in America today, it is believed to have held that distinction at one time. It was the horse of choice in revolutionary times, and later was ridden by a lineup of famous generals including Robert E. Lee (riding the famous Traveller), Ulysses S. Grant (Cincinnati), William T. Sherman (Lexington), and Stonewall Jackson (Little Sorrel).

The breed was first established in the Narragansett Bay area of Rhode Island from a mix of Scottish Galloways and Irish hobby horses. Until the Thoroughbred became firmly embedded in the lineage, they were referred to as Narragansett pacers. Somewhere in there, the Saddlebred got a touch of Morgan as well as Hackney.

FACTS

Located on 1,030 acres in Lexington, Kentucky, the Kentucky Horse Park is an educational theme park devoted to the horse. It includes a visitor's center, museum, research library, art gallery, and photo gallery. Visitors can take a leisurely guided trail ride or carriage ride through the park grounds. There are also educational programs and special events throughout the year. For information, visit them on their Web site at *www.kyhorsepark.com* or call 800-678-8813, or write to them at 4089 Iron Works Pike, Lexington, KY 40511.

In the early 1700s, the first Thoroughbreds to be brought to the continent were crossed with the Narragansett pacers. The pacer "disappeared" and was replaced by the American horse, now known as the Saddlebred. The American horse dominated the early horse show scene, which was first established in the mid-nineteenth century. A coal black stallion, Rex MacDonald, became so popular after an illustrious show career that he was idolized by the public and visited by U.S. presidents. Saddlebreds became favored as riding horses for their easy gaits (the rack, running walk, and fox trot), stamina, size, and the refined pedigree contributed by the Thoroughbred stock. The breed was first documented in a 1776 letter to the Continental Congress from an American diplomat living in France, who wanted to give a horse as a gift to Marie Antoinette.

The American Saddle Horse Association was founded in Louisville, Kentucky, in 1891, and today Saddlebreds still populate Kentucky's Shelby County, referred to as the "Saddle Horse Capital of the World."

Appaloosa

The spotted Appaloosa horse was depicted in cave drawings in what is now France almost 20,000 years ago. The Spanish brought this breed to North America, where the horse spread through the Native American populations in the Northwest, especially with the Nez Perce and Palouse tribes in Washington, Oregon, and Idaho. White settlers were said to have referred to them as "Palouse horses," thus their name. In 1938, the Appaloosa Horse Club was formed to preserve the breed.

Appaloosas are well-rounded horses; they are used in all equine sports, from jumping and roping to racing and trail riding. To be accepted in the registry, the horse must possess either a spotted coat pattern or mottled skin, and either white eye sclera readily visible and not associated with a white face or black-and-white striped hooves. If the horse's lineage is of Appaloosa stock but the horse does not exhibit these required characteristics, it can be registered as "noncharacteristic."

The Less Common Breeds

Andalusian

This was a significant Spanish breed in Europe from the twelfth to the seventeenth centuries and has been the basis for many breeds, including the Appaloosa. They are typically grey and of average height, around 15.2 hands.

Bashkir Curley

According to the registry for this breed, they have been in North America since the early 1800s. They are generally medium sized, but they can be pony sized or draft sized as well. Their coat is curly, as their name implies, and the curls get long in winter; the mane tends to split down the middle. They have been found to be "nonallergenic" to many people with allergies to horses and are used in all riding disciplines.

Cleveland Bay

Thought to have evolved in the seventeenth century, the Cleveland Bay peaked in popularity in the late 1800s in Britain, where they originally developed; it is now considered a rare breed, with less than five hundred purebred horses worldwide.

They were imported to the United States in the early 1800s, and Buffalo Bill Cody was said to have used them in his Wild West show. Cleveland Bays are, as their name implies, bay in color, stand 16 to 17 hands, and, because of their uniform characteristics, were often used as carriage horses. However, purebred and part-bred (often crossed with Thoroughbreds) Cleveland Bays make excellent mounts in all equine disciplines.

Fjord

The Norwegian Fjord horse is one of the world's oldest breeds; the original Fjords are thought to have migrated to Norway over 4,000 years ago. The present-day Fjord is believed to be descended from Przewalskii's horse and retains many of the same characteristics. The Fjord has distinct coloring, usually dun with black "zebra stripes" on its legs and a dorsal stripe that runs from its forelock through the mane down the back and through the tail. They are relatively small in height, averaging 13.2 to 14.2 hands, and weigh in at around 900 to 1200 pounds.

Fresian

Used in war during the Middle Ages, this breed also has been used as a draft horse; in fact, they were said to have influenced both the Clydesdale and Shire draft breeds. Fresians are black and have long feathered fetlocks, making them a very impressive animal.

Hackney

One of the oldest British breeds (dating back to the eleventh century), Hackneys are a mix of Thoroughbred and Arabian. They are mostly used as carriage horses.

Haflinger

These horses are golden chestnut in color with a long, white mane and tail. They were used heavily as pack horses during World War II, but now are popular in all types of riding.

Lipizzaner

This breed was founded in 1580 in Austria by the Archduke Charles II; the stallions were originally from Spain. They are grey in color and stand between 15 and 16 hands.

Horseshoes are considered lucky only if their open end faces up—facing down, according to folklore, is thought to make all the luck run out! Interestingly, until 1999, the horseshoe engraved on the Kentucky Derby trophy faced down. In 1999, they turned the horseshoe up for a special 125th anniversary edition of the trophy.

Miniature Horses

According to the World Class Miniature Horse Registry (WCMHR), miniature horses were thought to have been bred in Europe for pets for the children of royalty. And miniature they are! Under 36.5 inches tall, these little horses are exactly like big horses, only reduced in size. The WCMHR Web site (*www.wcmhr.com*) speculates that miniatures were first used in the United States in coal mining—their sturdiness allows them to pull many times their own weight. This horse is suitable for riding for children under 40 pounds. As the registry points out, while the size of these horses tends to influence people to treat them like dogs, they are, in fact, horses, and although perhaps more huggable than a full-sized horse, miniatures still need to be fed and cared for in the same manner as any horse.

Missouri Fox-trotter

This breed originated in the Ozark Mountains in the nineteenth century. Its four-beat gait is comfortable over long distances and at good speed. Fox-trotters can be of any color and range from 15 to 17 hands.

Paso Fino

Brought to North and South America by the Spanish conquistadors in the sixteenth century, the Paso Fino breed developed in Puerto Rico. Paso Finos have truly distinct gaits, which are not taught but natural to their breed. They tend to be on the small side, ranging from 14.2 to 15 hands.

Peruvian Paso

Peruvian Pasos and Paso Finos share a common heritage, but their breeding environment took them in different directions. Peruvian Pasos were bred in the harsh conditions of the mountainous regions of Peru and, therefore, are known for great stamina and gaits that are both comfortable for the rider and not tiring to the horse.

Rocky Mountain Horse

Founded in the Appalachia region of Kentucky, these medium-sized naturally gaited horses are exceptionally sure footed and were used to traverse the rugged mountain trails. Their breed association was established in 1986.

Tennessee Walking Horse

Founded in Tennessee, the Tennessee Walking Horse, or Tennessee Walker, is a mixture of Standardbred, Thoroughbred, Morgan, and American Saddlebred. They range in size from 14.3 to 17 hands and are light in weight at around 900 to 1200 pounds. They are found in all colors and are famous for the "running walk," a smooth, inherited gait unique to the breed.

Warmbloods

"Warmblood" is the collective name for various breeds that are a cross between a "cold-blooded" draft horse and a "hot-blooded" light horse (typically Thoroughbred or Arabian). They were developed in Europe but are now being heavily imported into the United States. Warmbloods are used extensively as show jumpers and in many riding and driving competitions. A few breed names you will run across are Dutch warmblood, Danish warmblood, Trakehner, and Hanoverian.

Draft Breeds

Belgian

The most common style of Belgian horse in the United States is the "modern style," which is longer legged than the old style. Belgians are used extensively among loggers and farmers. They average 16 to 17 hands, range from 1400 to 1800 pounds, and can be sorrel, roan, or chestnut in color.

Clydesdale

These big brown horses with flaxen manes and tails and fluffy fetlocks are best known as the Budweiser horses. The Clydesdale breed originated in Clyde Valley, Lancashire, Scotland, and were imported to the United States prior to the Civil War. Anheuser-Busch now owns the largest herd of Clydesdales in the world. Their breeding farms are located in St. Louis at Grant Farm (now a wildlife preserve, part of whose land was once farmed by Ulysses S. Grant) and near Los Angeles. The horses that haul the beer wagon are all geldings, stand at least 18 hands, and are bay in color with a white blaze down their face. Ten horses travel with the hitch, eight pull the wagon, and two serve as backups. The pair closest to the wagon are known as the "wheelhorses"; the next pair, the "body"; the third pair, the "swing" horses; and the front pair, appropriately, the "leaders." All of the Budweiser Clydesdale harnesses are handmade at the Santos Leather Shop in Massachusetts and cost over $10,000 each.

FACTS

The first Budweiser Clydesdales were presented to August A. Busch by his son in 1933, just after the repeal of Prohibition. The hitch hauled the first case of post-Prohibition beer from the brewery in St. Louis. The road show began when the hitch delivered a case to the governor of New York, who was instrumental in repealing Prohibition. While on the road, they did a little New England tour, then headed south to present a case of beer to President Roosevelt. Visit the Budweiser Clydesdale Web site at *www.abclydesdales.com*.

Percheron

Grey or black in color, these heavy draft horses run an average of 16 hands. The breed originated in France, around 50 miles southwest of Paris.

Pony Breeds

Connemara

This pony is considered Ireland's only native horse breed. It is the largest of the pony breeds, averaging 14 to 14.2 hands.

Fell Pony

Originating along the England/Scotland border, the Fell (mountain) pony is flashy, with feathered legs and lots of mane and tail, probably acquired from its early Fresian influence. They are under 14 hands but strong enough to carry an adult rider and are used extensively under harness.

Chincoteague Ponies

The Chincoteague and Assateague Islands sit on the mid-Atlantic coast, along the Delmarva Peninsula, where Virginia, Maryland, and

Delaware meet along the ocean. Visit this lovely part of the country and you will see small groups of wild ponies wandering Assateague Island. Although no one really knows how they came to live there, one version is that in the mid-600s, a Spanish galleon wrecked offshore, and ponies on board swam to safety and have roamed the island ever since.

The ponies graze on marshland grasses and browse on shrubs. The Chincoteague Volunteer Fire Department manages the herd and provides them with supplemental hay during harsh months as well as veterinary care when needed. The department has held an annual carnival since 1925, which includes the now well-known "swimming of the ponies" at slack tide from their home on Assateague Island to Chincoteague Island, where around forty colts and fillies are auctioned off to help control herd population and inbreeding and to raise funds to care for the pony herds.

ESSENTIALS

If you own a Chincoteague pony, you can register it with the Chincoteague Pony Association, P.O. Box 691, Chincoteague, Virginia 23336; 757-336-6917; *www.chincoteague.com.* You can also join the Chincoteague Pony Association, established in 1994, to help support efforts in preserving this national equine treasure.

The Chincoteague ponies were made famous by writer Marguerite Henry, whose 1947 *Misty of Chincoteague* tells the tale of a young girl and boy whose hearts are set on making the winning bid for the foal Misty. Henry and illustrator Wesley Dennis brought many favorite books to children's literature, including *Stormy, Misty's Foal; Sea Star, Orphan of Chincoteague; Brighty of the Grand Canyon;* and *King of the Wind: The Story of the Godolphin Arabian.* These books are still widely available in paperback editions.

Icelandic

The product of a cross between Germanic and Celtic horses brought to Iceland by settlers in A.D. 874, Icelandic horses are small, quick, hardy, and strong. They began to be exported in the 1850s. However, once exported, Iceland regulations do not allow them to come back into the country. These horses are late to mature and typically are not ridden until they are five years old, but they commonly live a long life. They come in every typical coat color and are best known for their unusual gaits, including the tolt (a four-beat running walk) and the flying pace, both of which are described by riders as "feeling like you are floating over the ground."

Icelandic horses were used for transporting goods and people across rugged volcanic terrain and mountains, and their sturdy, sure-footed breeding remains in evidence today. Despite their small size, their unique bone density is said to allow them to comfortably hold a 250-pound rider.

Shetland

This breed is probably what most of us imagine when we think of a pony. The height limit on the popular Shetland is 46 inches. They tend to be hardy and have good feet, and they are easy keepers.

Welsh Cob

The Welsh Cob was imported in the 1880s from the United Kingdom. The registry in the United States has four sections, with Section C, the Welsh Pony of Cob Type, being the rarest type of Welsh Cob in North America. The Welsh Cob is used in all riding disciplines.

Mixed Breeds

Some breeds are commonly crossed. Although you can never know for sure until the foal drops to the ground, these crosses have consistently good enough results to have warranted giving them a name and often their own registry.

- **Anglo-Arabian:** This horse is $7/8$ Thoroughbred and $1/8$ Arabian.
- **Araapaloosa:** The Araapaloosa is a cross between an Arabian and an Appaloosa.
- **Morab:** This mixed breed is a cross between a Morgan and an Arabian.

- **Moresian:** The Moresian is an often stunning mix of Morgan and Fresian.
- **Quarab:** I have personally seen results of the quarter horse/Arabian cross as petite, with either a Quarter Horse-type body or a tall and lanky more Arabian-type conformation.

Registering Your Horse

Listed in Appendix A, "Resources," are the associations that serve as the official registry for many of the breeds mentioned in this book. Many breeds have more than one association connected to them, varying from fan clubs to official registries for different aspects of the breed. If you buy a registered horse, it will come with registration papers that clearly note the breed association it is registered with. Also, some associations are "color" registries, and your horse may be "double registered," that is, registered both in its breed registry and the registry for its color.

ESSENTIALS

Being a member of the breed association of your horse makes you part of an instant equine community. Often included in membership is a magazine or newsletter that keeps you up to date on interesting information about the breed.

Color Registries

Some breeds have the main conformation characteristics of one of the common breeds but can be registered in a registry set up just for color. As stated previously, many of them, if they carry certain characteristics, can be double registered in both the breed association for the foundation horse type and the color breed association.

Paint

The paint horse came to North America with the Spanish conquistador Hernando Cortés in 1519. One of the sixteen horses that accompanied Cortés was a sorrel and white horse that bred with Native American mustangs, whose offspring was the first of the American paint horse breed. They became favored by the American Indians, and in the 1950s, a group dedicated to preserving the breed was formed.

QUESTIONS?

What does breeding stock mean?
Breeding stock refers to a mare or stallion that meets the eligibility requirements (e.g., through lineage) to be registered in the paint breed but does not exhibit the color trait of a paint. With careful breeding, these horses can be bred to consistently produce colorful offspring.

To be registered with the American Paint Horse Association, color pattern is essential, but there are also strict bloodline requirements that the sire or dam must be registered with the American Paint Horse Association, the American Quarter Horse Association, or the Jockey Club. Coloring of the paint must be a combination of white and any other coat color in the spectrum, and markings can be any size and shape and located anywhere on the body.

Following are the three coat patterns:

- **Overo:** There is typically no white on the back, the four legs are usually dark, the head often has a lot of white, and the predominant color may be white or dark.
- **Tobiano:** The legs are usually white, the head markings are often like that of solid color horses, with a blaze, stripe, strip, or snip, and the predominant color can be white or dark.
- **Tovero:** One or both eyes are blue, and there is a tendency toward dark coloring around the ears, flanks, and chest.

Palomino

The Palomino Horse Breeders of America registry describes the ideal coat color of the palomino to be "approximately the color of a United States gold coin." It also includes requirements for skin color, which must be "dark colored without pink spots wherever it shows . . . except for skin on the face, which may be pink where it is the continuation of a white marking." Further requirements are that both eyes must be the same color. The registry does allow the horse to have white legs and face markings.

Although a color breed, the registry also has conformation requirements: The palomino "must show refinement of head, bone, and general structure . . . and be suitable for carrying Western or English equipment. The horse must be between 14 and 17 hands when fully matured and show no pony or draft horse characteristics." The color can show up in almost any breed.

Buckskin

The buckskin color—cream with black points—can be found in most breeds. Other acceptable colorations include dun, red dun, and grulla, all having black points with a variation in the body color. The registry originated in 1965, and horses can be double registered in their breed association as well as in the buckskin registry.

Horse Colors

Some breeds not technically considered "color breeds" are nonetheless very color specific; Fresians, for instance, are always black. The colors that have registries were just discussed. Following are the other basic colorings of horses:

- **Bay:** Bay consists of a brown body with black points, that is, mane, tail, and legs up to the knee area.
- **Black:** It is rare to have a true black-coated horse; most actually are brown in the right light. But a black horse is simply all black.
- **Brown:** Body, points, mane, tail, and legs are all brown.
- **Chestnut:** Chestnut consists of reddish color all over, including the mane and tail.
- **Liver chestnut:** This deep brown color can be all over throughout the mane and tail or just the coat color.

- **Sorrel:** Sorrel consists of a chestnut body and legs, with flaxen colored mane and tail.
- **Roan:** Roan is a base color mixed throughout with white. A chestnut color mixed with white hairs is called a "red roan," and a black coat mixed with white hairs is a "blue roan."

Researching Pedigree

People most often trace bloodlines when they are thinking about buying a young horse and want to know what mares and stallions are in the horse's background so that they can get an idea of what the animal may ultimately look like as a mature horse. Pedigree is also important when planning to breed a horse. To increase the odds that you get the type of horse you want out of the foal, you first want to know as much about your mare's genetic makeup as possible. Then, once you've researched stallions and have one or two on the top of your list, the stallion's pedigree might tell you something about what the match between your mare and the stallion might result in. In a most simplistic example, if the bloodlines of your quarter horse mare show a predominance of Poco Bueno (a stocky-type Quarter Horse) and you are hoping to maintain that stocky foundation type in the offspring, you would probably want to stay away from stallions that show a lot of Thoroughbred lines in their pedigrees and stick with more stocky foundation types. Again, this is a very simplistic explanation—breeding horses is an art and science, and an inexact one at that!

FACTS

It is much easier to research pedigree if your horse is registered with a breed association (see Appendix A); otherwise, it may be difficult to find out who your horse's sire and dam are. For Quarter Horses, members of the American Quarter Horse Association can go to the AQHA Web site, enter the registered name of any horse, and for a small fee get an eight-generation pedigree. Most other breed associations also offer pedigree searches for a fee.

Above All Else, Enjoy Your Horse!

Owning a purebred horse puts you in touch with an equine community that shares many of your interests. People can get downright fierce in their devotion to a particular breed! But you certainly don't need to own a purebred to enjoy your horse—far from it. Maybe your horse is a cross between two breeds, in which case you can have fun learning about both and trying to pick out the characteristics of each that your horse exhibits. However, as long as she's healthy and has four good legs and feet, what breed she is will probably have little impact on your overall enjoyment of your horse!

CHAPTER 3
Anatomy

Knowing a little about how the horse is put together can help you understand when something is wrong and what the problem might be related to. Understanding the various systems can also help you understand proper equine management and avoid many problems. In this chapter I'll give you an overview on a horse's anatomy. You can also visit *www.horseinfo.webprovider.com*. This anatomy Web site has a menu of the different systems, including illustrations and links.

The Teeth

Horses have two basic kinds of teeth—molars and incisors. Like most animals, the incisors are used for biting off things (such as grass), and the molars are used for grinding up what they bite off before it goes through the rest of the digestive system.

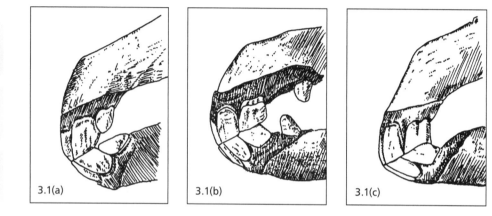

FIGURE 3.1(a):
One Year

FIGURE 3.1(b):
Five Years

FIGURE 3.1(c):
Fifteen Years

3.1(a)   3.1(b)   3.1(c)

The foal will begin to show teeth within a couple weeks of birth. Between the ages of two and five years, baby teeth begin to shed and are replaced by permanent teeth.

The horse has at least thirty-six permanent teeth—twelve incisors and twenty-four molars—and some horses have four wolf teeth (essentially premolars) and four canine teeth (behind the incisors). Wolf teeth can sometimes interfere with where the bit rests in the mouth, in which case they need to be removed. They have a shallow root and removal is a fairly easy process.

Underbites and Overbites

Also known as sow mouth (underbite) or parrot mouth (overbite), these malocclusions of the incisors are genetically based (breeding stock with these problems should be gelded or not used as broodmares). The most pressing issue that these abnormalities cause are uneven wear, especially if the molars are also out of alignment.

Galvayne's Groove

This groove starts at the base of the tooth, top and bottom, making its first appearance at around ten years of age. The groove grows out with the tooth and recedes off the bottom as the tooth elongates. At around age thirty, the groove disappears off the tooth.

FACTS

As much as 4 inches of the horse's tooth is imbedded in the jawbone. The horse's teeth keep growing out from that base throughout its life.

Tooth Wear

If the molars wear unevenly, they can develop sharp edges. As a result, the horse will lose food out of his mouth, have difficulty chewing, and perhaps even drool. Eventually, since he is not getting the full nutritional benefit of the food he is being given, the horse will lose weight, because he is either dropping it or passing it through his system before it is fully digested.

The adult horse's teeth should be checked annually for proper wear. An equine dentist will examine the teeth both visually and manually using a speculum to keep the mouth open. If he or she finds sharp edges from uneven wear, the dentist will rasp (known as "floating") the teeth with special tools made specifically for horses and bring the teeth all back to an even grinding surface again.

The Digestive System

Horses have a huge digestive system but a stomach capacity of only about 4 gallons. The horse in the wild eats continually, passing food through its digestive tract all the time, emptying out the stomach and processing the food through to elimination.

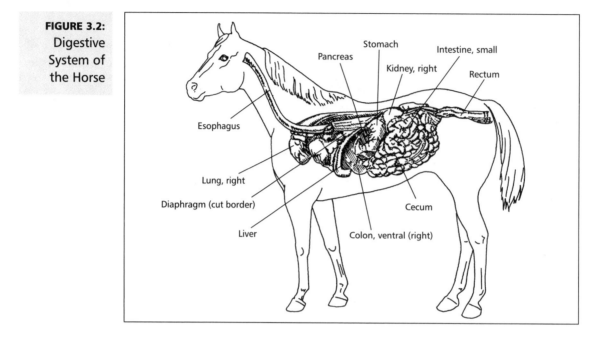

FIGURE 3.2:
Digestive
System of
the Horse

The domestic horses without access to pasture should have grain divided into at least two and perhaps three meals per day, depending on the quantity they are receiving (which depends on the level of work that is required of them). Hay can be a free choice, if possible, but again, it is more likely split up into three or four feedings a day. The main point is that the horse's digestive system is a large, complex machine that needs to be constantly processing food but not stuffed so full it can't do its job properly.

The Mouth

As with all animals, digestion begins with the chewing process, reducing food material to a size and consistency more conducive to the remaining digestive process. For the horse, however, not much actual digestion takes place in the mouth, although the process does help produce the significant amounts of saliva needed for digestion.

The Esophagus

This muscular tube is approximately 4 feet long. It moves the food from the mouth to the stomach in rhythmic contractions. The esophagus has a one-way valve at the entrance to the stomach that prevents the horse from vomiting.

The Stomach

The horse's relatively small stomach contains acid and pepsin, which break food down.

The Small Intestine

Approximately 70 feet long, the small intestine has approximately a 12-gallon capacity. Digested foods are absorbed and enter the bloodstream. Some of it is processed by the liver and stored as energy.

The Cecum

This critical apparatus holds a huge amount of bacteria. All ingested food passes through the cecum in a sort of side trip through the system. The bacteria break down cellulose (which the human body cannot digest) and produce fat-soluble vitamins that are absorbed and used.

Smaller, frequent feedings are best, otherwise, the stomach will move food before it is fully digested. This can mean that the horse isn't getting the full nutritional value of its feed, and also poses a greater risk of becoming impacted at one of those odd kinks and turns in the system.

The Large and Small Colons

The large colon has numerous parts (right lower, left lower, right upper, left upper, and transverse) and is around 12 feet long. It holds as much as 20 gallons of semiliquid stool. The small colon is a little shorter, at 10 to 12 feet long. In it, water is absorbed and stool is formed into balls.

The Rectum

Around a foot long, this is the channel through which the stool leaves the body.

The Muscles

The horse has muscles in every part of its body. Short thick muscles provide short bursts of speed, and long lean muscles are needed for both speed and endurance. Bulkiness and thick muscles are a desirable trait for horses shown at halter. However, since the thick muscling hinders movement, "halter horses" do not make especially good riding horses.

FIGURE 3.3:
The Muscles of the Horse

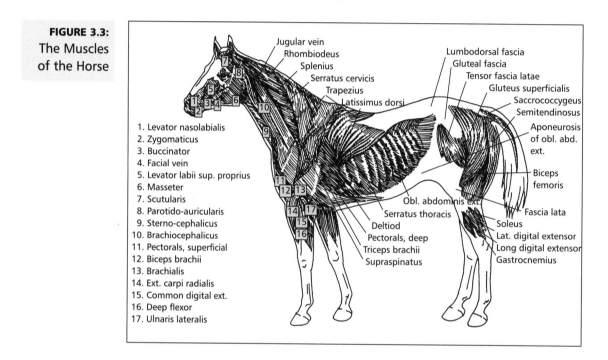

1. Levator nasolabialis
2. Zygomaticus
3. Buccinator
4. Facial vein
5. Levator labii sup. proprius
6. Masseter
7. Scutularis
8. Parotido-auricularis
9. Sterno-cephalicus
10. Brachiocephalicus
11. Pectorals, superficial
12. Biceps brachii
13. Brachialis
14. Ext. carpi radialis
15. Common digital ext.
16. Deep flexor
17. Ulnaris lateralis

Jugular vein
Rhombiodeus
Splenius
Serratus cervicis
Trapezius
Latissimus dorsi

Lumbodorsal fascia
Gluteal fascia
Tensor fascia latae
Gluteus superficialis
Saccrococcygeus
Semitendinosus
Aponeurosis of obl. abd. ext.
Biceps femoris
Fascia lata
Soleus
Lat. digital extensor
Long digital extensor
Gastrocnemius

Obl. abdominis ext.
Serratus thoracis
Deltiod
Pectorals, deep
Triceps brachii
Supraspinatus

ALERT

The contraction of muscles causes the production of lactic acid. Muscle fatigue results when there is too much of a buildup of lactic acid, causing a syndrome known as "tying up." Proper conditioning allows the horse to increase the muscles' ability to cope with lactic acid.

The Skeletal System

The horse's body is made up of 216 bones. The forelegs carry as much as 60 percent of the weight of the horse. By understanding the skeletal system of the horse, you can better understand how the horse moves and how movement may be hindered or aided when riding. For instance, in the diagram, you can readily see a huge bone at the shoulder just above and in front of the ribs. It isn't difficult to imagine that a saddle that rests too far ahead on the horse will interfere with movement of the shoulder structure.

FIGURE 3.4:
The Skeletal System of the Horse

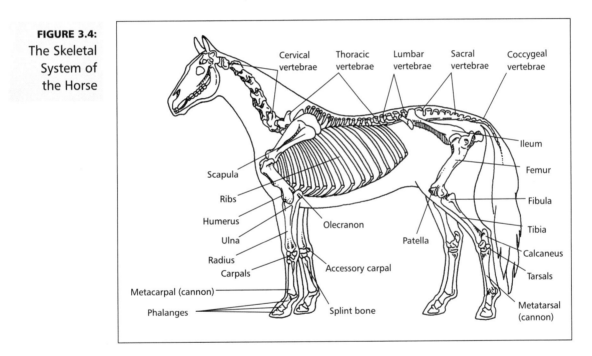

Here are some definitions relating to the bones. All of these parts of the bone are highly subject to injury.

- **Periosteum** is the layer of dense connective tissue covering each bone.
- **Joint** is the union of two bones whose position is maintained by ligaments, tendons, and a fibrous capsule.

- **Synovial membrane** is the connective tissue lining the inside of the joint.
- **Synovial fluid** allows for smooth movement of the joint.
- **Navicular bone** is a wedge-shaped bone in the foot that sits behind the coffin joint.
- **Bursae** are fluid-filled sacs between the tendons and the bones.

The Spine

The horse's spine is composed of eighteen thoracic and six lumbar vertebrae.

Arthritis

Arthritis is a significant problem in this athletic animal. The horse is inflicted with many specific arthritic conditions, including bone spavin (arthritis of the hock joint), osselets (arthritis of the fetlock joint), and omarthritis (arthritis of the shoulder joint).

X rays are used for arthritis diagnosis, and the typical treatment is pain-relieving medication and rest.

QUESTIONS?

What does conformation mean?
The overall structure of the horse is known as its **conformation**. Few horses, if any, have perfect conformation. What is considered good conformation depends a great deal on what you plan to do with the horse.

The Foot

The horse's foot is a complex and amazing apparatus. It not only holds a great amount of weight but also is able to withstand high impact from that weight. The hoof of a mature horse grows approximately a third of an inch a month. Proper trimming and shoeing by a good farrier when needed is critical to the horse's soundness.

FIGURE 3.5:
The Foot of
the Horse

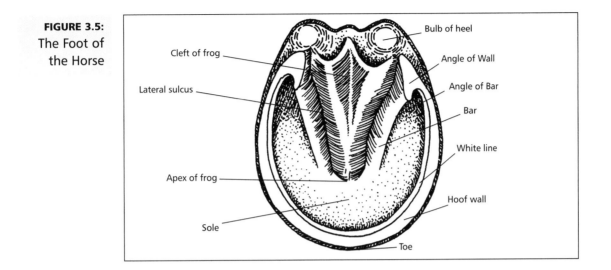

Bulb of heel

Cleft of frog

Angle of Wall

Angle of Bar

Lateral sulcus

Bar

White line

Apex of frog

Hoof wall

Sole

Toe

In Griffin and Gore's *Horse Owner's Veterinary Handbook,* an interesting comparison is made between the lower foreleg of the horse and the hand of the human:

- The knee or carpal joint in the horse corresponds to the human wrist.
- Everything below the horse's knee equals the bones of the human hand.
- Only three metacarpal bones are present in the horse (the cannon bone, splint bone, and fetlock joint, which equals the human knuckle joint), opposed to five in the human.
- The long pastern bone in the horse equals the proximal phalanx (the first bone in the finger).
- The outer insensitive laminae of the hoof corresponds to the fingernail.

FACTS

Horses have the unique ability to lock the stifle (see **FIGURE 3.7**), allowing them to relax the rest of their muscles and sleep while standing up without the possibility of falling down. This is possible because the horse has three patella ligaments in the stifle.

Shock Absorption

Five factors make possible the shock absorption properties of the hoof:

1. The digital cushion found deep within the foot
2. The hoof wall, which is the key structural support designed to take impact and spread it to the other shock-absorbing areas
3. The sole, which is concave and, therefore, doesn't impact the ground
4. The frog, a wedge of horn that is triangular in shape and presses into the digital cushion
5. The bulbs of the heel, which form the back of the frog and the bars alongside the frog

 **ESSENTIALS**

If your horse loses a shoe, keep a rubber protective boot on hand that slips over the horse's foot. You can save your horse discomfort and yourself lost riding time by protecting that bare hoof and calling your farrier immediately. These boots are also handy when you need to administer ointment to the hoof.

Vision

The horse's visual capabilities are unique and well suited to her needs. The uniqueness of the horse's vision contributes considerably to the horse's reputation for spooking easily. The horse's eye is not round, and therefore the retina and cornea are not equidistant from each other across the eye. In order to focus on an object, the horse needs to turn her head and focus with both eyes.

Another contributing factor to the horse's tendency to spook is that the placement of the eyes on either side of the head make the horse's vision largely monocular—she has one view of the world on the right side of her body and a different view on the left side. The horse can see as much as 350 degrees around her body, with a blind spot directly in front and directly behind. This independent vision allows the horse to be on the lookout for predators while grazing.

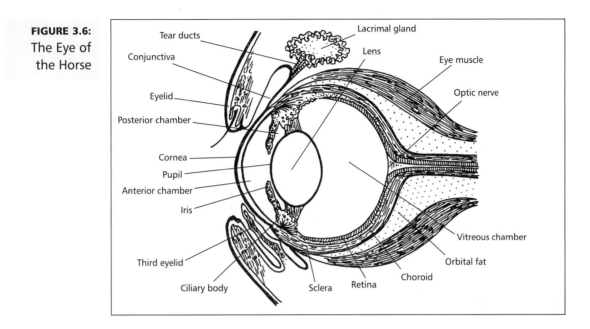

FIGURE 3.6:
The Eye of
the Horse

Labels: Tear ducts, Conjunctiva, Eyelid, Posterior chamber, Cornea, Pupil, Anterior chamber, Iris, Third eyelid, Ciliary body, Sclera, Retina, Choroid, Orbital fat, Vitreous chamber, Optic nerve, Eye muscle, Lens, Lacrimal gland

Well-Protected Eyes

Horses' eyes are surrounded by huge amounts of bone structure and set in a layer of fat that allows the eye to push back into a cavity, which keeps the eye well protected.

Problems

While the eye is well protected and eye problems are not prevalent, the horse can have problems with the eye, some causing blindness, that are similar to those of humans and other animals.

Conjunctivitis, an eye redness caused by irritated conjuntiva, is perhaps the most common and simple eye problem you may encounter. But red eye can be the sign of a more serious disease, such as an ulcer, so always be sure to check with your veterinarian.

The Respiratory System

The respiratory health of the horse is greatly impacted by equine management. Horses who spend a lot of time locked in closed stalls are subject to respiratory problems caused by constantly breathing urine odors. Anytime a horse is exposed to lots of dust—from hay, indoor arenas, dusty oats, and so on—chronic respiratory problems can develop.

Don't forget respiratory conditioning if you are planning a specific activity for your horse. Such conditioning can occur by gradually increasing the periods of trotting.

Heaves

Perhaps the most commonly known respiratory ailment is so-called heaves. Heaves is a chronic problem usually caused by dust and mold in the feed. Many horses who develop heaves either need to have their hay soaked in water before eating it or have to avoid hay altogether and instead eat commercially prepared complete feeds.

Pneumonia

As with humans, pneumonia in horses is caused by virus, bacteria, and foreign bodies in the lungs. Antibiotics may be administered and rest is typically prescribed. Your veterinarian will be able to make this diagnosis.

Skin

The best way to avoid skin problems is to help avoid broken skin (including lacerations from dangers in paddocks or stalls and abrasions from poor-fitting equipment) and, again, to practice a solid equine management program to reduce parasite exposure.

FACTS

Miniature pilorector muscles connect to the roots of the long hair of the horse's coat. When it is cold and these muscles contract, the long hairs stand up straight and trap air, which provides insulation. In winter, good grooming helps keep the coat free of mud that mats the hair and lessens its ability to provide this service.

The Skin's Job

The skin of the horse has all the same jobs as the skin of any animal:

- Skin provides a barrier to foreign objects.
- It serves as a huge sensory organ.
- It synthesizes vitamins.
- It provides insulation.

The Layers of the Skin

The skin has two main layers—the epidermis and the dermis—as well as a layer of fat just below its surface. Regular grooming helps the horse maintain a healthy hair coat by removing dirt and matted material and by increasing the production of sebum, an oily substance that helps the horse shed water and makes the coat shine.

FIGURE 3.7:
The Parts of the Horse

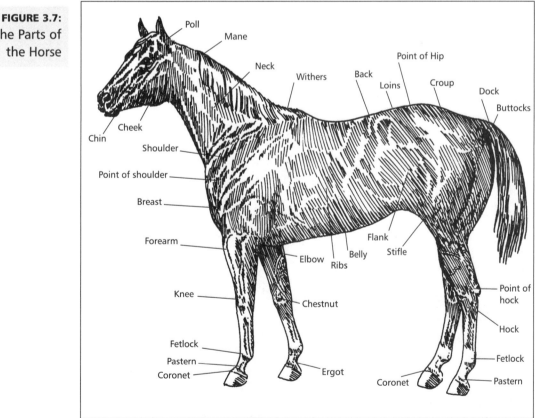

Knowledge Is Key

It would take several lifetimes to know and understand all the information that is currently available about the horse. However, take the time to learn at least the basics about how your horse operates. This knowledge will enable you to make better management decisions and help keep your horse fit, healthy, and ready to ride!

CHAPTER 4
Horse Behavior

Y our horse's behavior is perhaps the most important thing for you to understand and influence in order for the two of you to have the most satisfying relationship. How your horse behaves around you and in the barnyard is the key to your safety, as well as that of your horse and everyone who interacts with her.

This chapter covers the understanding of your horse's behavior as well as how to influence the handling of your horse (which is discussed in more detail in Chapter 11, "Handling").

Wild Herd Behavior

Horses are herd animals. In its simplest description, this means that in the wild, they would survive by roaming in groups. But herds are quite complex. They consist mostly of mares, called harem bands, who are serviced by one stallion that protects and defends the herd. The patriarch is the sole adult male horse in the herd; all the other males are young colts who will be driven out to live in a "bachelor band" when they are mature enough to become interested in breeding and represent a threat to the patriarch's harem.

There are also young fillies in the herd who will remain with the herd until they are either stolen by a stallion trying to start or increase his harem band, or are bred within the harem by their own father or by a new stallion who takes over the herd, which happens on an average of every two to three years.

QUESTIONS?

What is the flehman response?
The curling of the upper lip by a male horse in response to the scent of a female is referred to as the **flehman response.**

The dominant member of the herd, however, is a mare. This mare decides where the herd goes and, as the high-ranking member, gets first choice of food and water. Through a process of testing and retesting, all members of the herd will have come to understand and accept this as standard. If a member of the herd does not submit to the lead mare, the lead mare excommunicates the horse from the herd, driving him or her outside the group and leaving the horse vulnerable to predators and to finding its own food. The horse may learn and be accepted back, join a bachelor band if it's a stallion, or be scooped up by another stallion's harem if it's a mare.

In domestic horse life, stallions have the reputation for being dangerous and wanting what they want—which tends to be to mate with any mare in sight—whether or not there's a human being in the way. But anyone who has had mares knows that little compares with the bossiness of a mare, and that it in fact makes sense that a lead mare would boss the herd around!

The stallion keeps the herd together, and newcomers are not allowed into the established herd without the stallion's okay. With the mare and stallion dominating, all other members of the herd are part of a pecking order. As the herd dynamic changes—members die, foals are born, and youngsters age—the pecking order constantly adjusts. Age typically determines rank, with the youngsters being at the bottom, but as they grow older, these young horses constantly challenge and, thus, alter the status quo. In *Influencing Horse Behavior* (see Appendix A, "Resources"), Dr. Jim McCall puts it rather eloquently: "In the herd, the submissive must show respect to the dominant. The young must not invade the personal space of the elders. Higher ranking members of the herd are not to be ignored. Herd laws are consistent within all equine herds, only the individuals are different. This consistency gives the horse a sense of harmony. He knows how he fits into his world."

Domestic Herd Behavior

If you have more than one horse or keep your horse at a stable with other horses, you will have ample opportunity to see horse-to-horse behavior in action. Of course, the domestic "herd" dynamic is somewhat different from that of a wild herd. In the wild, the herd grows and changes according to breeding season, and there is a natural mix of younger and aging animals. In your backyard or at a boarding stable, the "herd" changes artificially, directed by humans according to a new horse bought or one sold, or a new boarder, and newcomers that need to mix into the herd often are of similar age, size, or even of the same sex as the existing herd members.

Nonetheless, watching groups of domestic horses interact can be the most fascinating part of being around horses. I could spend hours watching my three—an eleven-year-old gelding, an eight-year-old mare, and a four-year-old filly—sort things out in the course of their day together. The mare and gelding have lived together since the mare was six months old. The filly came into the picture when the mare was six; my mare has had a lot to say to the newcomer. The gelding just assumes the others know he's the elder statesman, and he occasionally lifts a leg or pins his ears as a reminder that nothing has changed, especially when one of the others thinks perhaps she might like to eat out of his hay pile. And that's just the tip of the conversational iceberg that takes place among these three throughout the entire day. Who gets to drink, who runs down the hill from the back field first and what position he or she takes when they get here, and how close they get to stand to each other are all under discussion, especially since the filly is constantly challenging her place in the arrangement.

Self-Preservation

The horse's instinct for self-preservation can easily control its behavior to a point that seems self-destructive. But it is so highly ingrained that the horse cannot help but listen to that nagging feeling if something seems to be threatening its very survival. The behavior a horse exhibits when concerned with its own survival can be very hard to understand.

ESSENTIALS   Learning about horse behavior and looking for the underlying reason from the horse's point of view can be fascinating and rewarding for both human and horse.

A friend who raises horses once had a yearling colt who shortly after he was weaned began to be more and more wary of my friend. The colt was in with a couple of other foals his age who were as friendly as all the other youngsters she'd raised over the years. Finally, she presented this horse and its growing problem to a horseman who was giving a clinic at her farm. He described the horse as having such a high degree of self-preservation instinct that things seemed threatening to him that didn't really bother most other horses. He showed the group watching him work with the colt how he would present himself to this horse and begin to change his behavior, teaching the young horse that he was a trustworthy human and not a threat. The horseman explained that most horses are so sensitive that they can understand when you mean them no harm, but that this particular horse's self-preservation instinct was so high that it ruled over his other sensitivities.

My friend expressed concern that many people would have instantly decided this horse had been abused. Yet I have known her for years, and the only "abuse" her animals get is an overdose of kindness!

Turning Horses Out Together

There is no denying that horse play can be very rambunctious, which is why people often are reluctant to let horses be loose together. Domestic horses, like wild horses, will establish a pecking order, and in determining their ranks, the scene can get a little wild with biting, kicking, charging, rearing, and other potentially harmful actions. Yes, horses can definitely hurt each other. But feral horses roaming in a "wild" state almost never injure each other. It is the domestic arrangement in which we keep horses that makes injury much more possible.

Horses would rather not be hurt, and most horses will wisely pay attention to each other's subtle signals and know when to avoid actual physical contact. A horse turned out with an established group of other horses will be completely aware at all times, reading the messages that the other horses are sending and acting accordingly. One would think that alone would be enough to ensure that you can stick horses together any time without them hurting each other. But there are at least two general things that humans do that mess up this natural order of things.

Not Enough Space

Horses, when turned out alone, should always have the absolute most space that you can carve out for them. However, when putting horses out together, a great amount of space is even more important. It never ceases to amaze me how far my mare will chase my filly to let her know where her real boundary line is. If the horse being chased has nowhere to go but over or through the fence to relieve itself of the situation, that is where the horse will go. But if there is ample space, then the lower-echelon horse has room to learn the lesson of boundaries and won't get hurt in the process.

FACTS

Imprinting is a specific desensitizing (and controversial) method used with a newborn foal. Robert Miller, DVM, has spent years developing the theory and technique of imprinting with horses. His technique involves handling the newborn foal extensively to accustom it to events it will encounter later in life. Imprinting is only as successful as the skill and knowledge of the person using it. Decide for yourself whether imprinting is right for your horses by reading Dr. Miller's *Imprint Training of the Newborn Foal* (Western Horseman, 1991).

Some horses don't put on a chase like my mare does but instead may back up and kick with both back feet at their opponent or lunge with bared teeth. If the space is big enough and there are no corners and small alleyways to get trapped in, the horse getting the worse end of the deal can stay out of reach of teeth or hind feet. But if the space is too small, the horse can easily be pinned in the corner of a corral and kicked badly. If given enough space, a horse's choice will almost always be to simply get out of Dodge as requested. And if the ample space they are in is a grassy pasture, most horses would be too occupied with their nose in the grass to spend much time getting in arguments anyway!

Socializing Horses, Especially When Young

Horse owners often make the choice to never put their horse in with another horse, for fear that they will hurt each other. Although this choice is understandable, a solitary life is, I think, very unfair to the horse. Horses crave companionship and interaction with their own kind. And even though they surely have some innate knowledge of the meaning of signals given off by other horses, the unsocialized horse often doesn't understand pecking order and the seriousness of the signals.

Many times horses hurt one another because two or more horses are suddenly thrown together. If just one of them is unaccustomed to being with other horses, problems will develop fast. For example, if an unsocialized horse walks over to the hay pile of another horse, the horse with possession of the hay, Ms. Dominant, will likely pin her ears, cock a leg, or give some other threat that says "I'm boss, this is my hay pile, and I'm not sharing." The unsocialized horse is not likely to understand dominant and submissive standings in the herd and, therefore, won't understand what the signals mean. If he keeps coming closer, a bigger reaction is likely to follow. When this happens, one of the horses could easily get hurt. And thus the cycle continues, because, of course, when people hear of events such as this, they are even less inclined to put horses together.

Horses in "rental"-type trail rides are usually pretty socialized, but they often haven't learned to control their actions when around humans. A dangerous situation can develop when, for example, a novice rider doesn't understand the warning signals that the horse is giving to another about following too closely. A good kick from the other horse can result, so always keep safe distances between horses.

Introducing Horses to Each Other

The best time to socialize horses is when they are young. When young, they love to play and do so mostly without seriously hurting each other. At the same time, they learn to read each other's signals and coexist peacefully. Of course, the dam will have taught her youngster some things, but that doesn't always translate into understanding the same signals from a horse that is not his mother. And a horse who has learned only from his mother may not know that it can be hurt, since the dam would typically not do anything to really hurt her offspring.

A horse that is well socialized will more easily be able to get along with a new horse or group of horses. But even then, to be fair to your horse, you should put it with other horses who are socialized as well. When I temporarily moved to the Minneapolis area, I boarded my mare at a large boarding facility. After she had settled in for a couple of days, I was fine with her being turned out with a group of other boarders. The pastures and turnouts were large enough, and none of the horses looked exceptionally banged up. My mare was well socialized, and I knew from watching her in the past that she was very good at avoiding trouble with other horses. The horses at this facility clearly were well socialized and were given the chance to live artificially like a "herd" even if for just part of the day.

When I bring a new horse home, I blend it into the established "herd" gradually over the course of at least four stages: I let them see one another, put them side by side in corrals, put the new horse out with one other horse, and put the group together. I don't care how many days or weeks this takes, I size up how each seems to be reacting to the other and move to the next stage accordingly. Here are the steps I recommend:

1. First, put the horse in a pen where there is no common fence line with the other horses. (I use my round pen, which I don't use for everyday turnout.) That way everyone gets to see and hear the newcomer, and the newcomer gets to check out its surroundings without the potential of trashing fences and getting hurt in the process.

2. After the yelling at each other and racing around the pen settles down, usually in a day or two, the second step is to move the new horse to a corral adjacent to the existing herd. My corral has an electric fence line around the corral board fences—mostly to keep them from chewing the boards all day—that helps keep them from getting too friendly over the wood fence. But it is still open enough for the horses to touch noses, squeal, and do all the other things they like to do for introductions, without the ability to actually strike each other. If the horses are stalled at night, add the step of putting the new horse beside one of the horses she will eventually be turned out with, preferably in stalls where they can at least see each other; this also gives them more chances to get accustomed to each other from a distance.

3. When they've settled down and can ignore each other, which usually takes a day or two, it's time to put at least a couple of them together. If the new horse is going to join an existing herd of more than one other horse, pull all of the old residents out into other corrals or stalls for an afternoon or two, and let the newcomer and just one horse get accustomed to each other. This really all depends on how they have acted thus far and what the personalities of the existing herd members are like.

4. Finally, when you do put them all together, set out piles of hay at a good distance apart to give them something else to preoccupy themselves with

besides each other. It can work like a charm—by the time they finish the hay pile, they look up and say, "Hey, it's you, the horse I've seen over the fence for a few days," and go off and have a drink or nap in the sun.

Inevitably they will check each other out, and some squealing and maybe even some striking and a little biting may go on. Typically, this sounds a whole lot worse than it actually is—they seem to wait until the second you walk around the corner of the barn to squeal and grunt at each other. You run back expecting to see slices of horse flesh hanging from one of the horse's mouths, but what you find is the two offenders looking at you and seeming to wonder why you suddenly reappeared.

FACTS

If you're a fan of the classic television show *Mr. Ed*, starring a talking palomino, check out *www.mister-ed.com*. This Web site includes sound clips, historical background, information about the cast, and any recent news mentions that the show has received. Also included is an episode guide of all of the 143 episodes broadcast between 1961 and 1966.

If after a couple of days, two of the group just won't leave each other alone, you may have to separate them or work on some new groupings.

Horses, like other animals, communicate by making sounds. These include:

- **Snort and/or blowing sound:** Horses tend to make a snorting noise—sometimes a short snort and other times an elongated sound—when they are afraid of something. This seems to make the horse appear even larger and more impressive to the potential danger.
- **Nicker:** This low, friendly rat-ta-tat-tat sound is one that horses use as a greeting.
- **Neigh/whinny:** High-pitched, long, and loud, a whinny is another greeting that can be used for long distances.
- **Squeal:** This somewhat unpleasant short high-pitched sound is the one you'll hear when two horses are getting to know each other.

- **Scream:** This sound happens in a true fight, often between competing stallions, something that we rarely witness in domesticated horse life.

Grouping by Age

Grouping by age range is much more logical than grouping by sex. Putting a very young horse—a horse under two years old—in with a group of older horses can have bad results. These youngsters can get hurt just because of their size differences. After the age of two or three, most horses (and definitely the stock horse breeds) tend to be of substantial size compared to adults and are a little less delicate. If at all possible and at the very least, make sure a young horse has a couple of companions of similar age in the group.

FACTS

Horses may seem "stupid" to the general public because they are known to exhibit fear of things such as rocks or a piece of paper blowing in the wind. My response to people who ask me if horses are stupid is that horses think and make decisions like horses. We humans smoke cigarettes despite dire health warnings and are reported in the daily papers for murdering each other for pocket change. So who are we to call horses stupid?

The Stallion Dilemma

Of course, stallions present a different issue altogether and clearly cannot run with mares with whom you do not want them to breed. I have, on the other hand, heard of many stallions who run with groups of geldings. However, these stallions have been very well socialized.

A Word of Caution

Keep in mind that this information represents some guidelines and some ideas that are based on what I or others have tried and found to work in grouping horses. There is always the situation that defies all "rules of thumb"—the horse living alone that actually prefers it that way, the foal who lives with a group of aged geldings that gets along just fine, or the horse that gets seriously injured in what had been for months a "perfect" grouping of horses. With horses, the unexpected truly does happen, and ultimately you are the decision maker when it comes to your horse.

Domestic horses are products of their environment and of whatever education they have received from humans. Their "education" is not just specific "training" but occurs every moment a human is interacting with them, from riding to grooming to just picking manure out of the paddock when the horse is in it.

Maybe your horse deserves a nice rub around the ears after a workout. But instead of him pounding on you like you're a post, maybe it would be a little nicer for the both of you if Rubby could look forward to a gentle grooming around the head and ears with a towel and a nice soft brush. And be sure you are doing the rubbing. The horse doesn't need to rub back; he can just relax and enjoy the attention. Let him rub later on the tree out in his pasture if he wants to.

Even if you've been giving your horse the wrong message all these years—if he's been rummaging around your pockets and nipping at you, flinging off the halter and rushing off to the grain bucket, knocking you out of the way to get to the hay pile, or moving off before you are even mounted and settled in the saddle—it's never too late to start teaching new messages! Although it's going to be harder to undo what has been done, horses are pretty smart and can learn new things if you perfect your ability to teach them. It's entirely up to you.

Learning the Signals

After observing horses and how they interact with each other, you can begin to understand some of the early signals that a horse might be giving. In other words, the horse almost always does something first that serves as a signal to an upcoming action. World-class horseman Ray Hunt has a now-famous line: "What happened before what happened happened?" That's the place you want to learn to be aware of. Before a horse can kick out with a hind leg, it almost always has to shift its weight off the leg it plans to kick with. If you learn to be aware of the weight shift, you will never have to worry about the kick. There's even most likely a step before that weight shift, like a glance back with ears slightly pinned. You can make good use of increased awareness in both handling and riding horses. Remember: Horses are experts at not expending any more energy than necessary, so they will most likely give you some signals. It's up to you to pick up on them.

Leading by Respect, Not Fear

Horses naturally look for a leader to tell them how things are. It is the way of the herd. In the horse/human relationship, it makes sense for the human to be the leader. Everyone stays a little safer that way, since sometimes what a horse thinks is the best idea—for example, to bolt for home across that major highway—often isn't in the best interest of both parties. (Of course, sometimes the human's idea isn't in the best interest of both parties either, but that is the topic for another book.)

FACTS

Clever Hans was a horse in Berlin whose schoolmaster owner, Wilhelm von Osten, taught to solve mathematical equations, answer geography questions, identify musical scores, and do other things that we don't associate with a horse's normal range of knowledge. A test was eventually conducted that determined that von Osten was giving signals to Clever Hans from a spot behind the horse. Unless you knew that horses can see almost completely behind them, you wouldn't have guessed this was taking place.

Being the leader doesn't have to preclude having a partnership with your horse. And it definitely doesn't mean you have to establish a relationship with your horse that is based on fear—in fact, that is exactly what you don't want. A horse can follow its leader either out of fear or out of respect, and to the novice horse handler, the outcome of either of these approaches may look the same. However, with experience, you will see that they are actually quite different. Of course, I absolutely advocate gaining your horse's respect; the lives, thoughts, and feelings of animals, to me, are no less valuable than those of humans. And you can feel that way about horses and still not let them walk all over you.

Some horses are natural leaders themselves; they can be the most challenging and the most interesting to work with. If you are a beginner, you will probably want to get some help with such horses. These horses seem to think, "Well, if this human isn't going to be the leader, then I am." A horse who seems a bit of a rogue in the hands of a beginner can be a gentle horse when handled by an experienced horse person.

To Move or Be Moved

Horses decide the position of other horse herd members and human members of their herd according to who the movers are. Higher ranking herd members do not need to exert much effort to get lower ranking herd mates to move out of their space (or to not move into it). Ears back or a leg barely raised can be enough.

If dominance is determined by who does the moving, the human needs to be the mover, not the movee. This is not easy—every interaction you have with your horse presents an opportunity to be moved. You always need to be aware of this, even when you are just going into your horse's paddock to fill the water tub.

I'm not at all suggesting that you need to be *aggressive* with your horse, but you may need to learn to be *assertive*. Pay attention to where your horse is when you enter his space and what he does as you interact with him. For instance, a common reaction of a young horse on a halter rope who is learning to lead and move around you respectfully is to drop his shoulder in to you and push you out of his way if he is confused by what you want. This is the kind of thing you need to nip in the bud immediately. If you move a step back when your horse drops his shoulder, he has learned a big lesson about his ability to move you. The horse with the type of personality that will take advantage of this kind of experience will present you with all kinds of related behavior to deal with. Even the most submissive horse will remember that he can simply move you out of the way when a real crisis comes up. (See Chapter 11 for more on this subject.)

If you watch a horse signal another horse to, for example, not get near a particular pile of hay, the first thing she might do is pin her ears a little and jerk her head at the other horse. Socialized horses know those early signals—and they will either continue and challenge the horse for her pile or, more likely, move off. After a few times, the horse protecting the hay pile will only have to pin her ears while still eating or lift her head, and the other horse will know that today is not a good day to share hay. You can learn to recognize signals (e.g., the drop in the shoulder or, eventually, even a look in her eye) and then redirect the horse from that potential action before she actually follows through.

How to Be Safe in the Group

You've safely integrated all the horses on your property or your horse in among the group where it lives. Now the human comes not only in with the horse but also within the group of horses. Uh oh.

First, if you feed the group all together, you are going to find pecking-order issues being duked out in squeals and grunts during mealtimes. I personally prefer to feeding my horses in separate pens and allowing them the benefit of eating their meals in peace. But if you choose to feed them all together, there are a couple of things to consider:

- The pecking order system will be in high gear at feeding time, especially about grain. The safest thing to do would be to set up your feeding area so that you can feed them without going in with the group. You are better off not being accidentally in the line of fire when Trigger tells Bucky for the umpteenth time that he eats from the third bucket from the barn wall. If you have to go in with the group and it is a little more unruly than you can handle, carry a flag (a 3- or 4-foot metal or fiberglass rod with a piece of cloth attached to one end and comfortable handle on the other) or something that can help you establish your personal space and help them learn that you are not to be mauled at feeding time.
- You will need to either spread hay piles far enough apart so that one horse doesn't guard three hay piles or use a bunk feeder large enough to accommodate the number of horses you have—and large enough to provide the appropriate amount of space they will need to eat it from the same feeder!

Ultimately, you need to set up your feeding space in as safe a way as possible. And you may want to consider those times when you need to have someone else feed the horses. I prefer to set up my place so that no one who is unfamiliar with my horses and my handling preferences has to go in with my horses and interact with them while they are loose. Instead, the feeder can do almost everything from the other side of the fence.

ESSENTIALS

If you can't watch horse behavior in real life, you might enjoy some of the following movies:

Black Beauty
The Horse in the Gray Flannel Suit
The Horse Whisperer
Into the West
Lucky Luke

National Velvet
The Red Pony
Speedy
White Mane
Wild Hearts Can't Be Broken

Herd Bound and Barn Sour

Because horses are herd animals and territory is important to them, most are bothered by being separated from their group or taken away from the barn. Some horses exhibit this displeasure so subtly that only the most experienced horse handler would even notice it. Others exhibit it so graphically that you can't help but notice—say, when you are being mowed down by a distraught horse dancing around on the end of a lead rope screaming for its pal or when you are on a runaway horse who comes to a screeching halt only when he reaches the barn aisle.

Chances are you'll experience something somewhere in between, and you might even attribute the behavior to another cause. Don't be fooled—the horse who plods along on the ride away from the barn but "jigs" on the ride home is not suddenly peppy for no reason.

The way to actually deal with barn sourness and herd bound behavior will come up in the chapter on handling, but the important thing is to learn to offer your horse the support she needs in order to be comfortable with you while away from her equine friends. She needs to know that you are nice to be with, that you have a keen sense of her need for a pecking order, and that when things aren't looking so great, she doesn't need to race back to the barn but can turn to you to help her through it. In order to succeed in having your horse have this kind of faith in you, you need to learn to be totally consistent, completely unwavering, and infinitely reliable in your support and in the boundaries you establish. You need to understand what is happening when barn sour behavior arises. Instead of being convinced by well-meaning advice to turn to new and bigger bits or changes in feeding programs, get to the root of the problem and up the level of your relationship with your horse a notch.

Stable Vices

Stable vices are basically bad habits that horses develop typically from being left in a confined area too long. People think that confined horses are bored, and to counter their boredom, they hang plastic milk jugs in their stalls or give them balls to play with or mount roller toys in the corner. Horses, in my humble opinion, do not get bored in the sense that people do. Horses develop stable vices not because they are bored but because they are frustrated and stressed about being confined; confinement is completely against their natural way of existing. They are large animals with nomadic lifestyles. They need to move that big body of theirs around at will. Horses who roam freely most of the time and get ridden regularly actually seem to enjoy some time snuggled up in a nicely bedded stall.

Here are some of the common stable vices:

- **Cribbing:** Cribbing is perhaps the most insidious, most well-known, and worst stable vice. When a horse cribs, it grips its top front teeth on some hard edge, usually the top of a stall door or a fence board, pulls back, and makes a grunting noise—and does it over and over and over again. This is an addictive behavior that, once learned, typically can never be eliminated but only controlled. The addiction has been discovered to come from a release of natural stress-relieving endorphins that the horse experiences each time it does this.

Horses can either learn to crib accidentally or they can learn it from the horse in the next stall or a paddock mate who cribs on the fence boards. Cribbing can be expensive—when a 1,000-pound horse pulls back on something time and time again, that something, be it a fence board, a stall door, or a feed tub screwed into the wall, gets a lot of stress. Cribbing holds numerous potential major health issues for the horse; for example, the front teeth will show unnatural wear. And some horses are more interested in their addiction than in eating.

Some people don't mind having a horse with this vice, but if you are in the market for a horse, I suggest you avoid a cribber. (Although cribbing doesn't affect riding at all, it is technically considered an unsoundness, and anyone selling a horse is obligated to tell you about this habit.) If you board your horse and notice a horse nearby cribbing, get your horse moved out of the cribbing horse's sight (and preferably earshot).

If you have a horse that cribs, or yours develops the habit, keep it outside all the time in an environment where there is little to crib on—electric fencing instead of board fencing; feed buckets loose on the ground, not attached to walls; a shelter that has no edges inside for the horse to grab onto, and so on. The most addicted cribbers will find amazing ways to satisfy their addiction. There are anti-cribbing collars you can buy; they need to be adjusted perfectly and seem to be effective.

QUESTIONS?

What is meant by sound and unsound?
If the horse is perfectly healthy, it is said to be "**sound.**" If the horse is temporarily lame or has some problems eating, it is considered "**unsound.**" Anything that adversely affects a horse's health is considered an "unsoundness." If the horse's problem is chronic, the horse is "permanently unsound."

- **Weaving:** This is typically seen in a horse in a stall. The horse stands at the door and weaves back and forth, back and forth, shifting its weight from one front leg to the other. This uneasy type of horse doesn't take confinement well. And the problem will escalate if he develops any lameness issues that require immobility, because weaving is almost impossible to control physically. So, if your horse starts to weave, you need to get the horse into a better frame of mind.

- **Digging/pawing:** This habit is as much annoying as it is anything, although it can cause uneven foot wear for barefoot horses on hard ground. Some horses paw anywhere in their stalls, sometimes digging up giant craters with both front feet. Some will paw right at the entrance to the stall, setting a nice booby trap for you to sink into.

Encouraging Good Behavior

When you earn a horse's trust, you have earned a lot. However, once you have it, you can't ever betray that trust—it's hard, but the minute you let someone talk you into trying that bigger bit or whatever, you jeopardize your horse's faith that you are consistent and trustworthy. Go with your good instincts, and if you feel unsure, enlist the aid of people whose instincts are similar to yours. This doesn't mean you should avoid exploring new ideas. However, using your good instincts as a guide will help ensure your horse's trust in you.

ALERT

According to Dr. Jim McCall, author of *Influencing Horse Behavior*: "Horses . . . do not build relationships on like but rather on respect. . . . You are going to have a difficult time training your horse [if] he perceives you as the submissive member of the partnership."

The behavior of a horse that does not trust you can look pretty ugly, and yet the horse is not to blame. Find some mentors in the horse world that you can turn to before you reach the point where you can't handle your own horse. A trusting, respectful horse in the hands of a trustworthy, respectful human is wonderful to behold and even more wonderful to experience.

CHAPTER 5

A Horse of Your Own

Now that you've had an overview of the different breeds of horses to choose from, know a little bit about the anatomy and physiology of these large and complicated animals, and have some sense of their behavioral traits, it's time to get a horse of your own! However, I hope you read this entire book before you start looking seriously.

There are many places to find horses for sale and many different circumstances under which to buy them—backyard sales, auctions, sale barns, and so forth. You will hear as many good stories as bad stories about each way of buying a horse, but there are some places that are better than others for a beginner to look. I'll tell you all the details in this chapter.

Deciding What You Want

Before you start looking, you should make a short list of some traits you would like in the horse you are planning to buy.

Age

A rule of thumb for a beginner is to stay away from horses under four or five years old. In actuality, there are lots of horses between three and five who are a lot better educated than many horses in their teens, and probably are a lot safer for a beginner, but such youngsters have been handled and started under saddle by very reputable people who work with horses at a deep level. You need to know who you are dealing with to trust a youngster to be a safe bet for a beginner.

Between five and ten years old, many horses seem to gain some natural mellowing (although this is far from always the case!), and it usually means the horse has simply had more experiences. But, ultimately, age is not the biggest factor for determining a horse's safety. There is a saying that a horse will always eventually rise up or come down to the level of her rider/handler; many twenty-plus-year-old horses are happy to run away with an unskilled rider if they feel unsupported in scary situations (which can include something as basic as leaving the barnyard).

FACTS

The Thoroughbred Man O' War was born in 1917, a product of careful breeding. He was first raced as a two-year-old on June 6, 1919, at Belmont, a race he won by 6 lengths. The chestnut colt was 16.2 hands as a three-year-old, and he lost only one race in his career. Although never a contender for the Triple Crown (he never ran the Kentucky Derby), he won both the Preakness and the Belmont and regularly beat world and U.S. records.

History

Even young horses can have passed through numerous hands. Find out what you can about how many owners the horse has had and about the circumstances of each sale. The horse's current seller may not know much or may not offer much of what he or she does know in order not to sour your outlook on the horse, but it's worth asking. Having too many owners can cause behavioral problems in horses, simply from having been handled inconsistently—or the horse may actually have changed hands often specifically because of behavioral problems.

Education

One of the most important things for you to know about your prospective horse is its level of education. Find out, if you can, who educated the horse as a youngster and who started him under saddle. How did it go? Who took care of the horse's education from there? And how was the horse educated? Was it trained with whips and spurs? Was it trained in the mechanical but effective approach of conditioned response? Or was it educated through a style of horsemanship in which the horse's natural instincts are used to the rider's advantage and the horse is taught through respect, not fear? Can you follow through with the method? If the horse will stop only if you dig spurs into its shoulders, are you prepared to do this? Or, better yet, are you prepared to spend the time and money for someone to re-educate the horse with you?

Color

How important is coloring? It may not be a good reason to buy a particular horse, but let's face it—it matters. Some people are attracted to paint horses and collect them for their color alone. It does help to like the color of the horse you'll look at every day, but when you finally find the horse whose temperament and education fits you, you won't even notice that it has pink polka dots.

Size

Size doesn't have to matter, but it can. Most people with large builds like to have a horse of some substance under them. A tall person typically would like the horse to be tall too. Short people can go either way. But a beginner rider who is short can gain a lot of confidence on a smaller horse. Believe me, it *is* farther to the ground on a tall horse than a short one!

Conformation

Buying a horse that is well put together makes a lot of other things easier too, such as shoeing and saddle fitting. Although you learned some basic information on conformation in Chapter 3, "Anatomy," an experienced horse person can really help you out. If you have an idea ahead of time that there is something specific you plan to do with the horse—such as jumping, dressage, barrel racing—look for conformation specifics that lend the horse to that activity. Any horse is suitable to do almost any of these things for fun, but if you intend to compete, your equine athlete needs to have some innate ability in your chosen event.

Cost

Maybe this comes first in your case or maybe your price range is wide enough that it is less of a priority. Chances are, though, you have a top limit of how much you can spend on a horse. Although there are some market standards, they are pretty loose—what you consider a trait that should bring the price of a horse down may be of no consequence to the seller. The seller will have his or her own reasons for setting a price, including how much they have invested in the horse for things such as training. Expect to spend from zero to $10,000 for your first horse, with anything in between being fair game. If your top price is, say, $1,500, there are many horses out there for you; it just may take a little longer to find exactly the right one.

Places to Buy Horses

Now that you have a general description in mind of the horse you are looking for, it's time to start scouting around.

Classified Ads

If you live in a horsey part of the country, you may find a lot of horses for sale in the classified section of the daily newspaper. If that isn't the case where you live, you won't get very far with a newspaper. However, you can find classified listings in any of the regional equine publications. Classified publications usually have a horse section. For instance, in Maine, there is *Uncle Henry's* (525 Eastern Avenue, P.O. Box 9104, Augusta, Maine 04332-9104; 207-623-1411; *www.unclehenrys.com*), which is a weekly classified listing that has categories for everything from antiques to snowmobiles, and includes livestock and, specifically, "horses and accessories." These listings are free to the noncommercial advertiser, and the magazine itself sells on the newsstand for $1.50 or by subscription. In New Hampshire, the state Department of Agriculture puts out *The Weekly Market Bulletin,* a weekly newsletter that contains classified ads that list horses. Most state agriculture departments have a similar publication. Keep your horse-to-be profile in mind as you read the listings and circle any that come close. Don't make calls on horses that don't fit one of the major points in your profile; it just wastes your time and money, as well as the time of the person who is selling the horse.

FACTS

If you are well connected in the local horse community, you may come across free horses. Many are given away because they have frightened their owners, or because the owner no longer has time or interest in riding, has tried to sell the horse without success, and feels badly that the horse is just hanging around. Just remember, horses are never given away because they are *too* well educated or too well behaved.

Most of the time the horses listed in the classifieds are backyard horses being sold by owners of one or two horses. You'll need to travel around your region a bit, from backyard to backyard, but this is a very legitimate and worthwhile way to scout for a horse.

Here are some phrases you may run across in the classified ads:

- **Broodmare only:** A broodmare is a mare that has soundness problems that prevent her from being ridden but don't prevent her from being used for breeding.
- **Companion horse only:** This horse cannot be ridden and its only use would be to mow the lawn or keep another horse company.
- **Good foundation; needs finishing:** This usually describes a horse who has had the fundamentals and probably is farther along than "green broke" but still is in the advanced beginner stage of its education as a riding horse.
- **Grade:** Grade describes a horse that displays the characteristics of a specific breed but whose breeding history is unknown and doesn't allow it to be registered.
- **Green broke:** Typically this means the horse has had a saddle on and tolerates being ridden but hasn't had many hours under saddle.

QUESTIONS?

What is a backyard horse?
A **backyard horse** is one that lives at the home of its owner. People can have more than one backyard horse depending on the size of their backyard. The term has been used to indicate horses of lesser quality, but that, of course, is in the eye of the beholder!

- **Husband horse:** A husband horse is a nice, calm horse that tolerates inconsistent riding, tends to take care of its rider, and is a horse you would be comfortable with as a beginner or part-time rider.
- **Prospect:** This is a horse that the owner feels has the potential to excel in a particular type of activity if it is educated to do so.
- **Rides E/W:** This horse has been ridden in both English and Western tack.
- **Ring sour:** This typically describes a horse that has been shown competitively for a number of years and is exhibiting signs of being sick of the show ring.

- **UTD on shots and worming:** This horse is up to date on its annual vaccinations and deworming program.
- **Willing over fences:** This horse has been jumped successfully (i.e., it doesn't tend to balk).

Breeders

If you are interested in a specific breed of horse, you will definitely want to visit reputable breeders within the range that you feel comfortable traveling. Also consider what you would be willing to pay to get the horse to you if you bought one (trailering is often charged by the mile). Buying from a breeder may be a bit more expensive than some other sources of horses, but what you get if you go to reputable people is the best selection of top-quality horses. Breeders often have young animals because, logically, they breed and sell the offspring. But many breeders, in order to keep a wide selection, sell on commission other people's horses within their chosen breed. You should bring someone more experienced than you are with you to a breeder, since breeders are professionals and experts, and it's important to understand what they are telling and showing you.

Auctions

There is probably a horse auction taking place somewhere near you on average of once a month or so. Check the regional horse publications. Horse auctions work like most auctions—people bring their horses, a professional auctioneer sells them, and a percentage goes to the auction house. The horse is led and/or ridden in front of the audience, and the highest bidder wins. Usually there are contingencies for vet checks and for you to test ride the horse, but you need to know these details before you hold up your bidder's number. If this method of buying a horse interests you at all, you should plan to visit a few auctions before considering buying. You can get great horses this way, but you need to have some experience or fully trust your advisor.

Sale Barns

Some horse facilities are set up in the business of buying and selling horses. They typically are not breeders and do not breed their own livestock or specialize in one breed of horse. They are an outlet for people who want to sell a horse but don't have the time, expertise, or interest to sell it on their own. Typically, the horses are a wide range of breeds at a wide range of ages and prices.

The Internet

Many horse sites on the Internet have listings of horses for sale. Many barns who breed and sell horses have their own Web sites. This can be a great way to narrow your search; you even can see photos of prospects. And it can give you a sense of what the horse market is like. But ultimately you should see the horse in person. So again, either limit your search to your state or region or be prepared to fly or drive some distance to see the horse. And you'll want your experienced horse person to come with you, which adds to the complication and expense of looking long distance.

Professional Trainers

People who educate horses for a living often know of horses that are being sold. Sometimes they have horses for sale themselves that are at their barn for further education, specifically in order for the horse to be more saleable. Making a few calls to barns where horses are trained may bring up a few prospects. Expect these horses to be on the higher end of your price range, since the seller is not only paying the trainer a commission but also paying for ongoing training and board while the horse is there for sale.

Equine Rescue Shelters

Getting a horse from a rescue shelter can be inexpensive up front, but less experienced people can find themselves with more than they bargained for. Horses often become rescue cases because inexperienced people bring a horse home and unintentionally let bad habits crop up that develop further into dangerous habits, making the owner afraid to handle the horse. The vicious cycle starts when the dangerous habit makes the owner so fearful of the horse that the horse never gets out of its stall, as that would require someone to lead it to the corral. Some owners stop feeding their horses because they are afraid to open the stall door at all. At some point, the owner, or perhaps a concerned friend or neighbor, calls the equine rescue and the horse is taken away (an oversimplification of the process, of course, but basically this is what often happens).

ALERT

Often what you are buying at a sale barn is someone else's problem. You often don't get the opportunity to discuss the horse with the owner. Reputable sellers won't sell a beginner a horse that the beginner can't handle, so it's important to learn who is reputable and who is not.

Shelters usually work with the horses first to bring them back to health, and some re-educate the horse in order to increase the odds of a successful placement. If you are experienced enough to carry through with the work the shelter has done or to re-educate the horse yourself, getting a horse from a shelter can be an extremely rewarding experience. Some horses just simply needed a little better handling from the start and are fine once they are under the care of different people.

Many rescue cases are horses who have chronic health problems and whose owners could no longer afford the care the horses needed or simply lost interest in them because they couldn't ride anymore. Navicular disease, arthritis, and chronic respiratory problems are just a short list of diseases that can make horses unrideable or able to take only light riding. (As you'll see in Chapter 10, "Beyond Conventional Health Care," there are some things that you can do to improve chronic problems like this.) It can be very rewarding to give these horses a home as a companion animal to your one riding horse, if you have the time, money, and energy to care for them.

Buying from a Distance

Horses are shipped around the country, even around the world, all the time, but a beginner doesn't need to take the time and go to the expense of buying from such a distance. There are lots of good horses within a few hours' drive of your own home. While it can be fun to search the country and go look at horses in distant states, you might wait to do that kind of thing until you are a more experienced horse buyer. Why not put the travel money into the horse itself, either to buy a horse further along in its education or to have the horse and/or yourself educated once you get her?

Bring a Trusted Friend

If you are new to horses, the most important thing you can do is bring someone who is experienced along with you. This trusted person needs to be someone who knows your skill level and preferably has nothing to gain or lose from the transaction.

ESSENTIALS

The best person to bring with you when looking at horses is simply a horse-savvy friend who has nothing to gain from the purchase except you talking *ad nauseam* about your new horse!

Some people bring their instructor along if they've been taking lessons for a while, or their trainer—the person they plan to have work with the horse for them (and, I hope, with the two of you together, too) when they first get it. Just remember that both trainer and instructor have something to gain in the long run; that doesn't make them a bad choice, but their opinions will be naturally based on their own ulterior motives, good or bad, no matter how unbiased they try to be.

Visiting Your Prospects

You've found a horse that fits all your criteria. You've talked with the seller, and everything she told you about the horse makes you even more interested in him. You've arranged a time to come and see the horse. What now?

First, line up that friend. If you are a beginner rider, bring a friend who would be willing to ride the horse for you. Do whatever it is you do—yoga, meditate, drink hot tea—to calm yourself so that you don't rush into anything. Definitely do not bring a horse trailer on your first visit! If the horse turns out to be exactly what you want, it helps to be prepared with a deposit, but it may be best to leave your money home the first time around.

Although you'd like to visit your prospect unexpectedly at some point, the first time you go will probably be at a time agreed upon by you and the owner. The owner will probably have the horse all buffed up for you, and in a stall or small paddock. She may even have the horse already saddled and waiting in crossties in the aisle. People selling horses spend a lot of time showing them to prospective buyers, so they might want to speed things along a little on your first visit. But during the second visit, when you are much more serious, maybe even ready to put down a deposit if all goes well again, tell the seller you want to see the horse caught and saddled, maybe even to catch and saddle the horse yourself.

Though a possibility, I doubt there is much in the way of drugging (i.e., tranquilizers or some other substance that temporarily masks the horse's ill behavior) going on in the horse-selling business. However, there are some mild calming substances or herbal treatments (which a seller is unlikely to tell you about) that can disguise some traits in a horse that might create a little surprise when you get the horse in your own backyard. Popping in unexpectedly to see the horse can be an educational experience.

In the excitement of the moment while visiting a horse you might buy, you can forget to ask some important questions. Refer to the following checklist when visiting prospects. Don't put your money down until you have at least learned the answers to the questions listed here!

General Background
___ How old is the horse?
___ How long have you owned her? Where did you buy her from?
___ Is she registered? (If so, ask to look at her papers. If not, ask what they know about her breeding.)

Riding Experience
___ When was the horse started under saddle? How did that go?
___ Who started her? (If it was a professional trainer, find out his or her name.)
___ What kind of riding has been done with her? Is there a special type of riding that she seems to do the best?
___ Who has ridden her? Beginners? Only experienced riders?
___ What kind of equipment has she been ridden in? (This applies to whether they used English or Western saddles as well as to whether they used special equipment such as draw reins, tie downs, and so forth.)

Health History
___ Has she had any health problems? Does she have any chronic illnesses? (If so, ask what you have to do about it.) Does she require any regular medication or special feeding?
___ What does she eat? How many times a day is she fed? Has she ever been on pasture?
___ Has she ever colicked? What was the reason for the colic episode? How was it resolved?
___ What is her shoeing/trimming schedule? Does she require special shoes? Can she go barefoot any part of the year? How is she with the farrier? (Ask whether you can call her farrier and talk with him or her about the horse.)

Handling/Stabling
___ How thorough is the horse's groundwork? Does she accept being tied? Has she ever been in crossties?
___ Has she been in a trailer? What kind of trailers has she been in? How does she load/unload? How does she travel?
___ What kind of fencing is she accustomed to? Has she ever been around electric fencing?
___ Has she been turned out with other horses? Turned out with other animals, such as sheep, donkeys, and goats?

Watch the seller ride the horse. If the owner/seller is unwilling to ride the horse for you, a beginner might take this as a reason to not buy the horse. A horse that is being sold because it is too much for its seller to ride is not the right horse for a beginner. If the owner has a broken leg (you might ask how that happened) then it is obvious she can't ride the horse for you. But under no circumstances should you—especially if you are not very experienced and perhaps even if you are—ride the horse before seeing it ridden by someone else, so that you can determine if your skill level is enough to handle what you see.

ESSENTIALS If you already have a riding helmet, be sure to bring it with you when you check out the horse. Most people allowing you to ride a horse on their property will insist you wear one anyway, so you might as well bring the one you are comfortable with.

When you are done looking at the horse and are ready to leave, give the seller a sense of your interest level. Don't commit to anything, but if you are still interested in the horse after the first visit, let the seller know that. Let her know at what stage in your search you are—"I really like Old Blue, but I've just begun looking, so it will be at least a couple of weeks before I get back to you" or "Old Blue seems pretty close to what I'm looking for, but there are two more on my list, so I want to look at them first." If you are definitely not interested, say so—"Old Blue is pretty, but when he bucked you off, I got kind of nervous."

If you are interested enough to worry about whether the horse will be sold while you look at your remaining prospects, ask if you can have first refusal on the horse. If someone else comes along who's interested, the seller will call and let you know that you need to make a decision. Many sellers may not be willing to do this, but it's worth a try, especially if you have looked at quite a few horses and Old Blue comes the closest yet to what you want.

The Prepurchase Exam

You've decided on a horse that meets your needs and appeals to you enough to make you want to have it in your backyard and tend to it two or three times a day, seven days a week, 365 days a year. Whether you want the horse checked over by a vet before you finalize the sale is up to you—the seller probably won't suggest it.

Prepurchase exams on horses are very common—it's sort of like a home inspection before buying a house—and all large animal veterinary practices have a standard exam they administer. If the seller won't allow a prepurchase exam (also known as a vet check), walk away. With horses, it is definitely a "buyer beware" proposition. If it's your choice not to have the horse checked by a vet, fine, but you need to know that you are taking a chance.

FACTS

Don't forget to do the following things with each of your prospects:
- Watch the horse being tacked up and ridden by someone else.
- Tack and ride the horse yourself.
- After the first visit, visit the stable unannounced to see your prospect.
- Look at the horse's registration papers, if there are any.
- Have a veterinarian do a prepurchase exam.
- If you have a serious reservation, don't buy the horse.

In a prepurchase exam, the vet checks the horse's temperature, heart rate, and other vital signs, and also performs some general lameness and range of motion tests. You may decide to have other tests done as well. For instance, if you are buying the horse with a specific performance activity in mind, such as jumping, you may want the doctor to X-ray leg joints, specifically knees and feet. If you are going to use a mare for breeding, ask the vet to look specifically at the horse's reproductive system in the prepurchase exam.

If you are looking for a performance horse, even if you are at the beginner level, you will definitely want to have it vetted. The basic exam takes around ninety minutes, and both you and the seller should be there.

It can be done at the seller's facility, or the horse can be trailered to a veterinary facility. Either way, the potential buyer typically pays for the exam and everything related to it.

The prepurchase exam is an assessment tool, not a pass-or-fail test. Here are the most important items to be informed about:

- Does the horse have a chronic illness or injury that isn't obvious to you, the layperson?
- If the horse has a known injury or illness, how severe is it and will it interfere with what you want to do with the horse? There are some things that come up that don't have any impact on how you plan to use the horse and, therefore, don't count as a reason to walk away. But keep in mind that if you decide to sell the horse in the future, a chronic injury or illness may make the pool of potential buyers smaller and the horse harder to sell.
- Does anything about the horse's conformation make it unable or unlikely to be able to do what you plan to ask of her? For instance, an underbite in the horse's teeth has nothing to do with her ability to jump; it can, however, decrease her ability to efficiently digest her food and, therefore, make it difficult for her to maintain weight, ultimately lessening her energy and stamina for jumping. The underbite may not be a reason not to buy the horse if everything else about her is what you want—age, size, color, temperament, price—but you should find out whether the horse will require any special tooth work or feeding either now or as she ages.

  The veterinarian will share the results of the examination with you and the seller, as well as provide you with a written copy. While the veterinarian is there, bring up any health questions you may have about the horse that are not covered in the general exam.

The Big Purchase

You've viewed your prospect being ridden, ridden him yourself more than once (unless you're buying an unstarted horse), handled the horse, and perhaps brushed him and led him around the barnyard. You can't stop thinking about him and talking about him. He's been checked over by a veterinarian and given a clean bill of health. You're ready to buy.

When you inform the seller of your decision, you will probably be required to give a good-sized deposit to hold the horse. When you are ready to take him to his next home, you will need to pay the balance in full, unless you have made other arrangements with the seller.

Getting Your Horse Home

Arranging transportation shouldn't be too difficult; the sellers may be able to deliver him to you for a fee, or perhaps you have an experienced horse friend with a trailer. (This is where it will help to know about the horse's trailering history, both loading and riding, and what kind of trailer he's accustomed to.)

If you are not yet ready to take your horse to his final destination, the seller may be able to board him for you for a short period of time; it depends on the situation. For example, a seller with a boarding barn may be happy to have him stay on as long as you pay to board him, but a trainer may need to get him out of the barn as soon as possible to open up a stall for a new student.

Registration Transfer

If he is a registered animal, there will be a transfer of registration papers. The breed associations all operate a little differently, but in general the current owner will send in the transfer information and then the breed registry will send the new papers to you with your name added to them. Or it may be that the owner (who may or may not be the seller) will sign the papers over to you, and then you will send them to the breed registry. Transferring registration is usually not very expensive. However, you should get this done immediately, as this is an important part of the monetary value of your horse. If the horse is not registered, a simple bill of sale including a description of the horse should suffice.

A Smooth Transition

Finally, find out what your horse eats; this is something you should ask when you are still looking at him. What the horse eats can tell you a bit about his temperament and how easy he is to keep. Be sure to stock up on the same brand and type of food before your horse comes home. Eventually, you will develop your own likes and dislikes when it comes to brands and types of feed, but for now you should feed him what he's been accustomed to.

If there are other horses in the barn in which he is going to live and you plan to change your new horse to what the others eat, ask the seller for a five- to six-day supply of the food he's currently eating in order to switch him over gradually. Or you can buy a bag and plan to switch him over the course of that bag of feed. (See Chapter 7, "Nutrition," for suggestions on switching food.)

Have a place prepared for him: a safe stall or shelter with fresh bedding, with a place to hang a water bucket and a feed tub, a mineral block, a supply of grain and hay, a wheelbarrow and manure fork, and a solidly fenced turnout area are the least you'll need for your backyard setup. Even if you are boarding your new horse, you'll need a halter and a lead rope and a few grooming supplies, for example, brushes and a hoof pick.

When you get your new horse to where he is going to live, let him settle in for a few days and get to know you and his new environment. If there are other horses there, he is probably going to be a lot more interested in them than in you. Don't throw a saddle on him the minute you get him out of the trailer. Spend some time with him, groom him, and allow him to settle down a little. Some horses adapt very easily and will settle easily into a stall with a flake of hay and happily munch and look around. Others are more easily unsettled and will be restless for a while, their senses on high alert, pacing their stall, and stopping to listen to every noise and look at every movement. Give the horse— and his new owner!—some time to settle into the place it is hoped he will call home.

Leasing

There is a way to acquire a horse without actually owning it, and that is through leasing. Sometimes the current life circumstances of a horse's owner—pregnancy, health problems, temporary relocation for a job, a new job that takes up more time—make it impossible for the owner to give the horse the attention it needs. Usually leases are "free" (i.e., they do not have a monthly rental fee attached to them), but just like everything else, there are a number of ways it can be done.

Why Lease?

One very logical reason to lease a horse is so that you can "trade up" as your skills advance, especially if you compete. Say, for instance, you plan to learn dressage. If you spend the time and energy to get to the top levels of dressage competition, you will probably go through three or four horses on your way there. The horse who is laid back enough to be a beginner dressage horse may not have what it takes to be the Grand Prix candidate you want when your own skill level gets that advanced. If you have the space, you can collect these horses in your barn as you progress up the ranks; more likely you will need to sell them and put the money toward your next prospect. However, if you lease the horse, you can simply give it back to the owner when you are ready to move on.

The Lease Agreement

A lease may have a stipulation that the horse needs to remain at either the owner's house or at the barn where the horse is being boarded. This is probably your biggest consideration, following whether your skill level matches the education of the horse. Be sure to sign a lease agreement, or at least a letter of agreement, outlining the following details of the arrangement, plus anything else that you can think of:

- Who pays for maintenance items such as shoes and vaccinations?
- Is there an end date? Leaving the lease open ended is probably not a good idea; it is better to make the lease easy to renew by inserting a

phrase that allows the lease to continue for the same period of time (one year seems logical) simply by having both parties sign new signatures on the existing lease.

- Where can the horse be kept? What kind of shelter is sufficient? You may think a run-in shed with 24/7 turnout is perfect, but the owner may expect the horse to be in a box stall at night.
- Can the horse be turned out with other horses?
- Are you allowed to trailer the horse to a horse show, trail ride, or whatever? Can the horse be trailered out of state? And kept overnight?
- What happens if the horse needs emergency veterinary care? Who makes decisions about that care, and who pays for it?
- What happens if the horse dies while it is under your care? Of course, no one wants this to happen, but it certainly could and has.

However the actual lease is set up, proceed with your decision-making process as if you were buying the horse—that is, watch the owner or someone else ride the horse, handle it, ride it yourself, and so on. If leasing is the route you want to take, your selection will be slimmer. However, since you are not going to own the horse, you may be willing to overlook some things. Many free leases end up with the lessee purchasing the horse, so keep that in mind too. Some people don't like to lease because they are worried about getting too attached to the horse and having a hard time giving it up when the lease comes to an end.

If you are a parent buying your child's first horse, follow all of the same advice given in this chapter. Don't mount your child with a horse beyond his or her abilities—even the most gentle horse is still a large and unintentionally dangerous animal.

Lastly, there are also "shared leases," in which you lease a horse, probably at a riding stable, with someone else. You each are assigned specific days, or even times, that you can ride the horse. Typically, the stable owns such a horse and is responsible for all its care but uses partial leasing to cover a portion of the horse's upkeep. This is a reasonable way for boarding stables that keep a string of lesson horses to have the lesson horse pay its own way. Be sure to do this with a responsible lesson barn, however; you don't want to find out that your mount is being leased to four people, used for lessons, and ridden five times a day, seven days a week. Also, make sure that there are not so many different people riding the horse that there is never any consistency in handling. Horses can develop some very bad habits from this kind of use; if this is the case, be sure the horse's bad habits are ones you can deal with.

Congratulations!

Soon you will realize your dream and have your own horse! Whatever you lack in experience now, be assured that as the years go by you will look back and amaze even yourself at how much experience you have gained. Taking care of a horse of your own will seem as natural a part of your daily routine as brushing your teeth.

CHAPTER 6
Stabling

Between this chapter and the last, you became caretaker of a horse. Now you need to keep her somewhere. You basically have three options: a boarding facility; your backyard; or the backyard of a friend, acquaintance, or neighbor. Each one of these options has its complications and its benefits, which I'll discuss in this chapter.

Choosing a Boarding Facility

The basic premise of boarding a horse is simple: You pay money to someone who has gone to the expense of constructing a barn that holds many horses, and that person takes care of housing and feeding your horse and of the everyday maintenance of the facility, including mucking your horse's stall. Simple? It can be. However, it can also be extremely complicated.

FACTS

Daily stall cleaning is important. Start by picking out the large piles, then sifting around the bedding for the scattered chunks, and then moving away the top part of the bedding and digging out the wet spots. About once a week (maybe more if your horse is in its stall for long periods of time), strip stalls of all bedding and let the stall air out for as long as possible. Sprinkle lime on the wet spots to reduce odors before putting down fresh bedding.

You do have several decisions to make when it comes to boarding your horse. Let's take a closer look at some of them.

Location

Your first consideration is probably going to be the proximity of the boarding facility to your home or perhaps to your job. When I bought my gelding, I chose to keep him at a place that was 50 miles from my home and office because I was extremely interested in the kind of horsemanship that went on at that facility and there was no place closer that provided the same environment. When I lived in western Wisconsin and worked in downtown Minneapolis, I chose to board my mare at a facility halfway between work and home. On the weekends, I didn't mind the drive, and during the week, I could stop by on my way home from work to ride, groom, or simply check on her. It is a good idea to first check out places near either home or work to make it easier for you to spend the most time with your horse.

Housing Arrangement

If you are a first-time horse owner, you may not have much of an opinion regarding how your horse is housed. But you will develop your own preferences over time. If your ideas change from what is offered at your current facility, you certainly can move your horse.

Facilities offer different arrangements, but the most likely scenario is that your horse will have a box stall in which he will spend a good deal of time. The larger the stall the better—10' × 10' is minimum; 12' × 12' is better; larger is even better, but that gets into great amounts of bedding. (Any facility trying to make a living probably won't want to spend the extra time, money, and real estate on oversized stalls—larger stalls means fewer stalls, and that means fewer paying boarders).

FACTS

Award-winning author Dick Francis published his first novel, *Dead Cert*, in 1962. Close to forty mystery novels later, he has made a successful living. With the racing industry as the backdrop, his worldwide bestsellers have been translated into over thirty languages. Easy to get hooked on and with plenty of backlist to keep you going, Francis's novels include such titles as *Field of Thirteen, Bolt, Wild Horses, High Stakes*, and *Blood Sport*.

The best arrangement for a horse is a run-in shed with twenty-four-hour turnout (see the following section for more on turnout), but facilities offering this are few and far between. It is mostly a convenience issue—it is much easier to feed horses and clean stalls that are all under one roof than it is to trudge through the weather to many outside run-in sheds. Some barns with numerous stalls under one roof are set up so that there are small turnout corrals off the outer wall of each stall, essentially creating a run-in situation. This, along with turnout in a larger area during the day when you aren't exercising your horse, can be the best of all. With this arrangement, your horse is near the tack room and riding arena, if there is one, but still gets 24/7 turnout, albeit in a small area part of the time.

Horses seem to be more content when they have at least some control over their situation—for example, being in the sun or in the shade, out in the snow or in a cozy stall with deep bedding.

Turnout

Facilities differ greatly in what they offer for turnout for each horse. You should know how many hours a day each horse gets out. In ads for boarding stables, you might read "half-day turnout," which means each boarder's horse gets approximately four hours of the day out of its stall—which is perhaps okay if you ride every day, but not nearly enough if you don't! Are they all turned out in a big pasture ("pasture turnout") after feeding in the morning and spend the day there until they are brought in for evening feeding and for the night? Do they get just two hours each by themselves in a collection of small paddocks? The more time your horse is out of its stall, the better. Is it important to you whether or not your horse gets turned out with other horses? You will need to make that clear to the facility manager.

QUESTIONS?

What does turnout mean?
Turnout refers to the period when your horse is out of the confinement of her stall and loose in a larger area—either outside in a corral or pasture, or in an indoor arena if the weather is bad.

The Facility Itself

Is there a riding arena? If you live in a cold climate where good footing is a concern during the winter months, and/or work nine to five, you'll probably want to keep your horse where there is an indoor arena. In exceptionally cold parts of the country like the Upper Midwest, you may even want to find an arena that is somewhat heated. If there is no indoor arena, does the outdoor arena have lights? Is it okay to use them? How early in the morning or how late in the evening is it okay for boarders to come and use the facility?

Find out how many boarders they take on. Are the riding areas big enough for the number of boarders? Are there trails nearby? (See the section "Keeping Your Horse at Home" later in this chapter for other things to consider when boarding, such as what to look for in stall floors.)

Type of Riding

The boarding facilities I have enjoyed the most have been those that have an eclectic group of riders of all different types of Western and English riding disciplines, from reining or barrel racing to dressage or jumping, from competitive riders to just plain backyard trail riders. But if you are interested in learning about a particular type of riding, you might want to find a facility where the concentration is on one particular kind of riding so that you can really expand your knowledge in that one area. A barn concentrating on jumping will probably have a nice cross-country jump course, some good low-level training jumps in the arena, perhaps include members of the local hunt club, and maybe hold some jumping clinics that you can participate in without having to leave the property.

The Boarding Agreement

It is a good idea to ask to see the boarding agreement that you will be expected to sign if you bring your horse to stay at the facility. You should note anything that you are expected to supply or do; also note when board is due and what happens if you are late with your board. (Having a horse in limbo because a facility refuses to release it until overdue board payments are made is a scenario that does happen.) Try to think of anything that you may have forgotten to ask about, such as whether there are specific times when you can use the facility; whether there are any other requirements, such as wearing a riding helmet; or whether there are any limitations on the number of riders allowed at a time in the arena, and so forth.

Read the agreement very carefully. If there is anything you do not understand, ask for an explanation. If there is anything you are uncomfortable with, don't hesitate to ask whether that particular point in the boarding contract can be altered—you never know unless you ask! Don't feel trapped into signing an agreement that you are uncomfortable with; there are plenty of other facilities available.

Other Boarders

Before signing on the dotted line, you should spend some time hanging around the facility, meeting some of the other boarders and watching them work with their horses. Ask them whether they like boarding there. Boarders come and go pretty regularly for all sorts of reasons (but if there is a huge turnover you might want to find out why), so if there's one person whose style you don't appreciate—maybe she's got a quick temper with her horse or maybe he seems to take over the indoor arena when he's riding—it probably isn't a reason to not board there. But if everyone seems to work their horses hard and then put them away dripping with sweat, or if people argue with each other about how to use the arena, then maybe the general atmosphere of the barn doesn't suit you. It's hard to know everything in a couple hours, but you should be able to sense any major problems. What you will most likely find is a congenial group of horse enthusiasts who welcome a new horse and rider into their fold.

Cost

Expect the cost to vary widely from facility to facility. I have heard of costs within a 35-mile radius of my New Hampshire home that range from $250 to $650 per month. The closer you get to more populated areas, the more boarding will probably cost. A 30-acre horse facility in a highly desirable real estate market with limited open land left, where housing developers are drooling over the fifteen houses they could build and sell on each two-acre lot, means the facility probably costs a lot to construct, and the monthly board will reflect that.

Services will cost you as well. Some facilities include riding lessons with board. Some offer such things as holding your horse for the farrier or vet, or blanketing against winter winds or summer sun. Some facilities offer deworming programs to keep all horses on the same schedule. Expect a higher cost for more amenities—such as a wash room for horses, a tack shop on the premises, a nice tack storage area with personal lockers, a heated lounge area, food to purchase on the premises, full bathrooms with a shower, maybe even a vet or farrier on the premises of larger facilities. There is a cost associated to the owner to provide these things, and in order for the facility to stay in business, the cost must be passed along to the boarders.

Other Details

Here are some other things to consider and ask about:

- Does the stable practice good safety habits? Look for a neatly kept barn with things such as water hoses coiled up and out of the way of horses and people. Aisles should be clear of debris and not used as storage areas. Grain should be stored in an area separate from the horse stalls, behind a latched gate or door, and neatly kept in rodent-proof storage bins. Although it is a barn and you can't expect to eat off the floors, a good sweeping of the common areas once a day and perhaps evidence of an annual cleaning of the dust generated from dirt driveways and arenas shows a commitment to quality in other areas as well. Also, find out whether the driveways are clear of junk and quickly cleared of snow in the winter.

Boarding stables may ask whether you want your horse to have his halter on or off while he is in his stall. In case of fire, it's easier to evacuate a horse with a halter on. But halters have been known to catch on something in the stall or even on the horse's foot when he scratches his head, injuring the horse as he struggles to break free. One alternative is a "break away" halter, which has a leather piece that will break when stressed.

- Are the stalls constructed safely and without protrusions that could injure your horse? Look for feeders for hay and grain that are appropriate to horses—they certainly don't have to be fancy but should be without sharp edges or holes. Are the stalls pretty clean on your visits? Stall doors should open and close with ease and latch easily. It's nice when boarding stables put name cards on each stall door telling who the horse is, what she eats, any peculiarities such as allergies or unusual habits (such as the ability to unlatch a stall door), and how to contact her owner in case of emergency.

- Are there good fire prevention measures, such as no smoking signs, fire extinguishers, and up-to-date electrical wiring? Is there an evacuation plan in the event of fire? Many stables offer owners the choice of having a halter left on their horse in the stall for quicker evacuation in case of fire or leaving the halter hanging on the door. Does anyone perform a night check, which can be as simple as a walk through the barn, peeking in each stall? Does the night check include an evening snack for everyone, or a topping off of water buckets? If it is a large facility that houses many horses and has lots of people milling around all the time, you might want to make sure that there is someone on the premises at most times and that the stable can be seen from the home of the owner or manager.

ESSENTIALS

For a comprehensive directory of hundreds of interesting and unusual horse-related Web sites that would be hard to find on your own, go to *www.haynet.net*. The directory is organized by categories such as "barn and farm equipment," "clubs and associations," and "harness racing." It also lists newsgroups, classifieds, and publications.

- Is there good security for your horse and your tack? You should be comfortable leaving your saddle there; otherwise, you'll have to tote it back and forth in your car or truck. If there is trailer parking space available, you could leave some things in your trailer, especially if you have a locking tack area. Find out whether other boarders are respectful of your things; they should not use them without permission (except in the case of an emergency, of course).
- Do the horses get ample water in their stalls and out in the paddocks/pastures? The stable should have a good plan for providing ice-free water in the winter. Look for clean water buckets and

containers that are large enough for the number of horses turned out in one area.

- Are there places in the pasture for horses to get away from flies or cold wind? A nice row of hemlock, spruce, or thickly planted shrubs will block the wind during the coldest times of the year if they are placed in the right spot; tall pines and hemlocks and other evergreens can provide some overhead shelter from light rain and snow. (However, see Chapter 7, "Nutrition," for a list of some common poisonous shrubs to avoid!) In the peak of fly season, horses need either a place to escape to or plenty of attention with fly sprays, sheets, and masks. Is the pasture run-in big enough for the number of horses turned out there? Typically, one horse can guard a surprisingly large area, leaving no shelter for any other horse. Horses can be switched around so that those that don't compete so much with each other can share.

- Will the facility add supplements to your horse's feed at your request (and expense, of course)? Some boarding stables charge extra per supplement per day; twenty-four horses that require an average of two supplements each added to their feed twice a day can add up to a lot of extra time for caretakers, so it's hard to blame them!

- What about those times when your horse needs medical attention? Can you pay someone to fill in for you if the horse needs to be walked three times a day for a week or have a bandage changed if you can't make it every day?

Keeping Your Horse with a Friend or Neighbor

Another viable and common option is to keep a horse with a friend who already has a horse or two. Usually the financial arrangements work great for both of you. Your friend will probably charge you a lot less than the going rate at the local boarding facility, since she is not in the business of boarding horses; she might charge just enough for her time and to cover the feed costs for her own horse(s).

Your friend, like at a boarding facility, would probably be the one doing all the work, since she will want to clean stalls and such according to her own schedule and standard of care, but there are many different arrangements you can make. If your friend is close enough to your home, you could share feeding responsibilities, say, one of you does it in the morning and the other at night. In exchange for fairly cheap (often referred to as "rough") board, you could offer to provide all your own feed and to muck your own stall, but of course, the owner of the barn will have the final say in how the arrangement is set up.

Dogs and horses don't always mix. Some dogs love to chase horses. If the pursuit is hot enough, they can chase them right through fences, causing all sorts of damage. And your dog can get hurt as well. So teach your dogs early on that the horses are off limits.

Advantages

There are several advantages to boarding your horse at a friend's house. For one thing, you have a built-in riding buddy. Also, during hay season, you can chip in and help each other bring in the year's supply. And you have someone to help you as you learn about caring for a horse if you are new to horse keeping.

Disadvantages

However, there are also many disadvantages:

- If this person has been a friend for a while, you could run into a disagreement that could end your friendship. The best thing to help avoid that is to try to be up front about everything and cover all possible bases before you bring your horse to her house.
- If the person was not a friend in the past, you may find you simply don't get along. If that happens, find a new place to keep your horse and move him as soon as possible. People who aren't fond of the owner of the barn are often less inclined to go visit their horses.

- In a setting more private than a boarding stable, you can sometimes feel like you are intruding when you want to go see your horse. For example, if the owner has extended family visiting and there's a football game in the yard, you might feel uncomfortable being there.
- You may not get a lot of the perks that a full boarding stable offers, such as access to a bathroom, a riding arena, and some of the anonymity that comes with the larger arrangement.

It all depends on the situation. Many people have multi-stall barns at their private home that board the horses of friends or neighbors. The barn is usually a bit away from the house and has a rustic bathroom, and the situation can work out just fine.

ESSENTIALS Take advantage of opportunities. For example, if your friend is at soccer practice with her daughter on Monday and Thursday nights, pick those evenings to spend some time at the barn on your own. If the situation works most of the time, find ways to work around the small problems.

Keeping Your Horse at Home

Perhaps you planned all along to keep your horse at your own home. This is the best arrangement of all! You get to decide everything about how your horse lives and to do things your own way. And you get to spend the maximum amount of time with your horse—if you have just fifteen minutes and can't fit in a ride, you can groom your horse without having to travel to do it.

Of course, when you keep your horse at home, you also will be doing all the day-to-day maintenance. This is a serious matter to think about ahead of time. Do you have the time to clean stalls, make trips to the feed store, hold your horse for the farrier, install and fix fences, and so forth? If you were traveling twenty to thirty minutes to the boarding facility, then perhaps you do have the time—that one-hour round-trip could have been used to do some maintenance tasks. But remember that you only travel to the boarding facility *if you want to.* If your horse is in your backyard, you can't skip feeding him for a day or two because you don't have the time or don't feel like it.

In the Zone

The first thing you need to know is whether zoning laws permit a horse to be kept in your neighborhood and, if so, whether the law includes parameters, for example, a certain number of acres per horse. Don't assume that it is legal just because someone up the street has a horse or two—the people up the street may be in a differently zoned area of town or have more acreage than you think. If you plan to relocate because you think you might like to have a horse around the house, be sure to investigate zoning laws beforehand.

Once you've established that is it legal to keep a horse in your yard, here are some other things to consider as you set up shop.

Give 'Em Shelter

If you plan to have a barn built, your options are limited only by the amount of space you have to construct your building and, of course, your budget. If you have a minimal amount of space, plan to have just one or two horses, and would like to leave most of the space for your horse(s) to run around in, consider a three-sided run-in shelter. Horses can live absolutely fine in this situation even in the most severe weather. If you expect two horses to use the run-in, it will have to be big enough for two horses to share, which can mean more space than you might think! Ideally, the run-in should have a standard stall space for each horse that will use it—that is, two horses should ideally have a run-in that is 12' × 24', or a 12' × 12' stall space per horse. The nice thing about this setup is that you could put a temporary panel down the middle and create two stalls with turnout areas for nighttime or emergencies.

The only problem with using just a run-in shelter is the inconvenience for the caretaker. It leaves no space to do things like groom or tack up your horse. You will need a space somewhere—a small garden shed nearby, some space in the garage, or the mudroom off your house—to store grain, tack, a wheelbarrow, and so on. And having just a run-in leaves no room for hay storage, so you will need to carve out a space somewhere for at least a one- or two-week supply of hay. If you have only one horse, this really isn't a huge issue, since your storage needs will be minimal.

FIGURE 6.1:
Run-in Shelter

There are plans for run-ins in numerous books on outbuilding construction, they occasionally show up in the horse magazines, or you can buy easily constructed prefab run-in sheds made from a frame of piping onto which you put a plywood shell.

Most other plans are bigger, more elaborate, more time-consuming to build, and more expensive, not to mention more time-consuming and costly to maintain. If you plan to build a full-fledged barn, you can go two-stall, four-stall, ten-stall, whatever you have the space and money for! A four-stall barn with a couple of stalls used for horses, one for a tack/grain room, and another for hay storage or as a spare stall if you need it for a friend (or a third horse), can be just the right size.

At this point, it can make a lot of sense to go to a builder who specializes in horse facilities, especially if you are new to horses. A local carpenter can work out just fine if you know exactly what to tell him or her to make the building safe for horses. Builders who specialize in equine shelters know the details of how high and wide the doorways need to be and how to safely install light fixtures for horses, and they are extra careful about picking up nails and taking care of all those little things that are hard to remember until you are in the midst of the project or, worse yet, after you are done. Equine barn builders offer everything from run-in sheds to multi-stall barns with tack rooms, washrooms, sprinkler systems, and overhead hay storage to indoor arenas with ten stalls, mirrors on the wall, and a heated viewing area. You can find builders who specialize in equine housing advertised in local and national horse magazines. If you see a barn you like in the area, stop and ask who built it.

FACTS

There are always things to repair or replace when you keep horses. Plan to have at least one extra water bucket, feed tub, and so on around to replace broken ones without having to make a special trip to the supply store. If something is wearing out, replace or fix it before it gives out. The more you keep up with things, the more you are in control—and the more free time you have for riding.

Using an Existing Structure

Maybe your property already has a little barn that has been used for horses in the past. If so, this can make your job a little easier. If horses were there fairly recently, it's likely the barn is in pretty good shape—but everyone has different standards for housing horses, so you'll want to check it out thoroughly to see if the building meets yours. If it was a barn used for a different purpose or even a different kind of animal, the first thing you need to do is examine it closely inside and out, looking for anything that might have been okay for a goat but that spells trouble for a horse. If you are new to horses, have a horse-savvy friend look the barn over with you.

Get rid of protruding nails, replace or cover glass windows that will be within reach of the horse (or a horse's flying hooves!) at any time, and look for anything that might cause a horse's hoof to get caught. Are there any electrical wires within reach of the horse's stall, or old rusted chicken wire, for example? Move it or block the horse's access to it. Be sure stall doors and such are high enough to contain a horse. Be sure stall doors and exterior doors open wide enough to get a horse in and out without the horse constantly hitting his hip on the doorframe.

Do not underestimate the strength of a horse! When building walls, hanging gates, creating fencing, or constructing anything that is to contain a horse, consider things like the horse leaning all its weight on the wall to scratch its hind end. Anything you build needs to be strong enough to take this kind of treatment from a half-ton animal.

FIGURE 6.2:
Floor Plan of a 30' x 30' Four-Stall Barn

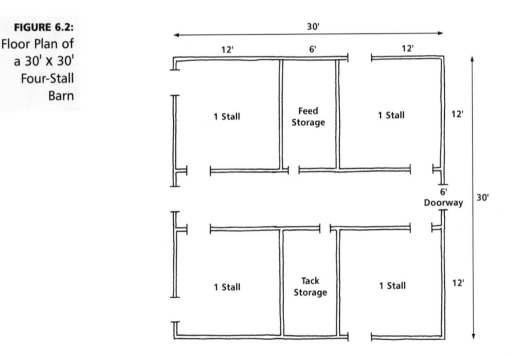

Another thing you should consider is the orientation of the building. The stalls I have created in my former cow barn are pretty open and have nice southern exposure. The advantage to this is that urine spots get baked by the sun for a few hours every day and dry out quickly. However, if your horse is in its stall a lot, you won't want the stall to bake in the sun all day and will want to be sure the horse has a shady area to retire to.

Flooring

There are basically three options for stall flooring: wood, concrete, or dirt.

Wood

Wood floors have the obvious disadvantage that they need to be exceptionally sturdy. Keep in mind that your horse isn't going to just tiptoe around the stall; the floor will have to be able to withstand the occasional jumping around of an excited horse or the thrashing around of a horse rolling in the nice clean bedding and hoisting herself to her feet again. Be aware of what is underneath—if it is an 8-foot drop onto a ledge of rocks, maybe it's not the best choice of a stall for a horse no matter how sturdy it is. Urine and manure will rot wood floors amazingly quickly. Although wood tends to be the least desirable choice for horse stall flooring, if it is clearly very sturdy, with a solid foundation underneath, and if you give it a little extra attention, they can actually be nice—because they can be swept completely clean. One thing to do is put down rubber mats or other synthetic floor coverings designed for use with horses. These help cushion the floor and, after being covered with some type of bedding, they prevent most of the urine from making contact with the wood, thus preserving the life of the floor. However, urine will still find its way between the mats, so once or twice a year, strip out the bedding, pull up the mats, wash down the floor and the mats, and let everything dry out in the sun.

Concrete

Concrete floors are definitely hard on a horse's legs, offering not even as much give as a wood floor. If this is what you've got, it doesn't make them unusable, but again, covering the floor with rubber stall mats and a deep layer of bedding to cushion your horse's legs will help. Rubber mats will also help if the concrete is smooth and potentially slippery. On the other hand, concrete does have two advantages: It holds up incredibly well, and it can be hosed down.

Dirt

Dirt floors are probably preferred over all others—there are no issues of being sturdy enough, they are fine for horses' legs, and, depending on the type of dirt, the urine doesn't settle on the surface for the horses to lounge around in. However, the urine does sink in, and dirt floors, therefore, do retain the smell of urine and don't have the advantage of being able to be hosed down. If stalls with dirt floors are deep inside the barn where they never get any sun or air circulation, the urine odor problem can be bad. Some people use rubber mats with dirt floors so that the urine soaks only the bedding, stopping at the mat and never reaching the dirt.

If the dirt floor does not get a lot of sun exposure, you will need to be extra diligent in cleaning out wet spots daily and perhaps strip stalls more frequently than needed with other types of stall flooring. Whenever you strip the stall and put down clean bedding, you can help the odor problem by spreading some lime or other odor-reducing products on the urine spots before putting fresh bedding down. And don't forget that urine odor is not just unpleasant; the fumes are bad for your horse's respiratory health!

Different Kinds of Bedding

Like most everything with horses, you will develop your own preference for the kind of bedding you prefer to keep in your horse's stall. Basically, the choices are sawdust, shavings, or straw. Sawdust can be the cheapest to use, depending on what part of the country you are in. In New Hampshire, a state that is 80 percent forested and has a significant logging industry, I can buy sawdust at my local mill for around $5 a truckload. However, availability is dependent on the mill's activity. Sawdust is easy to clean, since it slips easily through the manure fork, leaving the bedding in the stall instead of in the manure pile.

Bagged shavings are more widely available, both at mills and at your local feed store. Shavings bagged for use with horses consist of dry pine shavings; avoid other kinds, as they can contain shavings from wood that could make your horse ill if he consumes them. Bagged shavings can be an expensive route, but if you use good stall cleaning practices and get your horse out of her stall most of the day, you can get by on one or two bags a week.

Straw is another bedding alternative. It is often used in the stalls of foaling mares, since fine sawdust will stick to the wet newborn foal. Many horses will eat straw, but usually they only try a few bites before they decide it is not very palatable.

ESSENTIALS Both shavings and sawdust can dry your horse's feet. The key here is to get your horse out of its stall for as much of the day as possible for both its physical and mental health!

Many other types of bedding, chopped corn husks, for example, have come on the market. Some are synthetic. Some may be more available in some parts of the country than others, but none seem to have caught on as much as the old standbys of sawdust or shavings.

Fencing

There is a rule of thumb that recommends never bringing home farm animals until you have your fences up. Fencing is critical. For horses, electric fencing is often best, but you will probably find that you end up with a mix of fencing.

Electric Fencing

Electric fencing is probably the most commonly used for horses in the backyard setup. It is inexpensive, easily installed by even an amateur, and easily moved and reconfigured. To use electric fencing successfully, four essential ingredients are required:

1. **Fence posts:** These can be metal, wood, or fiberglass. You will need to buy insulators (the things you will string the electric wire on that keeps them from touching the posts and therefore grounding out) appropriate to the type of fence posts you use. Some fiberglass posts come with built-in insulators.
2. **Fence wire:** There are quite a few different kinds of fence wire. The more common types are barbed wire, twisted wire, flat tape, smooth wire, and high tensile wire.

    Forget about barbed wire for horses. Horses can get torn up when they get tangled in barbed wire, and it's just not worth it.

Smooth wire is common and comes in different gauges. The lighter gauges are easier to work with and just reel off the wood-slat jenny they come on. They are also more easily broken if a horse decides to test the fence's strength. In some ways this is better—if the wire breaks, the horse won't get tangled and cut up in it. But if you live near a busy road, getting cut up may be better than having the fence break, allowing the horse to run loose on the street.

3. **A fence charger:** Basically, electric, solar, or battery operated fence chargers are your choices. Make sure the charger is grounded properly so that if either the wire or the charger gets hit by a lightning bolt, it will run into the ground via an 8' × 10' rod that has a line running from it to the fence line.

4. **Training your horse(s):** Don't overlook this important part of using electric fencing. If your horse has never been housed in electric fencing before, it is important to teach him about it. First, make sure the fence line is highly visible. Then, take your horse into the fenced area on a lead rope. Walk the boundaries with him. I feel it is necessary for the horse to experience being zapped under controlled conditions. You can get him to stick his chest or nose on the wire by tempting him to lean across the wire with some grass or a handful of grain just on the other side. This may seem mean, but in order for electric fencing to be effective, you really need the horse to know that the wire means business. If horses have been fully introduced to electric fencing, you can feel comfortable with them behind it for the rest of their lives.

Board Fencing

White board fencing of the type that goes on for miles and miles in Kentucky racehorse country is beautiful, but my arm gets tired just thinking about painting it. People who use board fencing often also add electric wire to keep the horses from chewing it, so it becomes double fencing.

Vinyl

Vinyl fencing that resembles regular boards comes in two-, three-, and four-rail designs and averages around $4 to $5 per linear foot with posts included. Companies often offer lifetime guarantees against breakage.

Metal Panels

For small corrals, metal "pipe panels" that link together with pins can be convenient; the configuration can easily be changed and divided in new ways for different situations. Look for panels that are made for horses.

Water

As discussed in Chapter 7, "Nutrition," your horse will need access to fresh water, day in and day out, every season of the year. In the warmer weather, this is a piece of cake—just hitch up the right length of hose and fill a large container such as a muck bucket once or twice a day depending on how many horses you have, and their sizes.

ALERT

Carrying heavy water buckets can cause back and neck problems such as thoracic outlet syndrome. Lifting and carrying heavy things is a fact of life for horse owners. Learn good body mechanics and how to lift by using your knees to avoid putting a strain on your back.

If you live in an area that gets below freezing in the winter, getting water to your horse can be a chore. If you have electricity in your barn, there are many bucket heating options available. However, if you have only one horse, the expense and potential fire hazard of these heaters may not be worthwhile. It may be simpler to just bring the horse a bucket of fresh warm water from the house at each feeding time and to leave a bucket out for the horse during the day.

Feed Storage

Store your horse's feed in a place that is not easily accessible to the horse if she happens to get loose. Grain takes up little space—a garbage can in the corner of the garage can work just fine, with perhaps a shelf next to it for a container of supplements, a scoop, or other paraphernalia.

Hay also needs good storage space, free from dust and dampness, and definitely not open to the weather. With a horse eating about 150 forty-pound-sized square bales a year (of course, this varies widely depending on the horse), you should store at least a one- or two-week supply of five or ten bales at a time.

Manure

Don't forget to think about manure management before your horse walks onto the property! Your horse will start generating it immediately, and the supply will be constant.

There may be a gardener nearby who would just love to haul your manure away on a regular basis. Or if you can pile it in an accessible place, you can put a sign out by the road and allow people to stop and fill up their pickups. Of course, if you have your own garden, you may not want to give it away, but keep in mind that there's a never-ending supply!

Some communities have strict environmental regulations about manure disposal; some even require a concrete-lined pit. Check out any regulations your town might have. The key is to plan ahead, before the manure production begins.

Tack/Equipment Storage

You will have some storage needs for your tack and other equipment. If you have a horse trailer with a tack area in it, you can simply leave your saddle, bridle, brushes, and so forth there where they are always handy, whether you are on the go or not. If you have an existing building, consider where you could carve out some space to keep your tack. Be sure it is accessible to the area where you will tack up your horse—you don't want to have to carry your saddle (especially a Western one) a hundred yards every time you ride or stand in the rain or cold wind next to your garden shed to tack up.

Other pieces of equipment to be stored include a wheelbarrow and manure fork, a sheet or turnout rug if you choose to use blankets (even if you don't use them on a regular basis, it is good to have at least one around for emergencies and illnesses), and grooming supplies. These items do not take up an extraordinary amount of space, but you will be amazed at how quickly you begin to collect equine paraphernalia!

The Law

Now is as good a time as any to talk about some legal issues concerning horses. Ask people on the street to describe something about horses; right after "they're beautiful," they will most likely bring up "dangerous," "strong," or "flighty." It's true, if for no other reason than their sheer size and weight compared to humans, that horses are inherently dangerous. Combine that with a decision-making process and a reasoning largely unknown to us, and you easily have a recipe for disaster.

Many of us take that risk willingly. But getting hurt—stepped on, kicked, bucked off—is always possible.

ALERT

If you allow neighborhood kids to come around your horse, establish some ground rules—no hand feeding and no visiting when you aren't home—and have their parents sign release forms. You must decide how safe you feel your horse is and how many pony rides you want to subject him to.

The Release Form

Besides the boarding agreement discussed earlier, another contract you will often run into is the release. Any place where you board your horse or take lessons will require you to sign a release. Although it covers pretty standard things that you arc riding your horse on their property at your own risk or that you are taking lessons on one of the stable's horses at your own risk—you should nonetheless read a release carefully. Equine legal books often do not include contract forms because the authors (usually lawyers) realize that every situation is different. Therefore, stables are encouraged to tailor their release to their specific setup.

Occasionally, you may need to construct a release form of your own. For example, my property includes 90 acres with trails. Friends who come ride on their own horses are asked to sign a release, which I keep on file for all future outings. It can be uncomfortable asking a friend to sign a release form, but I figure any real friend is going to be happy to sign it. Also, I once took in a horse for a few days for a woman in an emergency situation, and I asked her to sign my release too, as it covers the topic of persons handling their own horse on my property at their own risk.

Equine Limited Liability Acts

We are known to live in a litigious society. Combine that with being involved in something inherently dangerous like horses, and the movement in states across America to pass equine limited liability laws is welcomed by horse owners everywhere. The laws are specifically designed to help horse professionals, from instructors to trainers, conduct their businesses with a public who is a little more legally informed about horse activity and a little less likely to file frivolous lawsuits. As many as forty-four states have an equine limited liability law, and more are adding, revising, and updating them each year.

ESSENTIALS   The Web site for the American Association for Horsemanship has a list of the states with a limited liability law and a link to each one (*www.law.utexas.edu/dawson/index.html*). Find out how horses are viewed legally in your state and become active in your state horse organization to help keep the horse industry viable.

Loose Horses

Legal issues commonly arise also in the area of loose horses. Simply put, one needs to prove negligence for a successful lawsuit—the owner would have to know that, for example, the fencing was inadequate or in need of repair. At the very least, Lady Luck could destroy the neighbor's garden; at worst, Thunder Bolt, running frantically down the road, could get hit by a car and cause harm or worse to the passengers, the car, and definitely to himself.

Don't dwell on the worst-case scenarios, but do understand some level of the law as it pertains to horses. While things happen even under the best of circumstances, you are responsible for keeping your horses in an appropriate setup. If you feel you can't do that, perhaps boarding for a while until you get your place properly set up is the thing to do, or maybe you need to wait a while longer to get a horse.

Decisions Aren't Always Final

Make your decisions about where to keep your horse using the same key decision-making process as you do everything else that is important. Keep in mind that boarding decisions can be changed, but if you don't feel good about a situation before you go into it, save yourself some headaches and don't do it.

If you are going to keep your horse at your house, it is important to have the basics in place before you bring your horse home. But remember, you will develop your likes and dislikes about things like fencing, feed, and even the types of buckets you use as you get experience, so don't buy everything at once. And keep in mind that things can be changed!

CHAPTER 7

Nutrition

Feeding the backyard horse can be a delicate task. As you discovered in Chapter 3, "Anatomy," the horse's digestive system is an amazing yet poorly constructed vehicle for processing the amounts of food needed by this large animal.

To cut to the basics, most domestic horses need grain, hay, and water to provide the essentials that their bodies need—water, energy, protein, carbohydrates, fatty acids, minerals, and vitamins. But each of those areas of horse nutrition have branches galore; if you mix in supplements, you can quickly need a computer program to figure it all out. This chapter will show you how to keep the feeding of your horse as simple as you can, while taking into consideration the regional deficiencies in your area and the individual needs of your horse.

First, There Is Water

Clean potable water provided in clean containers day and night, spring, summer, fall, and winter, is critical to the health and well-being of your horse. Without it, food cannot make its journey through the system, nutrients cannot be transported to and through the bloodstream, body temperature cannot be regulated, and waste and toxins cannot be eliminated. Without a steady supply of water, horses risk colic from food sitting in their digestive tract and fermenting or packing up and preventing the passage of manure. Water is vital.

According to James M. Griffin and Tom Gore, DVM, authors of the *Horse Owner's Veterinary Handbook*: "When deprived of water for two days, a horse generally refuses to eat and may show signs of colic. With ideal weather and good health, a horse might be able to live for five or six days without water."

How Much?

The average horse of around 1,000 pounds drinks around 10 gallons of water per day. That amount goes up or down according to the size of the horse. But it also increases if the horse works more than an hour or so a day. And if temperatures are extreme in either direction, hot or cold, the horse will require more water to replenish lost fluids and keep his interior temperature constant. Keeping fresh water in front of the horse at all times allows him to choose how much water he needs. At first you might find you are wasting water. The longer you take care of your horse, the more you will fine-tune how much is too much while still giving your horse free choice.

Providing Water

Unfortunately, providing horses with fresh water can sometimes be a pain. In summer and warm climates, it's fairly simple—hook up a hose long enough to reach your horse's stall and/or paddock, and fill 'er up. In winter and cold climates, the backyard horse owner finds herself with heavy buckets to carry, often long distances—if outdoor spigots freeze and the water has to be drawn from the house. Water remaining in buckets sometimes freezes solid before the horse gets to drink it. It seems never ending, but there are a few ways to combat this constant battle:

- **Heat tapes:** Heat tapes aren't used with the bucket itself but are wrapped around outside water spigots in order to use them throughout the winter and therefore cut down on carrying distance. Be very careful with heat tapes and any other electrical device that you use in the barn—any electrical appliance that runs most of the time increases the chance of fire. Follow the manufacturer's instructions exactly.
- **Hydrants:** A water hydrant is not much more than your typical spigot, except that it is designed so that when you close the hydrant handle, the water drops back below the frost line and prevents freezing. I am able to use my hydrant, which is located outside my barn (since most of the barn is above ground level) in below-zero temperatures.

FACTS

A rule of thumb for the quantity of water a horse needs daily is 1 gallon per 100 pounds of weight. Using this ratio, an average 1,000-pound horse will drink approximately 10 gallons of water each day. This amount varies widely, of course, and depends on many factors, especially how much exercise the horse gets. Lactating mares and hardworking horses need twice the average amount of water to compensate for fluid loss through milk and sweat.

- **Heated buckets:** These buckets resemble regular horse buckets but come with a double bottom that contains a heating element. A cord runs out from the back with a metal coil shielding the part of the cord that might come in contact with the horse. These buckets are thermostatically controlled, usually are around 150 watts, and are designed to prevent the water from freezing, not warm it. Most are also designed to shut off when the water level gets down to an inch or so. These buckets are a little expensive—between $30 and $50—but they are extremely handy and do their jobs well. However, it is usually recommended that you don't use extension cords, even though the cord that comes with them is only a few feet long. Your barn needs to have an outlet near the horse's stall, so you'll probably need to talk with an electrician. Again, follow the manufacturer's instructions exactly when using and operating these electrical appliances in barns and around horses.

- **Tank heaters:** If you have more than one or two horses, you probably will need something bigger than heated buckets. Tank heaters come in many designs, but they all basically float in a larger water tank and keep the water from freezing. They typically need pretty high wattage in order to keep all that water free of ice, so they can cost a little to run—but they can be worth it. If you have more than one horse, tank heaters are only helpful if the horses are all out together and have access to the tank, unless you can set up the tank so it is accessible from two paddocks. Again, follow the manufacturer's directions.

- **Insulated buckets:** One way to help with the frozen water situation is with insulated water buckets. These involve no electricity and are basically a giant thermos that helps water stay thawed. Most have an insulated float on the top that the horse presses on in order to drink. They are great for water in stalls overnight.

Do whatever you need to do and use whatever you are most comfortable with using to keep fresh water in front of your horse. It is critical that horses drink, especially in cold weather. But cold winter temperatures can be the most challenging, since some horses don't like to drink such cold water. Being in the Northeast, where the winter temperatures get pretty low, I offer my horses warm water in their stalls when I put them in for the evening.

Keep Those Buckets Clean

Plan to clean your water buckets regularly. If the buckets sit where they are exposed to the sun, algae and scum form quickly. Make bucket cleaning an easy task so that you won't mind doing it. Find your favorite bucket and water tub cleaning tool—a rag, a cookware sponge, a brush made just for bucket washing, a toilet bowl brush, and so on—and keep it handy (but out of reach of the horses). Once a week or so, round up all the 5-gallon buckets (include feed buckets), give them a good washing, and let them dry in the bacteria-killing sunshine.

Hay

Hay is the horse's most important foodstuff. The digestion of hay keeps the horse warm in winter, from the inside out, and provides the roughage to keep the digestive process moving along.

Hay can get complicated. It involves finding a source, determining what type of hay you want, figuring out how much to get, and making sure the supply you get is good quality.

If you board your horse, of course, you don't need to worry about most of this. However, you should be sure that your boarding facility does. When investigating facilities, don't be shy about asking to see their hay, what kind it is, if it is from fertilized fields, and where their supply comes from. Even if you don't know the best answers yourself, a good facility will consider these things important and know the answers to those questions about their own hay.

ESSENTIALS

Find the best deals on hay at *www.hayexchange.com*. This Web site lists every state, and hay suppliers list hay for sale under their state. There is also an online hay auction and information on hay analysis.

Finding a Supplier

One of nice things about having livestock such as horses is that it puts you in touch with the agricultural community. Finding and keeping a good hay supply will introduce you to local farmers. Before you bring your new horse home, look for a supplier and buy a decent amount of hay, depending on how much storage space you have. You should plan to keep at least a month's supply (around fifteen square bales per horse), which should give you a few extra bales in case you run late getting your next month's supply.

Ask other local backyard horse owners where they get their hay—farmers like good customers who pass their names along. On the other hand, if it was a bad hay year and supplies are low, horse owners can be reluctant to pass along their source!

FACTS

It's important to change grains gradually over a period of a few days. It's also good to introduce your horse gradually to the new season's crop of freshly cut hay. Make sure to have a few bales left from last year's supply when the new supply comes. If you don't have any older hay left to mix in with the new, take the extra time for a few days to feed the new hay in smaller quantities and more frequent meals spread out over the day.

The Grain Store

The grain store is certainly a place to ask about local hay farmers, and most grain stores usually carry baled hay. It is often high-quality hay, but their supply can be spotty, and it is probably going to be one of the most expensive ways to buy hay. If you have only one horse, then this may be a perfect source for you—you can get hay, shavings, feed, supplements, and any other supplies all in one monthly or twice-monthly shopping trip, and the additional cost is made up in convenience.

The Farmer's Barn

Farmers who have hay fields almost always end up with excess hay in the barn that they sell off over the course of the year. This method is usually a little cheaper per bale than the grain store. But the more the farmer has to handle the hay, the more expensive it gets per bale.

From the Field

The absolute cheapest way to get hay is out of the field during cutting season. Again, if you have one horse, this can be an easy method—you get on the local hay farmer's list and she or he calls you the morning they are planning to bale. A couple of round-trips with a pickup and you have your supply.

In order to take full advantage of the in-the-field method, you should have storage space for at least a truckload (about forty to fifty bales), but ideally, if you have room for three truckloads, you'll be set for one horse for the year! If you can get or store only one truckload during cutting season, at least you will still have paid less for part of your hay supply than if you got it all from the grain store or out of the farmer's barn in the middle of winter.

Delivery

You may also want to consider having hay delivered during the cutting season. However, there is an extra charge of anywhere from twenty-five cents to a dollar per bale on top of the out-of-the-field price. If you have more than one or two hay-eating animals and would have to make a million trips back and forth to the field, or you just can't work in the time to pick up your hay, this is a good compromise for getting your year's supply of hay in season.

ESSENTIALS

When you are transporting hay on the road, bring plenty of rope and take the time to tie the hay down well. Don't underestimate how much hay bales weigh—a tiny rope with a flimsy knot won't hold up to a pitching load of hay.

Some farmers offer to load it into your barn too, but again it will cost you even more for the workers' time. Some people have hay delivered monthly to their barn, which sounds like a nice arrangement; however, you are unlikely to find a supplier who will do this for the amount needed for one or two horses.

Advertisements for hay will have some terms and phrases that tell you something about the hay:

- **First cut:** This is the first cutting of the year; it includes any growth that has wintered over.
- **Second cut:** In northern New England, first cut is usually in late June and second cut in September. The second cutting is more nutritious, is shorter and softer grass, and is more expensive because it takes more of it to make a bale.

- **Alfalfa mix hay:** This often refers to a mix of grass hay that contains some alfalfa.
- **Horse hay:** Farmers will advertise hay as "horse hay," which typically means it is higher quality than the hay that people will buy for other livestock. For some reason, people seem to think it is okay to feed goats moldy hay, but any hay I buy for any of my animals is high quality, and certainly without mold, dust, or mildew.

Never lay a plastic tarp over your hay to protect it from rain and roof leaks. While the hay is curing, the plastic tarp will prevent moisture from escaping, and your hay will spoil.

- **Mulch hay:** Hay that has gone bad for whatever reason is advertised as mulch hay.
- **Never been rained on:** This statement typically refers not to hay bales getting wet but to the hay never having been rained on when it was laying on the ground drying and waiting to be baled.

The Haying Process in a Nutshell

Hay farmers check their fields regularly for growth. When the growth is sufficient and the weather forecast can confidently predict at least three days of hot, sunny weather, the fields will get cut. The cut hay lays in rows on the ground for two to three days to cure, or dry. Then, after a good day of drying in the sun and before the evening dew sets in, the hay is raked, baled, and removed from the field either by customers or the farmer.

Different Kinds of Hay

There are two basic kinds of hay that are commonly used with horses: grass and legume. And within each, there are also different kinds.

Grass Hay

Most backyard horses who are being used for recreational riding will do best on grass hay. It can be fed in reasonable quantities without the consequences of overeating that rich legume hay such as alfalfa can cause. Different kinds of grasses you will find as mixed grass hay include timothy, brome, orchardgrass, wheatgrass, bluegrass, and fescue. Some horses do have a preference, and there are some grasses that some horses don't like. So you may want to keep track of which hay your horse ate voraciously and which she picked at and wasted.

Legume Hay

Alfalfa and clover are legumes. The resulting hay contains more protein, essential amino acids, calcium, phosphorus, and beta-carotene than grass hays do. High performance horses do very well on alfalfa and need the extra energy it provides. Alfalfa may, however, provide a little too much energy for backyard horses that are ridden only a couple of times a week recreationally. Sometimes hay is part legume and part grass, which is a good compromise.

QUESTIONS?

What are amino acids?
Amino acids are the group of organic compounds that form the structure of proteins. Hay from alfalfa and clover is rich in amino acids and gives horses extra energy.

Hay Feeding Plan

Anytime you can spread your horse's meals into smaller more frequent ones, it is better for digestion. However, horse owners usually need to work to support their horse habit, so your horse is probably on the nine-to-five feeding schedule, where he gets fed half his meal in the morning before you go to work and half in the evening when you get home. While not ideal for the digestive function of the horse, thousands of horses survive just fine on this kind of schedule. Maybe you can find a neighbor to throw your horse a flake of hay in the middle of the day or a responsible neighborhood kid who would love to do that when she gets home from school in exchange for learning about horses or a small fee. The size of a flake of hay can vary almost from bale to bale, but the average-sized horse should be fed around

2.5 percent of its body weight each day, with at least half of that in the form of hay. For a 1000-pound horse, that is roughly 12 to 15 pounds of hay per day.

FACTS

A horse can deplete a pasture very quickly, eating the grass right down to the dirt and never giving it enough time to grow again. A rule of thumb for grazing pasture is an acre per horse. Even if you have one horse on one acre, it's best to fence it in half and allow the horse to graze on half for a week or two, then shut that half off and let it grow undisturbed while the horse grazes on the other half.

Grain

In the wild, horses live only on roughage, and they innately know how to get the nutrients they need by seeking out specific herbs and grasses—in other words, horses do not *need* grain to thrive. In the domesticated life of the horse, grain is more accurately a supplement, making up nutrients that your dry forage cannot provide. Except for the horse who cannot eat hay for health reasons, hay should be the main source of nutrition for the horse.

However, horses typically cannot eat enough dry, bulky hay in the course of a day to get the nutrition they need if the hay is of mediocre quality or the horse has a heavy workload. This is where grain steps in to fill in the nutritional gaps. In some areas of the country, horses are fed oats, corn, and mixes of whole grains. Most backyard horse owners rely on commercially manufactured horse feeds that have been designed to balance the nutrient intake when added to a recommended amount of hay.

Mixed Grain

Grain mixes can come with or without molasses (the addition of molasses gives the grain the designation of "sweet feed"). Manufacturers usually have many different mixes in their line of premixed grain. Oftentimes the major difference is in the percentage of protein. Some are actually "complete" feeds that, if forage is not available, could be fed as the horse's entire ration if given in sufficient quantities.

Organically Grown Grain

If you are interested in buying organically grown grain, there are a few companies who offer it. As with human food, organic feed is definitely more expensive than commercial preparations, and if you are interested in feeding wholly organically, you may have difficulty finding organically grown hay. This short list of feed companies may offer a supplier in your region:

- Blue Ribbon Organic Feeds, 530 W. Bambi Farms Road, Shelton, Washington 98584; 360-427-3208
- Organic Feed Company, P.O. Box 112, Dawson, North Dakota 58428; 701-327-4249
- Organics Unlimited, 34 Evergreen Road, Lebanon, Pennsylvania 17042; 717-273-1555
- Vermont Organic Grain Company, R.R. 1, P.O. Box 5, Bethel, Vermont 05032; 800-564-8125
- Also, organically grown alfalfa can be purchased from Rocking Diamond, Route 1, Selby, South Dakota 57472; 605-343-7056

What Kind?

You should pick a brand of grain that is easily accessible. When you buy your horse, find out what she is eating; if she seems to be doing well with it, you may as well stick to it. If you have other horses or the brand she was eating is not available through your nearby grain store, you can switch her to a different brand. You will probably find a similar mix in all brands. Always change gradually over the course of a week, mixing the new brand with the old brand, and gradually increasing the amount of the new until you've made a complete switch.

When a Horse Isn't Thriving

If you don't think your horse is thriving on a particular feed, talk with your veterinarian and your feed supplier. They can help you make some new decisions about grain choices and help you determine whether a supplement is needed for that individual. In making recommendations, they will consider his breed, size, age, living arrangement, and amount of use.

Of course, with your veterinarian, you should rule out certain diseases and illnesses that can contribute to poor digestion. Consider the following:

- Are his teeth in good shape? Have an equine dentist inspect and file his teeth if necessary. Sharp points develop from uneven wear, making it difficult to chew grain and causing considerable amounts of grain to drop on the ground instead of being ingested by the horse. (See Chapter 3, "Anatomy," for a more complete discussion of the horse's teeth.)
- If your horse is eating in a group, is he getting his full ration, or is another horse eating part of his meal?

FACTS

If your horse gets loose and finds the grain bin, she will happily eat until it is empty. Depending on how much was in the bin, she will almost definitely get colic as a result. A common rule of thumb is to keep grain behind three "locks." Lock one might be on the building the grain is kept in, lock two on the grain room door, and lock three on a horse-secured grain container (such as a garbage can with a locking lid).

Complete Feeds

Most grain manufacturers offer a feed that contains some roughage and can be fed as a complete feed without hay if fed in sufficient quantities. These complete feeds are very helpful in maintaining weight and proper nutrition in horses who have health problems such as heaves (a respiratory disease that is aggravated by the dust in hay—see Chapter 9, "General Health," for more details) or in older horses whose tooth wear has made chewing hay difficult. Complete feeds often come in pelleted or extruded (like dog food) form, but they also can come as loose mixes.

A horse who relies on complete feeds with no hay as her entire ration can be more prone to exhibiting unwanted behaviors, such as chewing wood. This results from the frustration caused by an innate need to eat roughage and simply keep busy.

Weight Control

Both overweight and underweight horses pose health problems. A horse that is slightly underweight is probably better off than an overweight horse. However, it takes very little—illness, overwork—for the slightly underweight individual to become too thin.

Overweight individuals tire easily, and obese broodmares can have breeding difficulties. Some horses, like people, easily gain weight and need to be carefully monitored for food intake. They may need to be taken off pasture and given a more controlled feeding program. The owner will have to take responsibility for getting the individual the exercise it needs to maintain a good weight. Keep close tabs on your horse's weight, and work with your health care team to address any underweight and overweight issues.

Feeding Differences

The nutritional needs of a growing horse compared to an adult horse who gets light work are very different. Horses need to be fed according to age and use. All grain manufacturers give recommendations on the bag or in supplemental literature. You can also talk directly with the feed sales representative. Following are the typical categories you will find.

Mature, Idle

"Mature" refers to the horse who is beyond growing age, which varies from breed to breed but is usually around four years old. The idle horse is one who is ridden only a couple hours per week and spends the rest of her time hanging around the corral. This horse does not need to be stuffed full of food! She often can exist on high-quality hay alone; however, always have the hay tested to be sure it contains all the nutrients a horse needs. If it does not, you will need to include grain in her feeding program. You might think you could simply add vitamins (see the supplement section), but most supplements are not palatable to a horse when fed by themselves, and need to be mixed with some grain.

Mature, Light Work

An adult horse of five years or older that is ridden three to five hours per week most likely will need some supplemental grain to meet his nutritional needs. Again, you need to be sure of the quality of your hay and consider your horse's individual characteristics to feed him enough but not too much.

Mature, Medium Work

The horse who is ridden five or six days out of seven days a week will definitely need to have his hay supplemented with a grain ration in order to get the proper amount of nutrients.

Mature, Heavy Work

The horse under heavy work, typically a performance horse ridden a few hours every day, will need to be fed hay, grain, and probably supplements. Her feeding program should be carefully constructed and constantly re-evaluated. The type and amount of feed the horse gets will depend on the type of work—jumping, dressage, eventing, trail riding—that the horse does.

Broodmares

The broodmare should be fed according to the information just given, except during two critical periods: in the last three months of pregnancy, at which time the fetus is under rapid growth, and while lactating. Otherwise, be sure she is fed with quality hay and grain as needed to supplement the quality of the hay. During the last three months of pregnancy, her need for protein, calcium, and phosphorus increases dramatically and will probably need to be given to her as a supplement rather than simply by increasing overall grain ration. Continue the same sort of regimen while the mare is lactating, but pay particular attention to the mare's decrease in lactation. As the foal begins to eat grain and hay more seriously (in two to three months) and heads toward weaning, begin to decrease the mare's feed accordingly.

The Growing Horse

Nursing foals, weanlings, and yearlings all need access to high-quality hay, often need to be fed grain to supplement hay, and may need supplements beyond that. And like all horses, these youngsters will need twenty-four-hour access to fresh water and mineralized salt.

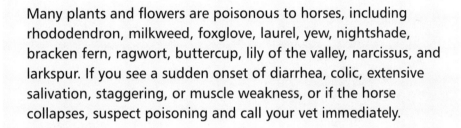

Many plants and flowers are poisonous to horses, including rhododendron, milkweed, foxglove, laurel, yew, nightshade, bracken fern, ragwort, buttercup, lily of the valley, narcissus, and larkspur. If you see a sudden onset of diarrhea, colic, extensive salivation, staggering, or muscle weakness, or if the horse collapses, suspect poisoning and call your vet immediately.

Supplements

Look in any equine supply catalog or tack shop, and the array of supplements you will find can be mind boggling. The catalog copy sounds appealing, and you can easily go a little overboard. You can also drain your bank account paying for these supplements and add a host of complications to feeding time by having to pull from a smorgasbord of supplement buckets.

Consult Your Team

As with all other health and nutrition concerns with your horse, turn to your horse's health care team—the veterinarian, holistic practitioner, farrier, feed suppliers, and you—to determine what, if anything, your horse might need for supplements.

Regional Nutrient Deficiencies

Sometimes a region has a known deficiency in a certain nutrient—for example, iodine deficiency is somewhat common, and in many areas of the Northeast, selenium is known to be deficient—and that is a good reason to supplement feed. The local extension agency or the U.S. Department of Agriculture can provide specifics about your area.

Salt Blocks

Salt and mineral blocks come in small bricklike sizes or large 50-pound blocks. If you feed commercial grain, your horse will probably get all the appropriate trace minerals she needs, so you could choose to use plain white salt blocks (the cost difference is insignificant). Hang one in every horse's stall and keep one in the paddock so that horses can always have free access to salt, which is a key mineral in their diet. Place the 50-pound block on a pan that keeps the salt block off the ground. If at all possible, keeping it under some sort of cover is also helpful, since it will deteriorate fast when rained on.

How to Feed Supplements

Most supplements come in pelleted form and gets added to the horses daily grain ration. (For "natural" nutritional supplements and a list of some commercially available types of supplements that you will run into on the feed store shelves and in catalogs, see Chapter 10, "Beyond Conventional Health Care.")

QUESTIONS?

What does esophagal choke mean?
This is a condition that is often caused when horses gulp down pelleted feeds too rapidly. To deter this, place a couple of stones or half a salt block in the feed bucket—having to eat around them makes the horse slow down.

Multivitamins

According to Griffin and Gore's *Horse Owner's Veterinary Handbook*, all vitamins except A and E "are synthesized by bacteria in the horse's large intestine." Only A and E need to be supplied through the diet, so giving multivitamins to a healthy, properly fed animal is probably overkill.

B Vitamins

B vitamins are often given to animals who are stressed and are showing weight loss and lack of vigor. B vitamins can come in quickly dissolving gel and paste form in an oral syringe.

Vitamin C

Like Vitamin B, horses make their own Vitamin C and do not need supplementation of this antioxidant unless they have a chronic illness or are otherwise compromised.

Supplements for Older Horses

Most supplements directed at older horses are to relieve arthritis and joint pain and include a glucosamine/chondroitin mix for joint flexibility (with names like Glucomax, Flex-free, etc). Some are digestive aids and include bacterial cultures, such as acidophilus, that are critical to digestion, since older horses often don't process their food as efficiently as when they were younger.

Mare and Foal Supplements

Most of these are basically multivitamins with electrolytes and trace minerals to boost levels in growing horses and lactating mares.

Hoof Growth Supplements

The horse's hoof is important. If the hoof is not growing properly, it probably wouldn't hurt to add a supplement to the horse's diet. However, as always, consult with your equine health care team, especially your veterinarian and farrier, to determine the need of supplementation of this kind. Hoof problems may also be caused by environmental factors, and it may be the bedding that needs to be altered, not the horse's nutrition.

Calcium and Phosphorus

Calcium and phosphorus are extremely important to the health of a horse. However, they also are dependent on each other, and their ratio is as important as their quantity. The perfect ratio is between 1:1 and 3:1, calcium to phosphorus, but should always consist of at least as much calcium as phosphorus. This can be an important issue if, for instance, you decide to add rice bran to your horse's diet. Rice bran is high in phosphorus and low in calcium, and so a calcium supplement would be needed to maintain an appropriate ratio.

Coat Supplements

These are supplements intended to enhance coat shine and maintenance and are usually fortified with fatty acids as well as other vitamins and minerals.

Colic Preventatives

These supplements contain high-fiber ingredients, such as psyllium seed husks, that are a natural laxative needed to reduce the potential for colic in horses who consume sand and dirt while feeding from the ground or on short pasture. These supplements are intended for prevention and are not to be used in the event of a colic episode, in which case you should promptly call a veterinarian.

Respiratory Supplements

These are supplements intended to help with respiratory problems. They range from cough syrup-like formulas to mixes of herbs and herbal extracts for nutritional support for horses with conditions that cause coughing and breathing problems.

Vitamin E and Selenium

These two nutrients are best given in combination. Selenium deficiencies are found in many parts of the United States. Too much selenium is toxic, but not enough can cause muscle deficiencies and a weakened immune system.

Keep It Simple

There are many more supplements and types of feeding and feeding programs that you will run across as you get more experience with horses. Always keep in mind that the horse's natural diet is quite simple. If you can keep your feed program simple while getting the horse the nutrition she needs, you will both be much happier.

CHAPTER **8**

Grooming

Grooming your horse is good for both her physical and mental health. It is a great way to interact with your horse in an enjoyable activity as well as give you the opportunity to check her over for nicks and cuts, skin problems, and other things you might not see unless you get your hands on her. You don't need to groom your horse every day—though simple grooming is one thing you can't really overdo!

Your horse will really appreciate it if you retrieve her from her corral and just groom her instead of always retrieving her only to make her go to work. Grooming a horse is also great exercise for you. This chapter tells you all about how to be hands-on with your horse.

Grooming and Riding

It is necessary to brush the dirt out of your horse's coat and to pick out her feet both before and after you ride—regardless of whether your ride consists of schooling in the arena or a hack out on the trails! Brushing the coat anywhere the saddle will come in contact with it is critical, but it is also important to clean the dirt out of the rest of the horse's coat as well, since the dirt will irritate her skin when she gets sweaty from exercise.

Upon return, you may want to hose your horse down, in the summer season. However, just use water; bathing her with shampoos after every ride can be detrimental to her coat. If it's not the right season for hosing off sweat, at least wipe your horse down with a towel in the sweaty areas and wipe off any mud or wetness from snow, puddles, or wet roads. Wipe her face and ears down with a damp towel too, since she will be itchy in those places. Take a few extra minutes to give her back a bit of a rubdown—your horse will definitely appreciate it. Once the sweaty areas are dry, brush her coat out thoroughly.

FACTS

If you show your horse, expect to become an expert at grooming. Competition in the horse show world is stiff, and you will want to give your horse every little edge to stand out in the crowd. Perfect grooming with every detail attended to is just one more notch in your favor on the judge's card. Even if grooming isn't an official aspect of a particular class, it never hurts to have the judge look favorably upon your team.

Grooming Tools

First, you should set up some sort of tote with the basic grooming tools you need to give your horse an average grooming. Inexpensive totes come in heavy-duty plastic of all colors. (If you have more than one horse and want to keep their grooming tools separate, you can color coordinate their individual tote and brushes.) Tote boxes also come in wood—you can have fun painting, staining, and decoupaging them any way you want.

Cotton socks with worn heels, deteriorated elastic, or whose partner has been mysteriously eaten by the clothes dryer make handy items to have in the barn. I keep a plastic grocery bag hanging in my tack room full of socks. Dampen them and use them to wipe your horse's face and ears. Clean bell boots with them. Wipe down the bit after a ride. The list is endless! Keep a second bag, bucket, or basket to throw the dirty ones into. When your supply of clean worn socks starts to get low, throw the dirty load in the laundry. If a sock gets exceptionally soiled, just throw it away.

Another handy thing to have is a grooming apron. The apron itself will protect your clothing from getting covered in horsehair, dust, and mud. If you get one with pockets in the front, it will be handy for holding brushes, a hoof pick, or braiding equipment.

Brushes

Curry Comb

Curry combs are typically made of stiff rubber, with a ring of pointed edges around the outside. They are used to brush the surface mud off your horse's coat. These brushes come in round or oval shapes and are designed to be used in a gentle circular motion.

ESSENTIALS

You can pick up very inexpensive horse brushes. But if you can, or maybe once you get beyond your startup purchases, buy good quality natural horsehair brushes. Nice brushes make the task of grooming that much more pleasant for both you and the horse.

Body Brush

A body brush is made of somewhat stiff fibers designed to really get down to the skin and brush dirt to the surface. Be careful not to get a brush with bristles that are too stiff, however; we're talking about an animal that can feel a fly land on its butt, so imagine how a really stiff brush feels! Instead, get a brush that's stiff but still flexible and learn to use the flick of your wrist to get that loose dirt to the surface.

Finishing Brush

This body brush is the last you'll use in your grooming routine. It is very soft and used to brush away the loose dirt while leaving a polished shine to your horse's coat.

Face Brush

Brushes for the face are very soft and come in different sizes. You will want a fairly small one to do the delicate areas around your horse's nose, eyes, and ears.

Mane/Tail Brushes

Mane and tail hair grows very slowly, so you should be careful to pull out as little as possible. If the mane or tail becomes knotted, use one of the products described in the next section to loosen the knots before you run a brush through the hair. You can buy a style of comb with teeth that rotate to help untangle knotted hairs without pulling them out.

ESSENTIALS

Keep all of your basic tools handy for grooming before riding. Fill a tote, bucket, or bag or hang a wire basket near the place you tack up with basics such as a curry comb, hoof pick, body brushes, mane and tail comb, and towel.

Hoof Picks

There are a few different kinds of hoof picks. They are relatively inexpensive, so you can try out different kinds and see which suits you best. My personal favorite is the kind with a thick plastic handle and a stiff brush on the other side of the hoof pick. The brush allows you to brush mud and dirt off the horse's hoof before picking it up and to brush off the remnants of what you pick out of the hoof.

Simple hoof picks come as steel picks with vinyl-coated handles of differing colors. Also common are hoof picks in a pocket-knife style that folds in half and is handy to carry in your pocket out on the trail.

Clippers

If you plan to show your horse, you will need a pair or two of clippers. Clippers come in many sizes; just be sure to buy ones that are intended for horses. They need to be sturdy and suitable for a horse's coat and mane hair. Have extra blades handy, since clipping coarse hair dulls them pretty fast.

To get your horse used to clippers, first let her see them, check them out, smell them, and feel them. Turn them on and let her hear them from a distance. If she is handling all of this well, she may be ready to feel them against her skin while they are on.

Normally, it would be best to have your horse on a lead rope for this kind of thing (not on cross ties) and to let her move as much as she needs to. It also helps to use cordless clippers so that you can easily move with the horse when she moves. When she stops moving, take the clippers away to let her know standing still was what you were looking for. Then slowly start again, working with the places on her body where she is okay with the clippers and moving to less comfortable areas gradually. It's worth taking your time; once your horse is comfortable with clippers, she should remain so.

ALERT

If you plan to clip your horse's ears, make sure you use clippers of an appropriate small size and get your horse totally comfortable with having her ears handled before you start trying to clip them.

You may choose to clip the winter coat on a performance horse to help him get less heated during winter workouts. There are different levels of clipping, and the level you choose depends on how hard your horse will work in the winter, how cold the winters are in your area, how much blanketing you want to do, and how much you want your horse to go outside in the winter. Types of clipping include:

- **Trace clip:** Just the areas on the lower part of the body from the middle of the side to the top of the legs are clipped.
- **Blanket clip:** A blanket-like area of unclipped hair is left on the horse's back from the withers to the croup.
- **Hunter clip:** The entire body is clipped except an outline of the saddle. (Set the saddle or saddle pad on the horse's back while clipping to serve as a template.)

If you bathe and groom your horse to prepare him for a show the following day, bed the stall with fresh shavings and blanket him with a light blanket. If you clip your horse, you will need to blanket him accordingly—for example, a full body clip in the northern climates in winter means heavier blanketing, both indoors and out. Blanketing also gives you a few other things to consider while grooming—for example, you need to watch for sore and chafed areas where the blanket rubbed the horse.

Other Tools

Shedding Blades

If your backyard horse is allowed to grow a nice winter coat, you should have a shedding blade around to help you in the spring when that coat really starts to shed. The traditional shedding blade comes as a long, thin metal blade with a leather handle on either end that can be folded and hooked to make a loop. The blade is smooth on one edge and has small teeth on the other to get that loose hair out.

A shedding and mud tool that is also useful is a flat rubber mitten with little bumps on both sides. This gentle tool lifts mud and loose hair, and you can really scrub at the mud without hurting your horse.

Towels and Wipes

Always have some clean towels around the barn. They are useful for any number of things, from grooming to first aid. White towels are good to have around for first aid use, since the dye in colored towels is probably not good for open cuts. A roll of paper towels, a container of shop towels, and moisturized hand wipes also come in handy in the barn.

Vacuums

Yes, you can buy special vacuum cleaners for horses that suck mud, dirt, and shedding hair off the horse or can also be used to blow dry the horse when he is wet. These vacuums start at around $200, but you can pay up to $500 for higher-level models with more features. If you show your horse or have more than one or two horses to groom, these can be time-savers. Otherwise, elbow grease and good brushes do the trick.

QUESTIONS?

What does hogging mean?
Hogging, also known as roaching, refers to a mane that has been completely shaved.

Bathing Items

Horses shouldn't be shampooed too often (although for the show ring, it's almost inevitable that they will be bathed regularly), but when you do choose to bathe your horse, there is a wealth of products to choose from. Shampoos can be moisturizing, can include a bracer that feels good after a hard workout, or can be conditioning and intended to make your horse's coat shine like never before. Some shampoos are specifically antifungal; others include fly-repellant products such as citronella. Shampoos also exist especially for grey and white horse coats.

Rubber mitt-style brushes are great for shampooing. They have short bristles on one side, hard rubber bumps on the other, and a hole on either side at the opening of the mitt that allows you to stick your thumb through to better hold the mitt.

Braiding

Braiding styles depend on the discipline—and, in fact, the need to braid at all depends on the discipline—but it can be a fun thing to do whether or not you compete. In general, the more braids you put in a mane, the longer the neck appears to be. Just a few thick braids make the neck appear shorter and thicker. Mane braids can be left hanging, tucked up into themselves in neat little bobs, or looped into the next braid in chain-like links. Braided manes are traditionally accompanied by braided tails, which can be left in one thick long braid or woven into tight, smaller braids.

Sweat Scrapers

Something as simple as a sweat scraper comes in numerous styles. First, you can choose between plastic or aluminum. There's also a squeegee-style sweat scraper similar to what the gas station attendant uses on your windshield, only curved. As with many things with horses, you will need to use a few different kinds to discover what suits you best.

Grooming Products

Many products exist to make grooming a little easier. Some just smell nice and make the horse look more polished; others have very practical purposes such as detangling manes or making braiding easier. Most of these products are available in a few different brands, the main difference often being smell. They can be expensive, so you may want to hang around a show barn for a couple of weekends to see and smell what people are using. Then you can make some choices of what to try and what you definitely aren't interested in before you make any purchases.

Mane/Tail Detanglers

These detanglers do their job well, and they usually smell just great. They come in spray or gel form. Although the spray is a little easier to use, I prefer the gel because it can be directed more accurately. Be aware that it is so slippery that you need to be careful not to get any on the saddle area! And if you get it on your hands, you will find it difficult to keep reins from slipping through your fingers.

Coat Gloss

Coat gloss is used to make your horse's coat shine. These are topical enhancements only and don't have any deep-seated effects on coat health. For more lasting effects, you need to find supplements designed specifically for that purpose.

FACTS

In an interesting twist, a product that has long been on the market for horses—Straight Arrow's Mane and Tail shampoo and conditioner—became so popular with horse people that they began to use it on their own hair! The company caught on to their product's secondary use and got FDA approval to market the shampoo and the conditioner to humans. Now it can be found on drugstore shelves.

Hoof Dressings

Horses in the show ring have their toenails polished. Black has always been available, but now you can choose copper, silver, and many other colors of hoof! Be careful that the product you choose doesn't have a drying effect, especially if you choose to remove it with hoof polish remover. Ask your farrier her or his opinion, especially if your horse has less than perfect hoofs to begin with. And typically, as with anything, if used excessively, hoof dressing may cause problems.

Grooming How-To's

Body

To give your horse's coat a thorough grooming, follow these steps:

1. Begin with a curry comb of your choosing and brush up loose hair and underlying dirt. If the horse is shedding, use a shedding blade first and get as much loose hair as possible out before you begin brushing. Use these tools only on the horse's main body, not in areas where bones stick out, such as in the flank or shoulder area, and not on the legs and face.
2. Use your stiffest body brush and brush out all the loose dirt and hair that the curry brought to the surface. Use this brush to get the mud

off the horse's legs. Don't forget under the mane. Brush gently but firmly, using a flicking motion as the brush leaves the horse's body to help lift up the deeply embedded dirt.

3. Use the soft finishing brush to brush out any remaining hair and dirt and to give your horse's coat a nice shine.
4. Finish by rubbing down your horse's coat with a clean, soft towel.

As you groom your horse, look for cuts, parasites, or other skin problems. Be aware of any tenderness he may exhibit as you brush him. While picking out his hooves, look for any bruises or sensitivity in that area, especially if you picked out a stone or stick that was caught in his foot.

Hooves

Pick out your horse's hooves both before and after riding. Doing so before you ride allows you to pick out anything that might bother the horse's feet on the ride. Doing so after riding allows you to inspect for and remove any stones or pieces of sticks or anything else that the horse may have picked up and gotten stuck in its hoof while on the ride.

Reserve a small, fairly stiff brush (maybe one of those cheap ones that you bought with your startup grooming supplies that has since been replaced with a high-quality natural bristle brush) to remove the dirt and mud from the outside of the hoof.

Pick up a foot and use your hoof pick to gently dig the packed dirt, manure, and bedding out of the grooves (bars) around the triangular-shaped protrusion known as the frog. If your horse is shoeless, the rest of the dirt will pop right out. If your horse has shoes on, which he probably does, then you will also need to remove other packed dirt that has stuck to the inside of the shoe. In winter, the shoe will also have a pad, which is designed to pop the snow out of the hoof. If it doesn't, digging frozen snow out of your horse's hoof can require a little muscle.

Braiding

If you are as inept with hair styling as I am, buy yourself a little braiding kit that comes with rubber bands and a three-pronged fork that splits the hair into three even sections for easier braiding. The kits are available at most tack shops, are inexpensive, and come with instructions.

Bathing

First of all, if your horse isn't properly "halter broken" (see Chapter 11, "Handling") you might as well forget about a bath and spend your time doing some groundwork. Good halter breaking is critical for introducing things such as hoses to horses. You should understand how to let your horse move and at the same time be able to direct that movement to support her and help her understand that the hose is harmless. If you can't do this, you are wasting your time and making things a lot more stressful for your horse than they need to be.

FACTS

I don't condone shaving your horse's whiskers, but if you're going to show your horse, especially at halter, you will need to succumb to this practice. You can use small electric clippers designed for these delicate areas, or some people use disposable human razors, especially for touch-ups. Don't shave the inside of his ears; this hair keeps out dirt, water, and insects. If his ear hair is long and unruly, you can tidy it up with a small pair of scissors.

If you plan to bathe your horse for the first time, don't just turn the hose on her. As with anything new to a horse, take the time to introduce it to her slowly. In so doing, you will save her some stress and save time in the long run. Get plenty of length of hose out. If you have a hose attachment that offers different spray types, choose one that is shower-like—you don't want to drill holes through the horse, though you do want her to feel it. Turn the water on just a bit and begin by spraying the ground near her. Don't do this long enough to frighten her, just to let her know that this "thing" exists; spray the water on her feet and lower legs and let her know that this noisy thing isn't going to hurt her. Keep working up the body and stay at each level until she accepts it. It may take a few sessions, but if you introduce the hose gradually and in a manner fitting to her, she will come to enjoy bath time.

If you aren't using a hose to bathe your horse, assemble the things you will need to bathe her—buckets of warm water, brushes, a sweat scraper, and, depending on the temperature, a light blanket—before you get your horse on the scene. Where you bathe your horse depends on the setup of your barn. If you board, most large facilities will have a specific washroom; one big advantage to this is that there will probably be heated water available. Also, wash areas tend to have cement floors (with rubber mats to avoid slippery footing), which means the ground beneath you doesn't turn to mud while you are bathing your horse.

ESSENTIALS

For tips on grooming your horse, book suggestions, links to other interesting grooming Web sites, and an e-mail discussion list, check out *www.geocities.com/showgrooming.*

You will find it a bit difficult to get a dry horse's coat wet—the way the water runs off is proof in action of how well designed they are to withstand the elements! Once you get her wet, squeeze a thin line of shampoo the length of her body and give her a little shampoo massage. Do one side at a time and rinse it thoroughly before moving on to the other side—leaving shampoo behind to dry into your horse's coat is worse than never having bathed her at all.

The best way to get soap out is to use a hose directly on your horse. Once the horse is thoroughly rinsed, start on his upper body and use the sweat scraper to scrape the excess water off. When you wash the horse's face, use warm water (no soap), a wash cloth, and a little elbow grease. Never get water down a horse's ears.

CHAPTER 9
General Health

Horses seem to be at once very healthy and very delicate. A constant supply of water, quality hay, and supplemental grain when appropriate, combined with lots of turnout time, does more to keep a horse in good health than almost anything else you can do. The well-maintained horse can withstand hot summer or cold winter temperatures, and the physical conditions under which they can thrive range from cushy box stalls in barns rimmed with stained glass windows to a three-sided shed in the middle of a rocky pasture.

But when things go wrong, they can go wrong in a big way. The more you do to prevent horse health problems, the less it will cost the horse in stress and potential lifelong health issues, and the less it will cost you in both time and money.

The Horse's Environment

Chapter 6, "Stabling," and Chapter 7, "Nutrition," offer a lot of information about keeping your horse healthy. Here are some key environmental factors that also contribute to the general good health of your horse:

- Pick manure from stalls and turnout areas at least once per day, more often if there are more than two horses out together. Horses who stand in accumulated manure and breathe in urine odors are susceptible to hoof diseases, chronic respiratory problems, parasite infestations, and a host of other secondary problems.
- Keep areas clear of debris and fences in good repair to avoid physical injury to your horse. Horses can get into enough trouble on their own without your contribution. Fix damaged items—loose fence boards, down electric fence wire, protruding nails—as soon as you see them. If you don't, your horse will surely find them, and that will lead to the most devastating consequences!
- Lock up grain and keep stored hay out of your horse's reach if possible. Close off any areas that aren't safe for a horse to walk in, and keep such areas free of tempting things, such as hay bales, which will lure them into that area.
- Use fencing and equipment designed for horses. Never underestimate the strength of a horse—if you use chain link panels that are made for dog pens, they simply will not withstand a 1,000-pound animal who leans all his weight on it to scratch his very itchy behind.
- If something seems a little dangerous, it is—and it is ten times more dangerous when you add a horse to the picture!

Learn about Good Health for Horses

Start by reading this book, of course. But you will want a few references on hand in the event your horse seems ill. (See Appendix A, "Resources," for a list of veterinary manuals.) Although you should always call a vet when your horse is not well, you also should have something to refer to before the vet arrives.

Your Horse Care Team

I believe in assembling a diverse team of equine-knowledgeable people to help you with your horse's care. This team has many members including you, at least one equine veterinarian, a farrier, an equine dentist, a holistic practitioner, the stable manager if you board your horse, and your group of horse-owning friends.

You

You are the most important person on your horse's team. You not only administer the most care to your horse—preventive and acute—but also pick the other team members—so the success of your team is mostly on your shoulders. You know your horse the best, especially if you keep him at home, and you choose when and if to call in those other team members.

Rarely is money not a factor in making decisions about horse care. It is up to you to decide the level of expense you can handle for your horse and the different horse-related things that may come up. It can be a good use of funds to spend some money up front to educate yourself in equine health, nutrition, and first aid; this is a good way to save yourself from having to call the vet for every little malady but still be able to do the right thing by your horse.

ESSENTIALS   The Web site of Sara Caldwell, D.V.M., who specializes in horses and goats, is *www.horse-vet.com*. This nicely designed site has lots of good basic information and includes numerous useful links.

Veterinarian

Your choice of veterinarian may be limited to who is in your area. If you have a few options, you are fortunate; you may find that they each have an area—for example, reproduction or surgery—that they tend to be more specialized in. You should have one veterinarian who will come to know your horses.

Farrier

Perhaps your farrier will spend most of his or her time simply putting shoes on your horse. However, health problems with the foot can be common, and you should have a farrier who is willing to respond to an emergency and who is knowledgeable in foot health as well as in tacking on a shoe. Most people doing farrier work for a profession have educated themselves in foot health as well as shoeing. In fact, the equine veterinarian's education consists of very few hours on the foot, unless it is the student's specialty area.

FACTS

Your farrier will be a critical member of your horse's health team. You will see the farrier for general maintenance more regularly than any other member of the team—on an average of once every eight weeks. It's important to find someone who you can work well with and whose approach to your horse matches your own.

Equine Dentist

All equine veterinarians are knowledgeable about the horse's teeth— general maintenance and wear and tear. But the teeth are second in importance only to the foot. And just as you wouldn't expect, ask, or even want your veterinarian to trim and shoe your horse, it makes sense that neither would you ask him or her to examine and work on her teeth. A sound practice might be to have your veterinarian check and "float" your horse's teeth (that is, rasp away sharp points) in the spring when he or she administers spring vaccinations. Then, in the fall, you can make an appointment with an equine dentist who also can be used for any special problems throughout the rest of the year.

Although the practice of equine dentistry is becoming more common, equine dentists are not widespread; the ones that are out there are typically extremely busy. Start your search before the need for one arises. Let the dentist get accustomed to your horse with a maintenance check; don't wait for a dental emergency to find a dentist and introduce your horse to dentistry for the first time.

Holistic Practitioner

If you are interested in using homeopathy, herbs, energy therapies such as Reiki, massage, acupressure, and acupuncture in your horse care program, you should find a knowledgeable practitioner (probably more than one) to join your health care team. Read more about this in Chapter 10, "Beyond Conventional Health Care."

Stable Manager

If you board your horse, the person who feeds or leads your horse out to the paddock and back to her stall every day will know a lot about your horse's normal behavior and when she is acting abnormally. He or she may be your first line of defense when it comes to realizing your horse needs health care.

Horse Friends

The group of friends with whom you ride will also be an important part of your team. They are the ones to call to exchange information about a new feed or a place to buy bedding or any of the other ins and outs of owning a horse. They will be your moral support when your horse is ill or lame and while you are working through the sometimes complex process of figuring out just what is wrong. Conversely, you will be an important part of their horse care team as well.

Finding a Veterinarian

Find a local large animal veterinarian before you even bring your first horse home. It's nice to have an established relationship with the vet who has been to your place for routine vaccinations, etc., before you need him or her to come in an emergency situation. If you don't have a horse trailer or the horse can't be transported, it will be comforting to know that the vet already has some idea of how to get to your place.

Finding an equine veterinarian shouldn't be too difficult in most parts of the country. You can simply look in the phone book—if you don't find a large animal veterinary practice listed, call the small animal hospital and ask for a referral.

Once you locate a vet or two, you should get some feedback from horse owners who have used that practice. Stop by a place with horses and ask who they use or whether they know about a particular vet. Or go to a large facility and ask there. Don't ask just one person, however; ask at least three so that you can compare experiences and come to your own conclusion.

After you make a choice, call his or her office and set up a farm call. Ask if you can stop by to see the facility (there is probably a barn set up for surgery and follow-up care). How these inquiries are handled can tell you a lot about the practice.

FACTS

Here are the four important vital statistics to know about the horse:

1. Temperature: between 99 and 101 degrees Fahrenheit
2. Pulse: 30 to 40 beats per minute
3. Respiration: 8 to 20 breaths per minute
4. Capillary Refill Time (CRT): 1 to 2 seconds for blood to return to blanched tissue

While these statistics are average for the mature horse, you should establish a baseline that is normal for your horse.

If everything sounds good on the phone, make a visit to the hospital. You should find a neat, clean facility with professional staff who know how to answer your questions. If the first visit by the vet to your barn goes well and all other things check out, you've got yourself the beginning of a long-term relationship!

Establish a Baseline

If you just bought your horse, you may have had a vet check (see Chapter 5, "A Horse of Your Own") performed. The results of this exam can give you a baseline with which to begin to know your horse's health—a standard from which she may veer off. You would have gotten a temperature, respiration, and pulse report.

Don't attack your horse with a rectal thermometer the minute you get her home, but do learn how to perform such procedures so that you know how to do them and your horse will be accustomed to them before she is actually ill. The best way to keep your horse healthy is to get to know her inside and out.

Vaccinations

Annual vaccinations are the most basic part of health maintenance. Besides the universal diseases, your veterinarian will know others that are common to your area and will recommend vaccinations accordingly.

If you have travel plans that include crossing state lines, tell the vet which states you will be going through and what your final destination is; there may be diseases common to those areas, and some vaccinations may need to be given weeks ahead to offer effective protection. There are other concerns when traveling across state lines; for example, a health certificate is required. So check with your vet beforehand. A few of the most common diseases for which vaccinations exist are listed in the following sections.

E/W Encephalomyelitis

Also known as sleeping sickness or blind staggers, this disease is carried by mosquitoes and has a high mortality rate. Signs of infection are excessive depression and high fever. Vaccinate annually and sometimes twice annually in areas where mosquito season runs well into the fall.

Tetanus

Horses are very susceptible to tetanus, and their environment—old barns, rusty nails, manure—readily supports this bacteria that affects the nervous system and for which successful treatment is difficult at best. Again, there is an effective annual vaccination for tetanus. If your horse suffers a deep puncture wound, your vet may administer a booster tetanus vaccine at the time of the trauma.

Rabies

Unfortunately, rabies is a problem throughout most of the United States. This horrible disease of the central nervous system has an outcome of certain death; it is not one to mess with—for their sake and for yours, since rabies is communicable to humans (from contact with the saliva of an afflicted animal to an open wound). Statistics are not high for horses contracting rabies, but those who live in open situations and/or have access to pasture are prime candidates, since they come in contact with skunks, raccoons, bats, and other common rabies carriers. There is no need to get paranoid about rabies; vaccinating your horse annually is an easy and worthwhile precaution.

It is up to you to halter break your horse thoroughly enough for him to be gentle to handle. A vet should be able to give your horse a simple physical, administer annual vaccinations, and draw blood without difficulty. However, don't let any practitioner handle your horse in a way you don't approve of.

Equine Infectious Anemia (EIA)

Currently, there is no vaccination against EIA, though there is treatment for symptoms, which can be chronic. The so-called Coggins test requires the drawing of blood, which is tested for EIA. Although proof of a negative Coggins test is required for a horse to cross state lines and is also usually required at all horse shows and other events where horses congregate, this test has drawn a lot of controversy of late. If a horse tests positive, most states require the horse to be either quarantined or destroyed. Some horses test positive and are considered carriers but never exhibit clinical signs of the disease (which include fever, loss of appetite and weight loss, anemia, and muscular weakness). Again, these horses are either destroyed or quarantined. The controversy comes from the fact that since a small percentage of all horses in the country get tested, the ones that do—typically those that travel for shows and other events and need to produce a negative Coggins test for admission to the event's grounds—are thought by some to be unfairly penalized. It's another one of those things that will play itself out over time.

Potomac Fever

This disease was first diagnosed in the Potomac region of Maryland. It can, however, occur anywhere in the country. Your veterinarian will know whether there have been incidences in your area and whether or not horses in your area should be vaccinated. If contracted, the disease needs to be treated immediately, or it can become quite serious. Symptoms begin with the horse going off his feed, followed by severe diarrhea.

Lyme Disease

Carried by ticks, Lyme disease has become a concern in humans, pets, and livestock. The use of tick-controlling fly sprays can help prevent this disease, particularly in spring, when ticks are most voracious. The very tiny deer tick is the culprit in the spread of Lyme disease. Vaccinations are becoming available for humans and dogs; perhaps horse vaccinations will soon follow.

QUESTIONS?

What is azoturia?
Also known as "tying up" or "Monday morning disease," **azoturia** refers to the cramping of a horse's large muscles.

Strangles

This inflammation of the upper respiratory tract causes swollen lymph nodes that often abscess and break, contaminating the area and making other horses susceptible. Strangles is highly contagious and hearty, making a horse infectious for as long as a month, and any areas he has infected can remain so for long periods of time. Nasal vaccinations now exist for strangles. Because of the disease's persistence, vaccination makes sense if you do a lot of traveling that exposes your horse to other transient horses.

Healthy Teeth

The condition of a horse's teeth is critical to his overall well-being. The domesticated horse is fed in such a way that he does not wear his teeth evenly, as he would in the wild while grazing on pasture all the time. Add to that having to hold a bit in his mouth. By domesticating such an animal, we have made ourselves responsible for some things that nature would normally take care of. (See Chapter 3, "Anatomy," for a section on the anatomy of the horse's mouth and tooth structure.)

It is important to have an equine dentist look at your horse, but they are very busy and expensive. I take a two-step approach:

1. In the spring, I have my regular equine veterinarian check my horses' teeth during the "spring shots" visit; the vet looks for sharp edges and loose caps. Tooth maintenance is always important for good digestion. Also, here in the Northeast, spring begins our heaviest riding season, and a look at the teeth can prevent bit discomfort.
2. In the fall, before we go into the cold winter, I have my horses' teeth checked again by an equine dentist; that way I can be sure that the extra feed I am starting to give them to keep warm in winter is going to be used efficiently.

In order to effectively examine the horse's teeth, your practitioner will use a speculum. Speculums come in many designs; they all serve the function of keeping the horse's mouth wide open so that a thorough visual and manual examination can take place and teeth can be easily accessed.

ESSENTIALS

The dental speculum is used to prop open the horse's mouth for inspection of the teeth and mouth and to perform work on the teeth. They are usually made of metal and are held open in a variety of ways. Expect your equine dentist to use one to do a proper examination.

You should be prepared with a couple of buckets of warm water for rinsing tools and rinsing the horse's mouth during dental work. The most

1. Appaloosa

2. Paint

3. American Quarter Horse

Illustration by Orren Mixer

4. Tennessee Walking Horse

Photo Credit: Stuart Vesty

5. Connemara Pony

6. Thoroughbred

7. Fresian

8. Percheron

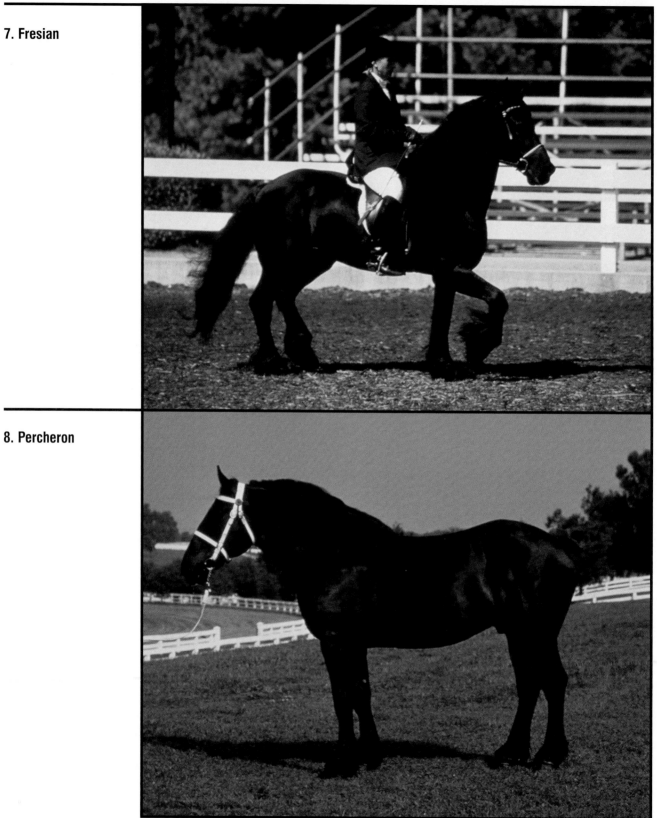

9. Shire

Photo Credit: Sharon McLin

10. Arabian

11. Norwegian Fjord

12. Foundation Quarter Horse

13. Morgan

Illustration by Jeanne Mellin

14. Belgian

15. Shetland Pony

Photo Credit: Carrie Rudeen

16. Saddlebred

**Photo Credit:
Jamie Donaldson**

common thing the dentist may find in the examination are sharp edges that have been created by uneven wear of the teeth. These can make it difficult to chew and cause inefficient digestion of feed; they can also cause ulcerations of the mouth lining that cause the horse to lose interest in eating.

Lameness

The causes of lameness can be external or internal. The center of the problem is usually in either the leg or the foot. You may or may not know what caused the lameness. Common lameness problems are typically seen in horses who are subject to a lot of foot stresses such as abrupt changes in direction, landing from jumps, and so on, as well as in overweight horses or breeds like the quarter horse, who have often been genetically manipulated to have heavy muscular bodies supported by small legs and feet. Navicular diseases cause changes in the tissues and supporting structure of the small navicular bone in the foot. A farrier can help make the horse more comfortable. Although horses can be used once they have developed a navicular disease, such use is often limited.

Obvious Causes

If a horse suddenly becomes lame, the first place to look is the foot. Check the foot on the lame leg for a nail, stick, or stone. If nothing is there, begin to check the rest of the leg for tender spots, swelling, or warmness, which is a sign of inflammation. At the tender site, look for an abrasion or puncture wound. An abrasion would probably have to be significant and, therefore, very visible to cause lameness, but puncture wounds can be extremely deep and hard to detect. A puncture wound as high as the shoulder could cause lameness as well.

You may have witnessed your horse fall, get a leg caught under or in a fence, go through an unsafe wooden structure, or fall getting out of the horse trailer. Although these accidents can cause serious and even permanent lameness, sometimes it is a comfort to at least know what the cause was.

Minor lameness from obvious causes is fairly manageable. If you saw the incident happen, administering arnica (see Chapter 10, "Beyond

Conventional Health Care") immediately can be very effective. However, its effectiveness is thought to be lessened as time passes. So if you didn't see a crash, misstep, or fall, it may be too late for arnica to help significantly (though it won't hurt, either). You might want to administer phenylbutazone—also known as bute—an anti-inflammatory pain reliever, for a day or two to help relieve the horse's pain. However, bute is a drug and needs to be prescribed by your veterinarian, who will want to see the horse first. The thing to be careful of with bute and other pain-masking drugs is that they can make the horse feel good enough to move around too much. If the horse can remain calm in his stall for a day or two, bute combined with limited mobility may be all that is needed.

Mystery Lamenesses

If a mystery lameness doesn't respond to bute and stall rest within a day or two, call the vet. Make sure the bute has passed through the system—it normally takes twenty-four hours—and that the lameness is evident again by the time the vet comes, so that he can see the lameness in action.

Lameness is a serious issue under the best of circumstances, but when you have no idea what has caused it, getting your veterinarian on the scene as soon as possible can make the difference between short-term layups and chronic lameness. Your vet may want to take X-rays or perform a nerve block test to zero in on the real issue.

ESSENTIALS

To pinpoint lameness problems, your vet may want to administer a nerve block test. This diagnostic tool numbs an area of the leg to see if the lameness disappears when the horse cannot feel pain from the affected area.

Laminitis

Like colic, laminitis is one of the things horse owners hear about a lot. By definition, laminitis is inflammation of the laminae in the foot (see the illustration of foot anatomy in Chapter 3, "Anatomy"). It is typically used interchangeably with the term *founder,* but founder is actually a result of laminitis that has progressed enough for the coffin bone to rotate, resulting in a chronic condition caused by permanent structural damage. Horses who have foundered can be kept fairly comfortable through drugs and corrective shoeing, but they will only be able to withstand extremely light riding, if any at all.

Common causes of laminitis are overeating grain or lush pasture and postpartum infection of the mare, both of which cause enterotoxemia. Following are the signs of laminitis:

- Hot feet caused by increased circulation
- Rapid pulse in foot area
- Preference for laying down to take weight off feet—when all four feet are involved
- Leaning back on its hind end to relieve the front feet or holding her front legs out in an odd stretched position—if just the two front feet are involved

Laminitis and founder are conditions that will require your farrier and veterinarian to work together to treat the horse.

Colic—the Equine "C Word"

While horses do get cancer, the frightening "C word" in the horse world is colic. Almost everything you do for your horse has some effect on the horse's potential for colic. Feeding schedule, food storage, the feed itself, access to fresh water, stress, hard riding, no exercise, trailering, administering medications, feeding on the ground, escaping, and overeating—you name it and colic can be the result!

What Is Colic?

Colic is simply a stomachache. It can be many different kinds of stomachache—gassy, not gassy, causing diarrhea, or causing constipation. But what may simply be a stomachache in many other animals is a life-threatening condition for the horse.

Colic is not a disease in and of itself but a symptom of some other problem. It may be an external factor such as overeating or bad feed, or it may be caused by something internally such as a strong heat cycle in a mare, a parasite infestation, or even a tumor. The cause may be obvious— you found your horse in the grain room halfway finished with what was a full bag of grain. But if it is something less obvious, it can be difficult to find the cause. If the cause is chronic, either colic will occur again or some other symptom will arise.

What Are the Signs of Colic?

The signs of colic can be many; this is where it is important to come to know your horse's usual behavior. Being a picky eater can be a normal thing for one horse but a colic warning sign in another horse who normally eats with relish. Other things to watch for include the horse not passing manure, grabbing at her sides with her mouth or kicking at her stomach with her back legs, exhibiting restlessness in her stall, sweating excessively for no apparent reason (such as hard work or extremely hot temperatures), or laying down for a long period of time and not getting up when you encourage her or rolling.

What Do You Do for a Colicky Horse?

The first thing to do is alert your veterinarian. If you just started to see signs of colic, you may not think it is necessary for him to pay a visit yet. However, your vet will want to get in on the scene as soon as possible—addressing colic immediately can mean the difference between a simple bellyache and a life-threatening situation. (See the sidebar for a list of questions your vet is likely to ask.)

If the horse is not passing manure, there are a few things you can do to encourage this. First, try getting the horse out and walking around. This will serve to keep the horse from laying down or rolling. If the horse's stomach is impacted with feed that won't pass through, rolling can cause the intestine to twist, which is absolutely to be avoided. In a mild colic episode, getting the horse moving can stimulate her system to cause her to pass manure.

Another strategy is to load the horse into a horse trailer. This can be just the stimulation he needs. Even though my mare walks calmly into a trailer, she is still on edge and almost immediately passes manure when she gets in. If your horse does not load well, even simply asking him to load can be enough. However, if your horse is really afraid of getting into a trailer, do not add this stress to the already existing stress of colic.

Pain-relieving medications such as Banamine are often administered to relieve the pain of gas colic and can help relax the muscles enough to help the horse release gas and/or manure and relieve the colic episode. But administer medication only if you have lots of experience or the veterinarian recommends it. If the drug masks the symptoms, the veterinarian will not be able to make an accurate diagnosis and suggest a treatment regimen.

FACTS

Here are some questions your vet is likely to ask during an exam for colic:
- When is the last time the horse ate?
- Has the horse gotten loose? If so, what might she have eaten?
- Is the horse passing manure?
- What is the horse's temperature?
- Is she nervous and pacing or standing in a corner hanging her head?
- Is she laying down a lot? Has she rolled?
- Is she grabbing or kicking at her sides?

Chapter 10, "Beyond Conventional Health Care," covers other treatments you can administer while waiting for the vet to arrive. Reiki, massage, and other energy therapies can help relieve the colic and relax the horse and make him more comfortable while waiting for an assessment of the situation.

Deworming

Because they eat from the ground and often on less than lush pasture, horses are subject to being robbed of nutrition and having their digestive tract damaged by many different kinds of parasitic worms. Your veterinarian will have a suggested deworming program. Because different parasites thrive in different climates, soil, and conditions, you should follow a deworming schedule recommended for your area. Most of the medications are the same, but one area of the country may need to administer them on a different schedule than another.

The best defense against worms is prevention. Clean manure out of the horse's area as often as possible. Of course, it isn't feasible to stand behind the horse with a manure fork, but picking out stalls daily and paddocks once or twice a day is ideal. Fresh manure is the perfect environment for flies to lay their eggs, which, if left in the paddock, can be ingested by the horse.

Following are the most problematic worms that affect horses:

- **Small and large strongyles:** Both are bloodsucking worms that attach themselves to the intestine and can cause anemia and ulcers.
- **Pinworms:** These live in the large intestine and can cause irritation around the rectum.
- **Roundworms:** Roundworms can cause intestinal blockage if the buildup is large, but regular deworming typically keeps the population within tolerable levels.
- **Tapeworms:** These are not too common in horses. However, when present, they steal nutrients and, like any worm infestation, large numbers can cause anemia, wasting, and colic.
- **Bots:** Bot flies lay little yellow eggs on the horse's body; the eggs are ingested and cycle through the body passing out through the manure, where the fly emerges and the cycle repeats itself. Like all worms, they are nutrient robbers in high quantities.
- **Lungworms:** Rare in horses but usually associated with donkeys, lungworms live in the lungs.

The best thing to do is have a sample of your horse's manure tested and then deworm accordingly. A simple inexpensive test will detect most worms, but tapeworms and a few others can be detected only by a more expensive test whose results take longer to return. Most horse owners find this cumbersome and simply administer a scheduled deworming program, typically every other month. Don't neglect this important aspect of your horse's health. Or instead of feeding your horse, you'll be feeding a parasite population!

To treat worms, most people use paste dewormers that come in syringe-like tubes. All you have to do is spin the little dial up to the proper weight for your horse and administer the appropriate amount of paste onto the back of the horse's tongue.

Avoid administering paste dewormers around mealtimes. The thick paste stays in the horse's mouth for a while before it all dissolves and is swallowed. If the horse has access to hay after getting a mouthful of paste, he can use the hay to cleanse his palette by spitting out the worm medication-soaked wad of hay. Also, after you deposit the medicine in the horse's mouth, lift his chin up for thirty seconds or so to avoid having a wad of paste drop out onto the ground.

Fly Control

The first line of defense against flies is getting fresh manure away from the barn. (Manure management is probably the most important thing you can do for the health of your horse.) From there, you will need to deal with the flies themselves.

Many spray products are on the market. Each control some flies better than others. Large facilities often have built-in fly spraying that operates on a timer. You will more likely be out there in the paddock spraying your horse down once or twice a day.

Follow the instructions on the bottle for how much and how often to spray your horse. As with deworming medications, keep an eye on the horse for an allergic reaction, usually in the form of hives, to a certain fly spray. Some products that didn't bother a horse last year may cause hives this year, so don't be complacent just because you have used the same fly spray every year.

Using Fly Sprays

For years, I simply brought the spray bottle out to the paddock and sprayed the horses down each morning. At some point, after watching the spray settle on their hay and having it blow back into my face, I decided that this was not a good idea. Now, I reserve a brush especially for fly spray; I set the brush down and spray it directly, and then brush the horse. This method seems to avoid having spray land just anywhere, including in my lungs. You can also use a face mask.

Small biting flies of different varieties really like to get along the horse's belly midline, in their ears, right at the top of their foretop, and in other places the horse can't reach. Be sure to protect these places.

Never spray fly spray on the horse's face. Spray it on a mitt or a small brush reserved exclusively for this purpose and carefully apply it to the horse's face, avoiding his eyes.

Nonchemical Methods of Fly Repellant

Garlic powder in the horse's feed is said to help control biting flies. It doesn't reduce the population per se, but at least the flies don't land. This is a messy method of fly control, although perhaps not more messy than fly spray! Springtime Products sells garlic powder by the tub specifically for this purpose. You will need to introduce it to your horse's feed gradually and a few weeks before fly season kicks in. Garlic powder is also said to boost the immune system and enhance coat condition.

You can also buy mesh fly sheets that cover the horse's body but are light and not hot in warm weather. Another tactic is to put your horses in stalls during the times of day when the flies are out in force—typically midday to dark—and leave them out overnight when the flies are not as bad.

Your Equine First Aid Kit

Don't wait for something to happen before you gather some basic first aid supplies. Having a first aid kit on hand can be the best insurance against having to use it! Know what is in the kit and what each item is for. In cold climates, keep any liquids, lotions, or paste medications somewhere warm but handy. Like all medications, be sure your equine meds are kept out of reach of pets and small children.

You can buy ready-made equine first aid kits in tack shops and from horse supply catalogs. Although items can be less expensive when purchased à la carte, the container itself offers a convenient way to keep everything together. Kits also often include a laminated information card about basic first aid. Once you figure out what kinds of bandages and other supplies you like best, you can tailor your first aid kit to your own preferences.

If you assemble your own first aid kit, here are some items to include:

- A few different kinds of bandages
- A traditional quilted leg wrap
- Tube of antibiotic cream
- Iodine
- Hydrogen peroxide
- Vet wrap
- Rubber and/or latex gloves
- Thermometer, either digital or heavy-duty ring top with string attached
- Scissors
- Adhesive tape
- Hand wipes
- Banamine, bute, "bute-less," or other equine-approved pain relievers

Also, keep a cold pack in the freezer and, depending on how adventuresome you are in your equine self-care program, keep a supply of different size needles and syringes on hand, as well as a vial of antibiotics (make sure they are up to date), epinephrine (for allergic reactions, and only under the advice of a veterinarian), and perhaps some B vitamins. See Appendix A, "Resources," for a list of veterinary manuals.

Surface Wounds

You can clean these yourself with warm water and an antiseptic solution. If the wound is bleeding, dust it with a blood coagulant.

Deeper Lacerations

You should probably call your vet immediately for deeper lacerations to determine the need for stitches. Puncture wounds need to be carefully examined to ascertain if any part of the object is still lodged in the wound. Puncture wounds are exceptionally susceptible to infection, as dirt gets trapped and the airless environment provides a perfect breeding ground for bacteria. Your vet will be able to thoroughly clean the wound and will probably prescribe a precautionary course of antibiotics.

Hives

Hives show up as raised bumps usually all over the horse's neck and body. In and of themselves, hives are not a serious issue and rarely even itch, although they look like they should. However, they do indicate a reaction to something. Figure out what has been introduced to your horse—a fly spray, a supplement—and avoid that product. Hives are common in the spring, when horses are losing their winter coats. If your horse has a good case of spring hives, your vet will hold off on spring vaccinations until the hives are under control.

QUESTIONS?

What does proud flesh mean?
A wound that won't heal produces scar tissue that protrudes from the wound area. This scar tissue is commonly referred to as **proud flesh**.

Eye Wounds

One spring my mare decided to give me a round of eye wounds to care for. I never found out what caused them, but one eye swelled up quite a bit. A month or two after the eye cleared up, she did it again, though less drastically. In both cases, the vet administered a green dye that allowed him to check for foreign objects in the eye. Then, I was to administer a topical pupil dilating ointment once a day for three days as well as an antibiotic ointment twice a day for a week to ten days.

I allowed her to go outside with a fly mask on to block the light, and she had full access to her stall so that she could get out of the sunlight if she chose. After a couple days, she sure hated to see me coming to poke ointment in her eye, but everything cleared up nicely both times. And she hasn't had an eye problem since.

General Health for the Geriatric Horse

It is hoped that your horse will be blessed with a long and healthy life. Horses commonly live to their late twenties and even thirty-plus these days. If your horse reaches that ripe old age, you can be proud of your equine management skills. By this age, the horse may be able to be ridden lightly—say, a little pony ride for your five-year-old nephew or a trip down to the mailbox each afternoon—but most likely will no longer be rideable.

The ailment you will most likely have to deal with is arthritis. With medication and/or support from natural products such as glucosamine, your elderly equine can probably be kept comfortable. For the arthritic horse, you need to be concerned with his ability to get up after laying down for a little nap or taking a little roll. If you stall your horses, give the older horse as large a stall as possible; some movement helps alleviate stiffness. And if he is getting either picked on or jostled around too much, you may find it necessary to separate him from the younger horses.

The other ailment you will most likely have to deal with is digestion. Old horses have worn teeth that just don't work like they used to. Many commercial feeds are designed especially for senior equines. They are typically more palatable and are easier to chew. You may have to make an effort to keep enough weight on your horse. Try to avoid first-cut hay with the older horse, and give him later-cut hay, which is softer and more easily digested.

Keep a close eye on your old pal, especially during winter months if you live in the north. Offer him a few extras—warmed water, a blanket—to help him live a comfortable retirement.

Of course, ultimately, the older horse will present you with that heart-wrenching decision of when the time has come to euthanize him. If you can keep him comfortable and enjoying life, that's great. But when the horse spends most of his day in noticeable pain and no longer cares about the world, it's time to be good to your old friend. The unfortunate reality is that horses are large animals, and the disposal of their bodies is easier if preplanned. There are many options that you should discuss with your vet.

Prevention Is Key

The things that can befall a horse are pretty overwhelming. Rectal prolapse, bowed tendons, scratches—the list is endless. Unless you have several horses for several years, the chance that you will experience even a small percentage of these is slim. The best expenditure of your time and money and the best approach to benefit your horse is in learning about how to keep horses in good health and practicing good equine management and preventive measures.

CHAPTER 10

Beyond Conventional Health Care

E quine holistic practitioners—many of whom are veterinarians—consider the whole patient and not just the disease, condition, or symptoms. The goal is to understand the immediate problem and the contributing factors and then propose therapies that enable the horse to heal from within itself *and* prevent recurrences. As you'll discover, even in crisis situations such as colic and laminitis, when speedy veterinary attention is crucial, complementary therapies offer the horse owner additional strategies for better outcomes and recoveries, as well as preventive care. We'll review holistic approaches in three categories: body work, nutritional support, and energy work.

The Holistic Approach

Here are some suggestions for finding a holistic practitioner:

- Ask your vet or at local barns for recommendations.
- Check bulletin boards at tack shops, feed stores, health food stores, natural pharmacies, and herb shops.
- Contact holistic veterinary organizations, such as the following, to find local practitioners:
  - Academy of Veterinary Homeopathy (AVH): *avh@naturalholistic.com* or 503-569-0795 (Oregon)
  - American Holistic Veterinary Medical Association (AHVMA): 410-569-0795 or (fax) 410-569-2346 (Maryland)
  - American Veterinary Chiropractic Association (AVCA): *amvetchiro@aol.com* or 309-658-2920 (Illinois)
  - International Veterinary Acupuncture Society (IVAS): *ivasoffice@aol.com* or 303-682-1167 (Colorado)

QUESTIONS?

What is alternative medicine?

Alternative medicine refers to diagnostic and treatment systems (modalities) not commonly taught in medical/veterinary schools such as nutrition, herbal medicine, homeopathy, chiropractic, and acutherapies.

Complementary (or adjunctive or integrative) medicine: This refers to natural treatments used in addition to conventional therapies, usually under the direction of a holistic vet and sometimes encouraged by traditional vets.

Holistic medicine: Holistic approaches take into account a wide range of factors—all systems of the individual horse as well as its care and overall environment—to propose preventive and treatment strategies to improve health and well-being.

Body Work

Massage: Stress Point Therapy

The muscular system of the horse accounts for 60 percent of the horse's body weight and is entirely responsible for movement. It is also the seat of mobility problems such as some lamenesses and reduced range of motion and flexibility, which can diminish performance. Whether your horse is a competitive athlete or accustomed to leisurely trail rides, it's likely that at some point, he'll experience muscle strain and spasms. According to Jack Meagher in his book *Beating Muscle Injuries for Horses*, "Any muscle [or] any portion of a muscle which is not working for the horse is working against the horse—ACTIVELY. Restore proper motion to the malfunctioning part and the [horse] recovers effective performance."

Always consult a veterinarian any time your horse is ill or severely injured. If you're lucky enough to find a vet who knows and incorporates alternative methods, all the better for your horse.

Motion occurs solely because muscles move bones by contracting and folding over upon themselves. These folds then release so that the muscle can stretch to full length. Damaged, tight muscles cannot release completely. A muscle's ability to relax is reduced and concussive stresses are transmitted down the line to other muscles and finally to the tendons, which have limited flexibility and are thus vulnerable to serious, sometimes permanent, damage. Because the horse often compensates for a damaged part by increasing stress on a healthy part, restrictions in one area of the body can appear somewhere else. Adding massage therapy to your routine before you exercise your horse will help him maintain supple muscles and efficient motion and avoid tendon damage and torn tissue.

The basis of Stress Point Therapy, used for decades by sports therapist Jack Meagher, is to locate and relieve the tight muscle that leads to the muscle spasm that leads to restricted motion—*before* the muscle is torn. Spasms are areas of clumped tendinous attachment tissue that cannot release. They occur at the anchoring end of muscles, near the bone—the stress points that this therapy is named for.

Prevention of serious damage is always the goal. The release process uses direct pressure from your fingers to dilate capillaries, cross-fiber friction to separate knotted muscle fibers, and compression with the heel of the hand or a loose fist to allow the entire muscle to relax and release the original spasm before exercise. The book *Beating Muscle Injuries for Horses* shows maps of all the stress points and specifics on identifying and correctly treating spasms and restrictions. It takes you through the process of identifying where motion is restricted so that you can provide the release that restores elasticity.

Chiropractic

Chiropractors focus on the relationship of the spinal column both to organic systems (nerves, organs, and immune system) and to the biomechanics of movement. The key approach in chiropractic is manipulation, and the key to success is the skill and training of the person using the technique.

The laws of biomechanics require that each part of the body interact with others *precisely*. When one part in the equine body loses its specific relationship with its coworkers, thousands of pounds of force can adversely affect the system. Long-term misalignments may be apparent in uneven muscle development or weight-bearing capacities. Even tiny structural changes can result in discomfort for the horse and will probably show up under saddle or in exercise.

Chiropractors use palpation—checking for pain or asymmetries with their hands—and flexion of the horse's limbs and joints to identify problem areas in the skeletal structure. Adjustments are made manually using a brief thrust at specific locations or by manipulating the body of the horse to provide release in various joints. This should be a relatively gentle process, always without force.

Acupressure

Acupressure is an easy and rewarding therapy that you can use yourself to protect, repair, and promote the well-being of your horse. The benefits seem to be so vast and varied that you will probably want to devote more time than is possible here to learning the basic principles and developing your skills. Acupressure is based on the meridian system at the heart of Traditional Chinese Medicine (TCM). Meridians are pathways in the body along which flows the energy considered vital to health, known as *chi* (sometimes spelled *qi*). In TCM, it is thought that any block or break along a meridian causes a chi imbalance that may appear as illness or discomfort. Therefore, the goal in TCM—and acupressure—is to maintain or repair interruptions in energy flow.

FACTS

In TCM, the ear is considered a miniature representation of the entire body, making "ear work" useful to relax a tense horse or rebalance an injured or ill one. Ear work is also very relaxing for horses being shod or examined by a vet. Some basic ear massages involve gently rubbing the tips of the ears to help relax the horse and rubbing in circles at the base of the ear to aid digestion and respiration. Be sure to gradually get your horse comfortable about having his ears touched before using this method for relieving stress.

The meridian system contains twelve main meridians, each related to major organ systems. Other points outside the twelve meridians are also important to the strong flow of chi. Zidonis, Soderberg, and Snow's *Equine Acupressure: A Working Manual* is one good source for point location and provides a comprehensive overview and guidelines to using acupressure, including strategies for relieving many common problems.

Acupuncturists have used the Qi Gong Machine (QGM) in treatment for humans for years, and the device has now been proven very effective with horses. Equisonic QGM is designed specifically for horses. The machine emits low-level (infrasonic) sound waves in the 8 to 14 hertz range, at the opposite frequency range from ultrasound (20,000 to 100,000 hz). Studies have shown that during hands-on healing, qi gong healers emit frequencies in this range. Because tissues do not heat up and there are no side effects, the QGMs can safely be used by anyone. It has helped horses recover from fractures, laminitis, chronic and acute inflammation, sprains, tendon damage, colic, puncture wounds, and navicular disease.

The relationship between the acupoints and their effects may seem strange at first if you aren't used to Chinese therapies—the points used to relieve symptoms are often located at a distance from the apparent site of injury or illness. The spleen meridian, for example, which runs up the right hind leg and across the horse's barrel, is related to the immune system, the digestive tract, and muscles and soft tissue. This first point on the spleen meridian (SP1), located on the right hind heel, is said to provide the horse's essential body energy. Stimulating SP1 balances the energy throughout the meridian. SP6 relieves gastrointestinal imbalances, including chronic diarrhea; SP9 relieves stifle pain and enhances the immune system; and so on.

Basic acupressure is typically done by gently applying and releasing between 2 and 4 pounds of pressure with the thumb to stimulate points. Watch your horse as you work to see whether you need to reduce pressure. He should relax, not tense, with your touch. Often, the horse's lips, chin, or eyelids will quiver as relief flows. He may yawn repeatedly. Work both the left and right sides of the horse from front to rear and top to bottom. Significant improvements are often immediately apparent, making acupressure a valuable adjunct to other therapies, improving recovery time and outcomes.

Herbs and Nutritional Supplements

Herbs for Health

Herbal medicine was a primary base of veterinary care until the twentieth century. Today many pharmaceutical drugs are based on natural and synthetic versions of the active compounds in plants. However, there is more value to herbs than just their active chemical compounds, and often much benefit is lost in the process of isolating active ingredients for the pharmaceutical version. According to Dr. Andrew Weil, a well-known proponent of natural medicine, plant-based drugs can be more toxic than the natural form of the plant.

It is rare for horses today to have access to the range of plants their ancestors encountered in the wild or in country pastures, but if they do, they will instinctively select the botanicals that contain what they need. In her book *A Modern Horse Herbal*, herbalist Hillary Page Self says, "Normally, unless forced by starvation, [horses] will not voluntarily eat any fodder which will do them harm. Therefore be aware of this and be guided by it. If the horse is not enthusiastic about a particular herb, find an alternative one to feed." She also says that horses will refuse an herb they've readily accepted once they no longer require its support.

FACTS

Medicinal herbs can enhance conventional medical treatment, boost and support the immune system for preventive maintenance, and offer remedies for some common problems that plague horses and the humans who care for them. Most remedies are based on repeated observation of the choices animals in a natural environment make when they are ill or injured.

Herbs can be added to the horse's feed, used as simple topical remedies or as poultices for swellings, bites, or abscesses. As in other aspects of horse care, it's possible to spend a lifetime studying herbs and not have enough time to learn half of everything there is to know. However, there are great resources available from people who *have* studied extensively that you can use as references, if you decide to add natural herbal support to your horse care routine.

More and more health food stores and specialty shops offer a wide array of botanical options. A 1,000-pound horse requires about an ounce (30 grams) of the herb of choice a day, so it pays to find out whether your local vendor offers quantity discounts or bulk options. There are also companies that specialize in providing herbal blends that are already combined for use in specific circumstances.

There are herbal answers for a wide range of questions about equine health. It's important to educate yourself or to find a knowledgeable source to be sure you're helping your horse, not creating problems. Not all herbs are safe for long-term use or every situation. Also, remember that many drugs are based on botanicals, and some herbs will show up as banned substances in American Horse Show Association drug tests.

ESSENTIALS

Dried herbs are simple to store. Cold does them no harm, so you can keep them in the barn during the winter. Avoid direct sunlight and damp areas—a dry, dark place is best. Store them in a container with a tight-fitting lid such as a glass jar, or in a Ziplock bag.

Garlic

Dozens of recent studies have shown that ancient garlic eaters such as the Egyptians were on to something important. Garlic has been shown to lower human blood cholesterol and blood pressure and prevent heavy metal poisoning. It can even slow the growth of certain tumors. In the United States, it is most commonly fed to horses as an insect repellent. Horses excrete the sulfur from garlic through their skin, which keeps bugs away.

However, one of the most important uses for garlic with equines is colic prevention. Garlic supports the good bacteria so vital to digestion. Since antibiotics wipe out all bacteria, feeding garlic is valuable after conventional antibiotics are given to encourage the good bacteria to re-establish. Garlic also acts as an antibiotic and has been particularly effective with respiratory infections and for seasonal respiratory allergies such as hay fever. It can prevent wounds from becoming infected by stimulating the production of white blood cells to strengthen general resistance to infection and improve the immune system. Louis Pasteur, who developed penicillin, thought garlic was just as effective in some situations. Powerful stuff—and powerfully smelly, too—but nothing worthwhile comes without some sort of price!

Garlic can be fed raw if your horse will eat it (some won't, others love it) or in powdered or dried (cold processed to retain the key ingredients) form. Add it to your horse's feed gradually over the course of a week to get her accustomed to the strong flavor. A 1,000-pound horse can be given four to five large or six to eight small crushed cloves a day or between half an ounce to an ounce of powder or granules. (Be sure to tightly seal the lid on powdered garlic to prevent it from clumping in humid weather.)

If you are giving garlic for general wellness, add the garlic to feed for about six weeks or so and then reduce and eliminate the dose. Herbalist Hillary Page Self recommends that herbs be used not on a year-round basis but with occasional breaks in order to give the body the chance to take over on its own. If your horse seems to be at his best with garlic, resume using the herb after a break. Start adding garlic a couple of weeks before the season starts if your horse has allergies or if you use it to deter insects, and keep her on it throughout the period that gives her trouble.

Rosehips

The high concentration of vitamin C in rosehips is great for fighting infection and helping to restore health after a long illness. Botanical sources of nutrients provide the additional benefits, such as fiber, that supplements don't, making rosehips a good choice over a Vitamin C supplement. In *A Modern Horse Herbal*, author Hillary Page Self reports that she has found rosehips to be extremely effective in promoting strong, healthy hooves. Feed half an ounce of chopped rosehip shells a day.

FACTS

Dandelions are a rich source of vitamins A, B, C, and D and minerals like potassium, magnesium, and calcium. It is effective for liver or kidney disorders. Purchase the dried leaves or collect fresh dandelion leaves anytime during the season. Dig for roots in mid to late summer to get the best benefits. (Avoid collecting dandelions from lawns treated with chemicals, though.)

Slippery Elm

The powdered bark from the slippery elm tree can be used as a poultice to encourage wounds to heal (mix the powder with boiling water and let cool to encourage it to stick before you bandage). It helps internally, too, for digestive problems, including ulcers, and is typically gentle enough for even sensitive horses. Add 2 tablespoons to plain yogurt or honey and add it to the feed.

Nutritional Supplements

Humans are discovering the benefits of adding a wide range of supplements to their diets to support good health. The fact is that even if you eat organically grown foods, you might not be able to consume enough to meet your body's requirements for the nutrients cells need. And if the majority of the food you eat is commercially grown, the evidence is that modern farming techniques, based largely on synthetic fertilizers and single-crop fields, have stripped much of the mineral content from the soil and thus from the foods we eat. Processing also destroys many vital nutrients.

The same is true for horse feeds. And as mentioned before, horses have much more limited access to the wide variety of grasses and plants in the wild that would supply their needs. So what's an owner to do? Select the best food you can find and consider bridging the nutritional gap with specific supplements. The following are a few that have found their way into feed rooms around the world.

Antioxidants

When you leave iron tools out in the weather, they oxidize, which produces rust. A similar degenerative process happens in cells. In the metabolic process, the body produces oxides, which are known as free radicals. Antioxidants are key components in the free radical defense system. (Familiar examples of antioxidants are vitamins A, C, and E.) When all is going well, the balance between free radicals and antioxidants keeps cellular damage manageable. However, in times of illness and other stresses—including exposure to pollution, heavy metals, and chemicals—free radicals can overwhelm the body's immune system, leaving the horse vulnerable to infections and illness, perhaps even cancer. Supplemental antioxidants can help return stressed horses to health or prevent stress exposure from negatively impacting health. The body will use and store only the antioxidants it requires and eliminate excess levels. Ideally, your veterinarian can help you determine the best strategy for supplementation.

MSM

MSM (methylsulfonylmethane) is an organic sulfur used by the body to produce enzymes for digestion and antibodies to fight infection and to build connective tissue (e.g., cartilage, skin, and hooves). MSM, used in conjunction with glucosamine, is often recommended for arthritic symptoms to rebuild the cartilage that cushions the bones. It also supports the body to reduce allergic reactions. If your horse gets a case of hives, MSM can erase this allergic reaction.

Glucosamine

Osteoarthritis seems to go hand in hand with an athletic life. When the cartilage that lines the joints to keep bones from rubbing together deteriorates because of wear and tear or age, crippling pain can result. Often an arthritic horse will be stiff before warming up or may resist work that used to be easy for him. Arthritis was once considered incurable, but with the discovery of nutritional support like glucosamine and MSM, the effects of this degenerative disease can often be arrested, if not reversed.

Glucosamine can actually rebuild damaged cartilage, in contrast to anti-inflammatory drugs that mask the pain and therefore can speed up the process of deterioration from overuse. If you and your veterinarian suspect arthritis (if your horse has ever taken a fall, broken a bone, or is in his teens, it's likely), try glucosamine, additional vitamin C, and MSM. (It is worth noting that there is evidence that glucosamine HC1 is more absorbable than glucosamine sulfate.)

You should see a change in about a month. If it's effective, you can keep your horse on glucosamine the rest of his life; this is a substance the body produces naturally, and there are no known side effects from this kind of supplementation. Prices have come way down for glucosamine—you may find it costs about $5 a week to free your horse from arthritis pain. The supplier will provide the right dosage frequency and amounts based on your horse's weight.

Probiotics

Your horse's digestive health may be your primary concern as an owner. Colic is the number one killer of horses, and anything we can do to keep our horses from joining that club is worth knowing about.

Horses process feed with the aid of various digestive bacteria (intestinal flora). These friendly bacteria are greatly reduced in number when your horse is under antibiotic treatment or under stress caused by long-distance traveling, loss of a companion, a move to a new home, and so forth. Also, if you change feed (which should always be done slowly), new flora must develop to break down the new feed. Adding beneficial bacteria (probiotics) to your horse's diet can help him recover more quickly from an illness or difficult adjustment and reduce the chances of colic.

Horse-specific probiotics are widely available from feed stores and catalog suppliers, and dosage suggestions come on the package. Older horses or those prone to mild colic episodes may especially benefit from probiotics. In a pinch, you can use acidophilus made for humans and available at health food stores or pharmacies. Empty three to five capsules into some applesauce, mix, and add it to the feed twice a day for about two weeks. Your horse will eat it up, and the helpful bacteria will help him digest his food efficiently.

The list of dietary supplements is extensive, and as you become more involved with horses, you will find that you add them based on your horse's health and needs. You certainly won't need them all, and you may not need any if your horse is thriving and energetic. But we all age; as time passes, the body can't make or absorb some nutrients as efficiently. Of course, like with anything, we can get carried away with tubs of supplements and generate quite a brew to prepare at your horse's mealtimes! But used wisely, nutritional supplements could add useful years to your horse's life.

ALERT

If your horse's hives are unusually severe or aren't gone in a day or so, or if they get worse, call your vet immediately. Allergic reactions can be serious.

Energy Therapies

For thousands of years, Asian cultures have perfected techniques to improve the flow of life energy called *chi*. Energy practitioners enhance energy to improve total health through various remedies (homeopathics or Bach flowers), tools (needles, magnets, sonic devices, or lasers), or their hands, as with Reiki.

Acupuncture

Acupuncturists use extremely fine needles to release areas of blocked chi at specific acupoints along the meridians, as discussed in the acupressure section. Once normal energy flow is re-established, circulation of chi increases to stimulate the nervous system to restore normal function in the body system that was depleted. Another benefit of acupuncture is the release of endorphins, the body's own "feel good" chemicals. As a result of these benefits, horses generally find acupuncture quite soothing.

Acupuncture is often the treatment of choice for performance problems linked to skeletal issues (such as navicular disease, disk problems, arthritis, and inflamed joints). It has also proven effective for conditions such as allergies, nerve injuries, reproductive disorders, heaves, kidney failure, and liver ailments.

Acupuncturists palpate the acupoints to make diagnoses and determine the best treatment. Because a specific diagnosis is involved, acupuncture is considered the practice of medicine and can only be legally performed by licensed veterinarians. Many more vets are training in this ancient medical art, so it won't be impossible to find someone; if your vet isn't licensed for acupuncture, perhaps he or she can refer you to someone.

Homeopathy

Homeopathic remedies are gaining in popularity both with horse folks and veterinarians. Homeopathy has been practiced for about 200 years in Europe and the United States. The basic premise of homeopathic medicine is that "like cures like," a theory first proposed by Hippocrates, the father of medicine. A substance that in large doses would produce symptoms can, in tiny doses, alleviate those symptoms. Homeopathic remedies stimulate the body's defense system to cope with the problem in a way similar to how vaccines operate.

Homeopathic remedies are made according to strict FDA standards; the natural animal, vegetable, or mineral substance it is based on is present only at an electromagnetic level, which makes this branch of natural medicine difficult to understand, although its effectiveness has been proven over and over.

Homeopathic practitioners use individual symptoms and case studies to devise a strategy to treat chronic or complex problems. And because homeopathics are not drugs, they do not produce positive results in American Horse Show Association drug tests. Success may depend on the experience the practitioner has prescribing remedies, so work with a vet or practitioner who has formally studied this art for the best chances of success. However, simple conditions may be treated at home with specific remedies that are generally available through vitamin suppliers, pharmacies, or health food stores.

FACTS

New uses for laser therapy are being discovered all the time. The modern low-level laser has become an important adjunct to acutherapies. Also, owners can safely use lasers on acupoints, or to effectively stimulate the body to fight off infection, which can be especially helpful if the horse has a reaction to antibiotics or other medications or you need quick results and can't wait for herbs to take effect. One caution: Never shine a laser directly into the eye!

To administer a remedy, insert four to six pellets or tablets (based on your horse's weight) into an apple (carve a little hole in it) or dissolve them in a little water and squirt the liquid onto his tongue. Be careful not to touch the remedy, which will reduce its potency. You can also add the pellets or tablets to grain if your horse is leery of medications in general, although horses can carefully eat all of the grain in their bucket and leave the remedy behind if they desire. Only use the remedy until the symptoms are relieved and use only one type at a time. Store them in a dark, cool, dry place.

Here are some remedies you should have on hand to treat trauma:

- **Arnica Montana:** Everyone should have arnica on hand. It can practically erase bruising and inflammation after an injury such as a kick, fall, or sprain. It also treats or prevents shock in cases of colic or other trauma. It's superior to bute for relieving swelling, tendon strain, or muscle pain after a workout. Many riders keep it on hand for their own use as well! Use 30X or 30C potency right after an accident, one dose every fifteen minutes for an hour or so, then a dose every five hours, reduced to a dose every twelve hours until the pain and swelling are gone. Arnica gel is effective externally for swelling or bruising.
- **Rhus Tox:** Use Rhus Tox for sprains, tendons, or ligament injuries. Start with arnica, then change when the pain and swelling are reduced. Give one dose each morning until improvement is apparent.
- **Ruta Graveolens:** This remedy is particularly effective for tendons, ligaments, and joints. Start with a course of arnica and then change to a dose of Ruta Graveolens once or twice a day.
- **Aconite:** Use for sudden stress, shock, or panic, such as that caused by injury or colic. Dose hourly for up to four hours.

Keep the following remedies on hand to treat allergies:

- **Apis mellifica, Antimonium crudum, or Urtica urens:** Use for hives or other soft, fluid-filled swellings such as insect bites. Apis is also good for filled tendons. Dose hourly until swelling subsides. If you don't see results overnight or symptoms increase, call your vet—a severe allergic reaction may be occurring.
- **Mixed pollens and Arundo:** Use for summer airborne pollens if your horse is shaking his head or has a runny nose from seasonal allergies. One dose up to three times a day can give relief.

Here are some remedies useful for treating wounds:

- **Ledum:** Ledum is very effective for puncture wounds. Administer three to four times daily.
- **Hypericum:** Hypericum is good for punctures, muscle spasms, and after surgery. Administer three times a day.

Bach Flowers

Bach Flowers can be thought of as homeopathy for the emotions. Dr. Edward Bach developed flower remedies in the 1930s to help human patients restore the harmony between mind and body necessary for the well-being of each. Today many holistic animal practitioners swear by the power of Bach Flower remedies to help horses (and every other animal, not to mention humans) to reduce or eliminate negative emotions so that they can better cope with stressful activities or events. If your horse is traumatized, anxious, nervous, or fearful, Bach Flower essences can be used alone or as an appropriate complement to alternative and conventional treatments.

The power of these remedies comes primarily from flowers, though other botanicals and even minerals may be the basis for remedies. They work not on the cellular system but on the subtle energies of the body. They have no side effects; if you use an inappropriate remedy, it simply has no effect. There are thirty-eight individual remedies, plus the combination remedy known as Rescue Remedy. With the assistance of brochures available where you purchase the flower essences, select the appropriate remedy based on your horse's personality and behavior. For example, walnut is useful in helping horses cope with changing circumstances, as when moving to a new home.

FACTS

Rescue Remedy is the most famous of the Bach Flower remedies. It contains a blend of five flower essences specific to reducing the effects of trauma and shock. If your horse suffers a loss of a barn buddy, or has an accident or illness, this remedy can reverse shock (both physical and emotional) and panic. (This remedy is good for people too.)

To use remedies, put four drops on a sugar cube or carrot and feed it to the horse. You can also add about ten drops of one or two remedies to a small amount of water (spring water is best) in a spray bottle and mist around the horse's shoulders, neck, and face. Another option is to spray your palm and cup it lightly over his nostril for a few breaths, and then rub the rest on his muzzle. Remedies can also be added to feed. Rescue Remedy's calming effects can help in an emergency situation.

Magnetic Therapy

Magnets have been used in health care for centuries to improve circulation, oxygen absorption, and cell function. The theory is that the iron atoms in blood corpuscles respond to magnetism to enhance blood flow, which aids in the elimination of waste products and in cellular regeneration. A similar action is thought to carry calcium ions to broken bones. Studies on horses have shown increased blood flow and improved soft tissue function and bone health in the majority of horses tested. Magnetic therapy has been used effectively to treat fractures, wounds, joint problems, and sprains noninvasively.

Magnetic fields are created by the flow of energy between a north and a south pole in static magnets (think of the magnets holding your shopping list to the fridge). In Pulsed Electromagnetic Field magnets the field is created by electric pulses, but static magnets are more common and are found in the leg wraps, hoof wraps, and blankets recently developed for equine uses.

By following a few basic rules, magnets can safely be used by anyone. (As always in cases of serious injury or illness, call in a professional for evaluation and treatment recommendations.) Magnets should only be used for a few consecutive hours or, under vet supervision, a few days at a time. Equine product manufacturers recommend that you don't use magnets on open wounds or burns, on injuries that are less than forty-eight hours old or are hot, or over liniments or chemicals like fly sprays.

Magnetic therapy has been used to improve laminitis outcomes, heal abscesses, relieve inflamed hocks, improve hoof growth, and heal soft tissue injuries, as well as to help muscles remain supple after a hard workout and keep muscles warm between competitive events. This gentle therapy may very well help a horse with chronic conditions like inflammation or poor hoof health to regain a level of soundness.

TTouch

The Tellington Touch (TTouch) was developed by Linda Tellington-Jones Kleger from work she did with Moshe Feldenkrais in the 1970s. Feldenkrais developed a system of gentle, nonhabitual movements and manipulations (the Feldenkrais Method of Functional Integration) to redirect human body patterns that had been established in response to dysfunction, tension, or pain. These new patterns of movement were said to awaken unused brain cells and establish new neural pathways. People from all over the world used the Feldenkrais Method and found relief from pain and new freedom of movement. Some even recovered from paralysis. With TTouch, the primary goal is to enhance the health, performance, and well-being of the horse, as well as to foster communication and trust between horse and handler. It is recommended that the owner or primary handler of the horse be the one to use TTouch on the horse to increase the connection between them.

Here are the four basic TTouch techniques:

1. Stroking with your flat hand to increase circulation and calm the horse
2. Cupping the hand and using the fingertips to move the horse's skin in small or large circles one and a quarter revolutions
3. Cupping the hands and patting the horse over the entire body to stimulate blood circulation
4. Taking up a roll of skin between the thumbs and fingers and sliding it along the muscle surface in straight lines

TTouch for horses incorporates stretches, mouth work, tail work, and ear work to release tension and increase the horse's sense of security. TTouch is often part of a program that includes ground exercises and bodywork called TTEAM (The Tellington-Touch Equine Awareness Method). These techniques promise to increase willingness, horse-human rapport, and athletic performance. Tellington-Jones

Kleger also has a riding component based on her thirty years of experience.

Learn about TTouch techniques from Linda Tellington-Jones Kleger's books (see Appendix A), videos, and nationwide clinics. You can also check out her Web site at *www.tellingtontouch.com.*

Reiki

In many hospitals (for humans) in the United States, Reiki is now offered by trained nurses to surgical patients. It's been found that procedures generally are more successful and recoveries more rapid and easy when the patient receives this gentle therapy before, during, or after surgery. In the past decade, as more horse owners and holistic practitioners have discovered the benefits of energy therapy themselves, they have gone on to share improved recovery rates and well-being with their animals, too.

Using their hands, Reiki practitioners boost the body's own energy flow to open pathways where chi may be blocked. Once students have been attuned by a Reiki master, they find that suddenly they can sense areas where energy is blocked; these areas feel warmer than surrounding areas, in response to the greater draw of energy there. Hands-on energy work requires no diagnosis, because the body will simply take the energy it needs from Reiki treatments to re-establish healthy chi movement throughout the body. As internal energy resumes its vital flow, healing can begin.

If you get the chance to watch a Reiki session, check it out. Generally, a treatment lasts forty minutes to an hour, depending on the horse's needs. Reiki soothes emotional unrest as well as helps a horse recover from physical illness or injury. The response from a horse as the energy pathways open can be dramatic. The eyes close and the head drops. The horse may yawn or work its mouth. His breathing deepens and often gut sounds increase (making Reiki useful in treating the early stages of colic). The horse's entire body reflects the deep level of relaxation taking place, usually within ten to fifteen minutes. Some horses even fall asleep!

Reiki won't replace your veterinarian, who you should always call immediately in an emergency, but it could make a tremendous difference in your horse's recovery in an emergency or chronic situation, for example, when you are awaiting the vet for a colicky horse. It can help minimize sprains and strains (especially in conjunction with homeopathics and cold hosing or ice), maintain chiropractic adjustments, soothe sore feet—the list goes on.

ESSENTIALS

The best thing about Reiki is that anyone can do it. In about a day, a Reiki master can give Reiki to you, your horses, and your pets. Reiki givers also receive energy when giving it, making Reiki an all-round win-win situation.

Take Control with Alternative Therapies

As you can see, alternative therapies often give horse owners some ability to help their horses in chronic and acute situations, and they definitely increase comfort for the horse. While you probably won't be using all of these techniques, you may find a few particularly helpful depending on your situation. While I can't emphasize enough that these treatments do not take the place of your regular veterinarian, they might help you see your veterinarian a little less often! Of course, you should always let your vet know what you have been doing on your own and seek his or her advice and that of a licensed practitioner when you are unsure or just learning.

CHAPTER 11
Handling

When it comes to horses, handling is everything. Your safety and often the horse's safety depends on your understanding of the best ways to handle your horse. The basics of handling revolve around something known as groundwork—that is, working with and educating your horse on the ground opposed to in the saddle. Much of what good groundwork consists of will clearly translate into things that are also useful when riding your horse. In this chapter I'll give you the basics on how to handle your horse.

Why Is Good Handling Important?

As you learned in Chapter 4, "Horse Behavior," the horse's world revolves around the need for order and understanding of his place in that order. *Where* he is in that pecking order isn't the important thing to your horse, but *knowing where he is* on that ladder is important to his peace of mind. So if you and your horse are attached by a lead rope and he decides you aren't running the show, he will put himself in charge—and he will lead you. I suspect it won't take long before you become concerned that your horse's decisions often aren't in your best interests or his.

I've been to many clinics where handling practices are taught and seen many a horse—both young and old—lead her handler into the arena or round pen to begin their lesson. It's a sorry sight and an unsafe situation as well, but it's encouraging to see that the owner has decided it's best to learn a new way of being with his or her horse.

QUESTIONS?

What does conditioned response mean?
Conditioned response is a training approach in which a horse (or any thinking animal, including humans) is conditioned to respond to the same stimulus the same way every time she confronts that stimulus.

It is definitely the person on the end of the lead rope that can make a difference; the same horse in the hands of two different people acts very differently. When I decided to get back into horses again and bought my two-year-old gelding, he dragged me around all summer. I worked hard to establish my leadership role, but what I was offering wasn't sufficient for him. However, the person I bought him from could handle him much better than I could! The handler was clearly the factor. Although it was all quite frustrating, I appreciate this horse who gave me a clear reason for wanting to find a way to interact safely with horses and attempt to become the kind of person that a horse could look to for support.

What's with the Left Side?

Many myths surround why it is traditional for most of what we do with the horse to be done from the left side. The most logical one comes from the need to mount on the left because of the position of the soldier's sword in battle. Well, most of us aren't using our horses in battle or carrying swords when we ride, so forget this "left side only" nonsense! The idea that this is some hard and fast rule has created many one-sided horses.

Yes, you'll find most halters attach on the left and saddles rig up on the left, but there's no saying you can't adjust those to operate from the right. Even if you don't go to that extreme, it pays to be mindful of working both sides of your horse. A good handler who wants to build a solid reliable horse will be sure his or her horse is as "two-sided" as possible, exposing it to new things from both sides and not doing everything from the traditional left. You could, for example, put the saddle pad on from the right side.

Interestingly, horses are often more pushy on the left side than they are on the right. That's because the left is where they are usually handled the most and where they have learned to be able to push their human handler around!

Handling the Young Foal

Good handling needs to start the first time a human comes into contact with a foal. This doesn't mean you need to halter up a three-day-old filly and drill her with groundwork exercises for two-hour stints. That is absolutely not a good idea. But what it does mean is that every time the human interacts with that filly—halter on or not—that interaction needs to be handling that is conducive to desirable behavior.

No matter what the foal's age, it does not need to step on you, knock you out of the way, or otherwise consider you something not to be considered. Each simple interaction can teach the foal to be yielding and step away from your pressure, not resist, brace against it, or move into it. One touch and one step is the first building block, negative or positive. Even simply scratching the young horse can be not only an enjoyable experience but also an educational one. By continuing to scratch only when the foal is behaving himself and moving him away (very important— don't let him move *you* away!) when he is being obnoxious about it teaches him that only respectful behavior gets respectful and generous behavior in return.

FACTS

Clicker training is a popular dog training method that has become popular in the horse world too. It involves repeatedly asking for a specific action, rewarding the performance of that action with a treat, and marking the desired action with a click from a little clicker box or even a click of your tongue. The click is then used to recall and reinforce that action. There are books, videos, and clinics that offer the correct method of doing this type of conditional-response training.

Although typically a very young foal does not need to be led (she will follow her mother anywhere), if you do need to lead her, run the lead rope around her rump to help encourage forward movement and better avoid setting up a pulling match. You might as well avoid pulling matches with horses, because even a foal will win.

These are tiny steps taken over the six months or so that the foal is a suckling. Once she is weaned and more independent, it is time to take all the steps you've set up since birth and begin to build on them. Again, this doesn't mean taking a young horse and training on him and drilling him for hours each day. Let the horse be a horse for a while—once he is under saddle, he will spend the rest of his life working for you. So having the first two or three years to just play seems like a fair deal.

Groundwork in Earnest

There are a couple of things, in my experience, that I have found to be the keys to being able to safely maneuver a horse on the end of a lead rope.

Keeping Their Distance

Beginners are usually taught to lead their horse by standing to the horse's left and holding the lead rope right at the clip, where it attaches to the horse's halter. I have come to believe this is dangerous. First, this tight grip on the horse is just one more way we confine this large animal and satisfy our own need to restrict his movement. Second, if the horse does spook at something from the right side, he has nowhere to go but on top of the handler—he can't jump forward because his forward movement is blocked by the tight hold on the lead rope.

QUESTIONS?

What is groundwork?
Groundwork is teaching your horse at the end of a lead rope. Many of the things you teach him in groundwork are transferable to the saddle.

Give the horse his own space! Teach your horses to lead a foot or two behind you—you can walk either directly in front or off to one side or the other. If the horse spooks from either side, he can jump without jumping on you. If he spooks forward, the freedom you are giving his head allows him to jump ahead to either side of you, which is what he will choose to do—if you've taught him that running you over is unacceptable under any circumstances. If you don't want your horse to run over you, you must first earn his respect. In the wild herd, the horses on the lower rungs of the pecking order would never dream of pummeling a higher-ranking individual. But some domesticated horses are more bold than others and look to challenge the pecking order status quo. You need to show these individuals more presence than you might need to show others. If your horse doesn't tend to challenge your position as leader, you can probably just send some energy up the length of the lead rope when he comes closer than you want. Don't keep henpecking him though; send just enough energy up the lead rope to match his eagerness. He will soon learn the rules of appropriate distance.

FACTS

In order to effectively handle a horse, you need to show something called "presence." If you are small, you need to make yourself seem larger than you are. Conversely, if you are large and have a booming voice, you may have too much presence for the more timid horse; you may find that horse will act defensively because he perceives you as a threat. Learn to have more or less presence, whatever the situation requires.

For the more bold horse you will need to do what it takes for him to understand that you mean what you say. In the words of Ray Hunt, "Do as much or as little as it takes to get the change you are looking for." This doesn't mean you should beat on your horse (this isn't about submission but about leadership and safety), but it may mean a bop on the end of the nose with the lead rope (or more!) for the more bold horse. If your car is on the tracks when you see a train coming, you will step on the gas as hard as it takes to get that car off the track in time to avoid that train, I imagine. If your horse learns to run you over, that bop on the nose or whap with a jacket or whatever you choose will seem pretty mild compared to hoof tracks up your back. If you feel badly, then think about how little good you would be to him when you're in the hospital recovering. If you get the horse as a youngster, you can teach him enough about respect so this won't happen to begin with. If you are trying to change behavior taught to the horse by other people, the more effective you are, the quicker the change will happen and you can both be happier.

Stepping over the Hindquarters

This is perhaps the single most useful move your horse could know. The goal is to have your horse learn that if you turn her head to the right and liven up some energy with your hand, arm, or the end of the lead rope (or eventually your mind), she is to step her right hind foot underneath her in front of the left hind foot, and step her whole hindquarters to her left—and vice versa for the left. This move not only expands your horse's bend and flexibility but also makes it possible, for example, to step your horse out of a corral full of other horses clamoring to get out or to step her into her stall and turn her to face you while you latch the stall door—the list of places this step comes in handy is endless. And, as with all other groundwork you do, this move is pretty useful when you are riding as well!

Yielding to Pressure

Your horse should understand to yield to pressure not brace against it or fight it. When your horse thoroughly understands this, you should be able to simply place your hand on her side with meaning to get her to step away from it. If she accidentally steps on her lead rope and pulls on her head, she will back up away from the pressure and free the lead rope rather than fight against it and rip it out from under her foot.

The only time it is safe to tie your horse is after she gains a thorough understanding of yielding to pressure. Understanding how to yield to pressure will also be helpful if she gets caught in, say, fence wire; there is a much better chance that she will not struggle and really hurt herself but instead wait to be released. Yielding to pressure means that when you go to put your horse's halter on, she will drop her head and help you get it in the right place, not throw her head up as high as she can and make it more difficult. If you need to back her up one step, you can ask for one step; when you get it and release the pressure, one step is all she'll move. True yielding is not a conditioned-response thing; it is truly meaningful to the horse.

Never learning to brace against pressure but yielding instead gives your horse a frame of reference that will make her so enjoyable and safe to be around that you will find it difficult to understand why everyone doesn't want their horses to operate this way.

Confinement

Humans seem to spend a lot of time concocting ways to further confine horses—stalls, paddocks, halters, bridles, cross ties, bits, side reins, tie downs—the list is endless, and it is expanded and refined all the time. Following are the two best things you can do for your horse from the beginning of your interactions, whether you are raising a foal or starting with a newly bought horse of any age:

1. Consider his mental fitness as important as his physical fitness. A horse with a calm mind will be able to listen to you and learn from you. I believe many people concentrate on fussing with a horse's body because it is more accessible and therefore a little easier to figure out. If you don't understand the horse's mind, then I hope what is in this book can inspire you to find some good help in increasing your understanding.

2. Develop a mutually respectful relationship that allows you to trust your horse enough to give her some space. If the horse has to be on the end of a lead rope, then at least she can have 2 or 3 feet of rope instead of being gripped at the clip. Many people can't give their horses that much space because the horse will constantly be diving for grass or prancing around. This is where it is your job to teach the horse that dragging you around the front lawn is simply unacceptable. I suspect most people with children are pretty quick to teach their kids that dragging mommy by the hand through the grocery store to the candy aisle is not the way they want them to behave. Why they don't want their 1000-pound horses to learn a similar lesson about respectful behavior is a mystery to me!

So give your horse a better life by teaching her to be respectful, which in turn allows you to trust her, which in turn allows you to stop trying to confine her so much. A horse who knows she can move if she absolutely has to is more likely to be okay about standing still when you want her to. Once you learn enough to not be so intent on confining your horse, you will breathe a sigh of relief and so will your horses!

Everyday Handling

Entering a Stall

The two main issues that come up with entering a stall are the horse who does not want to be caught and the horse who mauls you when you enter with his meal. Both of these behaviors are the result of small incidents that build up into safety concerns. Be aware of the small incidents and don't let them get any further than that.

Bringing Breakfast

To teach your horse to be respectful of you when you enter his stall with his feed, you need to have a picture in mind of what you would like your horse to look like when you enter. I suspect most of us would be content if our horses stand back from the door, face us, and wait patiently for us to put their feed in their buckets and hay racks.

First, keep in mind that this can be a lot to ask of a horse in the domestic environment. We confine them to a space not much bigger than their bodies, sometimes for extraordinary periods of time. Then we regulate their eating, a process totally opposite of their wild instincts of roaming and grazing twenty-four hours a day. No wonder they are a little anxious when we arrive with their meal!

FACTS

The twitch has long been a means of restraint for the horse. By squeezing the thick layer of skin on the end of the horse's nose with a twitch, you are giving the horse something else to think about besides that shot or worming medication you are trying to administer. The twitch is used in an area known to be an acupressure point, and one that releases natural pain-relieving, soothing endorphins that help the horse relax in general.

The Benefit of Respect

As mentioned earlier, if you spend as much time working with your horse's mental being as with his physical being, you will be one step ahead of the game. Your horse may still be anxious to get his grub, but teaching him a respectful way to act when you walk in the stall will make life a bit easier. The basic premise is not to enter the stall with the horse's food until he is a living example of that picture you have in your mind of him standing away from the door facing you. It may take a couple of weeks to teach the generally respectful horse. The less respectful, more bold horse may take a little more encouragement for that ideal picture to shape up. You may need to actually physically ask her to back away from the door by placing your hands on her and asking her to step away from your pressure. For a very assertive horse, you may need to actually halter her before bringing her food in and then ask her to back away from the door. Do only what it takes to get that picture you want—don't do too much and risk frightening the horse!

Feeding a horse treats by hand is perhaps fun for the human, but few people are capable of feeding a horse by hand without setting up obnoxious and pushy behavior in an animal with a very powerful jaw and head. If you want to feed your horse treats, put them in her food bucket!

Catching Your Horse

In the Stall

If your horse turns his head into a corner and his rear end to you when you want to catch him in his stall, you have allowed something to shape up here that can be very dangerous. You need to be experienced enough to know the fine line between what is enough to get a change and what is too much for the horse. If things have gotten this far, get that trusted experienced friend to help you. Your intention is to change the horse's mind about which direction he wants to face, and you definitely do not want to frighten the horse.

A horse who is afraid of your entering her stall can put you in a very dangerous situation, and you can easily make it worse. In fact, you can turn this into a vicious circle—the horse turns its rump to you when you enter its stall, so you feel you need to do something about it. But if you do too much, the horse will react even more defensively (he may kick out). Remember, although horses can find their stall to be a place of comfort, they can also feel very trapped. Their natural instinct to flee is not available to them in any way. The next instinct—to defend themselves—is the only thing they have. If sufficiently threatened (remember, "sufficiently" is different for each horse), they will position themselves to kick you or, less likely but still possible, lunge at you with teeth bared. Either event is unpleasant at best, for you and for your horse.

When you and your experienced friend work with this horse, the object is to get the horse to turn to face you. Your horse should be ready and willing to be haltered when you enter the stall, and this is what you are trying to teach him. Do not expect the horse to turn and face you all at once. Look for small signs that he is making an attempt at figuring out what you want and that he feels okay about doing it. Look for an ear to turn in your direction or even for him to simply turn his head but not his body. Step back away from the horse the minute you get any sign he is becoming willing. By taking the pressure off him, you will give your horse the signal that his reaction is right and that you are giving him the physical and mental space he needs to make the turn.

Outside the Stall

The horse who is turning her butt to you in the stall is having the same problem as the horse that can't be caught in the corral or pasture, only the size of the space is different. The corral or pasture is probably less dangerous for you (although people have a remarkable ability to get themselves in danger with horses), since the horse has a place to go to get away from you and doesn't have to be so defensive. But all that space will be exhausting and perhaps make it frustrating and get you working from an angry place—which is never a good thing with horses.

ESSENTIALS

Don't get too cocky about your relationship with your horse—all horses will have days when kicking up their heels with their friends will seem a better idea than anything you have in mind! But if you have built a solid relationship, you will actually find this more entertaining than frustrating.

The horse who respects you and considers you supremely important (a tall order but a noble one to work toward) will give you her attention when you step into her space—corral, pasture, or stall. She has learned that being with you is a pretty darn good place to be, maybe even as good as being with her pasture buddies. A horse with which you have built this kind of relationship will position herself to be caught when you step into the corral rather than turn away from you. She may even go one step further and walk toward you.

Do Your Homework

Before you ever get to the point where the horse is in a larger space and you want to catch her, you should spend some time working on this in a smaller space such as a corral or round pen. If the horse eludes you, then let him work for his avoidance. Keep him moving around the pen and, every once in a while, take a backward step and see what you get. If the horse stops, great. If he stops and turns his head toward you, even better.

Your ultimate goal is for him to stop and turn his whole body toward you. This is the sign that he is ready to be caught, and you had better be ready to take this opening and catch him. If you don't, your horse will think maybe this isn't what you want, and you will lose your opportunity, making the next try even harder.

When you offer a step back for the horse to stop, there are a couple other things that might happen as well. Here's a series of "ifs":

- If the horse stops when you take the pressure off, step back another step or two and see whether you can get him to turn his head.
- If you get that, take another step or two back from his head and move in toward his flank to see whether that will draw on his head enough while putting pressure on his rear to get him to step his body around away from you and face you.
- If you get this, you are probably golden.
- If at any of these stages he walks off, that's fine. In fact, encourage him to take a trip or two around the pen, and when you think he's thinking about how he'd maybe like to not be doing this (maybe he holds an ear in your direction), give him another opportunity to step in. You will probably get his whole body this time.

This whole process can take ten minutes or ninety minutes and is worth working on a few times when you don't *need* to catch your horse.

FACTS

A "flag" makes a good extender for your arm and can add to your presence when working with your horse. Use a length of stiff wire a few feet long with a piece of bandana-sized cloth attached to the end. Make sure the end of the wire is bent over so it can't poke your horse, the handle is comfortable and easy to grip, and the flag is not so heavy that your arm will tire.

Reminder

Always bear in mind that a horse can kick out a lot farther than you think. It is a good idea to let the horse know you are coming up behind him. Talk to him or, if you are going from the front of the horse to the back, keep your hand on the horse all the way around so that he can know where you are. The traditional logic has been that if you stay close to the horse's hind end, a kick won't have the full impact. Or if you are back almost far enough, you'll only get the tail end of the kick. DO NOT put yourself in the line of fire. A flag is useful as an extension of your arm so that you won't get within kicking distance; but in a confined situation like a stall, it may frighten the horse too much. Get help until you have enough experience to confidently handle these kinds of situations (and by then, you'll find them coming up less and less).

Picking Up the Feet

Teaching a horse to have her feet handled is something that needs to start taking place early in the horse's life. This can be done gradually and starts with good handling in general. People think they are having trouble picking up their horse's feet, when the trouble is in other parts of the horse's handling and in his attitude toward humans; if these problems are addressed, the horse's feet handling problems clear up too.

To teach a young horse about having her feet handled, forget about the feet for a while. Instead, while grooming the horse, start grooming the legs and getting the horse used to having her legs touched and worked with. Using grooming to get the horse accustomed to having his feet worked with is common sense. This is a good start.

The Front Feet

Getting a horse's foot lifted off the ground can be quite tricky (it's that self-preservation, always-be-prepared-for-flight thing!). Often the front feet are easier to pick up than the back, perhaps because the horse can keep better tabs on you when you're in front of her. The human may also be more at ease with the front legs because they aren't the ones you get kicked with. Getting stepped on or pawed at or shoved out of the way is not a pleasant experience either, however. So be aware of what the horse is capable of doing when she feels she is being pushed to her limits.

Stand beside the horse's leg facing the rear of the horse. Run your hand down the leg, and when you get toward the hoof, gently pull or squeeze or do something simple that might cause the horse to lift her foot. Hold the foot up for *just a couple seconds* and put the foot back down. The key here is to put the foot back down before the horse snatches it back. Set the horse up to succeed—don't hold the foot so long that she simply can't stand it any longer. That just isn't fair.

ESSENTIALS

Greg Eliel is a Washington-state-based clinician who has several clinics around the country as well as at his ranch in Washington. His Web site at *www.gregeliel.com* not only includes his clinic schedule but also contains some well-written and helpful tips and advice on great ways to work with your horse.

If she doesn't let you pick the foot up the first couple of tries, work at it in small increments and build on those—be satisfied the first few times with her shifting her weight, the next with her flexing, even if she doesn't actually lift her foot. Eventually, you will get the foot up.

And when I say put the foot back down, that is exactly what I mean—put it down. Don't just let go unexpectedly and have the horse's foot bang to the ground. If you do that, you'll find the horse reluctant to let you pick her foot up again. And if she does, she will snatch it away in anticipation of her foot banging to the ground. Give your horse this bit of respect and make sure your farrier does too!

The Back Feet

The back feet are similar to but different from the front feet. Again, stand beside the leg facing the rear and run your hand down the horse's leg to the hoof. Squeeze or gently pull to get the horse to lift her leg. When you first start to pick up back legs, just get the hoof off the ground, hold it for a second, and place it back down.

Eventually, you will work toward holding the back leg up and out, using your thigh to help support it. However, you should also be teaching your horse to hold up its own weight while one foot is raised; your farrier will expect this also.

Your Horse and the Farrier

It is your job to get your horse accustomed to having her feet handled, not your farrier's. Don't forget to gradually get her to lift one foot off the ground for longer and longer periods of time. With this kind of exposure, your farrier should have little problems trimming your horse's feet.

Add to your foot work a simple simulation of shoeing by gently tapping on the outer edge of the horse's hoof with something like the hoof pick. Although this is helpful, nothing quite replicates the experience of having shoes nailed on her feet! Your farrier might be able to show you some positions to practice to help your horse become accustomed to this handling before the farrier adds the complication of shoeing.

Some horses never have a problem with shoeing. More typically, horses simply need a few shoeings to get accustomed to this experience. With astute handling from both you and your farrier, your horse will soon learn to stand quietly.

Trailer Loading

Ah, the horse trailer, often the bane of the horse owner's existence. With a little work on your part, trailering your horse can be a walk in the park. After attending numerous horse clinics where good handling was taught, and where trailer loading demonstrations were always amazing, I have come to enjoy teaching horses to load onto trailers.

Choosing a Trailer

You will develop your own preference for the type of horse trailer you like. I opt for the open-box-style stock trailer with no ramp—called a "step-up." It is simple without a lot of elements to break and work around. And it is capable of being used for many other things besides moving horses. I have hauled bales of hay, goats, sheep, and motorcycles, to name just a few things.

Most simple trailers are bumper-pull trailers, where the tongue of the trailer hitches onto a ball on the back of your vehicle. Bigger trailers have gooseneck hitches, which require a connector in the back of your pickup (the nose of the trailer actually extends into the pickup and attaches to the connector). Another major difference is whether the trailer is constructed of steel or aluminum. Aluminum trailers are lighter in weight and don't rust, but they are much more expensive than steel trailers.

You can choose to tie your horse in the stock trailer or let her go loose. For long distances, being loose can help their leg circulation. Or you can tie the horse while driving and untie her while you are stopped at a rest area. You can also haul more than one horse in a stock trailer—some are big enough to have a door separating two stalls, front and back. My first trailer was just a 10-foot single box; if I needed to haul two horses, I would tie them side by side, just as they would be in a two-horse trailer. However, with the stock trailer you typically don't have a divider between the two horses tied side by side, which can prove a problem if the two horses don't get along.

The two-horse trailer has a straight stall arrangement, with one horse on the left and one on the right, and usually has at least a partial divider between them. If you haul only one horse, that horse should go on the driver's side (or if you haul two different-sized horses, put the heavier horse on the driver's side). Two-horse trailers typically have a manger in the nose that holds hay. This manger can prove dangerous if your horse is not comfortable in the trailer and gets frightened and leaps forward. One nice feature of two-horse trailers is that they usually have some storage space for tack or feed at the front under the manger.

The Ultimate Test: Load Her Up!

Loading a horse onto a trailer is the ultimate test of how well you've refined all the groundwork you've done with your horse thus far. If you have done a thorough job, trailer loading should go pretty smoothly. If your horse is the easygoing, forgiving type, your groundwork may not even have to be all that thorough! If the horse is overly concerned and not as easily trusting of your intentions, you will have to spend a little more time refining your groundwork before you get to trailer loading.

When loading young horses or any horse for the first time, it's wise to have someone around in case you get in trouble. You want someone there in case of a problem, but not actually helping—this is your deal. Make sure the person is patient and respects your approach to handling your animals.

Make sure the trailer you use is exceedingly safe—that there are no sharp protrusions to get cut on or odd places for a lead rope to get caught. It shouldn't make much of a difference if the trailer has a ramp or is a step-up type.

Before loading her up, put a halter on your horse. Make sure that it has a fairly long lead rope—12 feet is okay, but 16 feet would be better. I suggest putting a bag of hay in the trailer not as a bribe to get her in but as a comforting thing to greet her when she does climb all the way onto the trailer. If the hay bag offers one more incentive for her to climb in, great, but you should in fact be careful not to entice her onto the trailer physically before she's mentally ready to be there.

Lead your horse to the trailer and let her check things out. Have the gate open and let her look and smell inside. As long as her attention is on the trailer, let her do this investigating. If you sense that she is becoming interested in things outside the trailer, do what it takes to return her attention back inside—send some energy up the lead rope or actually lead her back to the entrance if you have to.

Basically, as long as her attention is on that trailer, everything will be quiet and calm. If her attention leaves the trailer, things will get busy. If you have done your groundwork well up to this point and your timing and consistency is good, she will soon figure out that the trailer is a good place to be, as that's where things are calm and peaceful.

ESSENTIALS

> If you are new to the concept of groundwork and need some ideas for things to do, Buck Brannaman's book *Groundwork:The First Impression* and his video, *From the Ground Up*, covering things such as trailer loading and halter work, might be helpful. See Appendix A for details.

Don't Rush!

Once she is calmly looking inside, ask her to take a step up by gently tapping her on the rump with the end of the lead rope. *Don't rush this stage*. The last thing you want to do is have the horse thinking of the trailer as a peaceful place, and then ruin that idea. You should neither expect nor want her to go all the way in at this point. If she puts her two front feet in, let her soak on that idea for a second, then ask her to back out before she decides to back out herself. Do this a few times until you feel this is solid. If yours is a two-horse trailer and she has no other way out of it but backing out, you will want to do this step several times until you are confident that she knows the way out is by backing up.

The next step will be getting all four feet onto the trailer. If she puts all four in but backs right out, that's okay. If she rushes out a little excited, calm her down, rub her, talk to her first, then ask her to step onto it again. Don't expect her to walk right up onto the trailer and settle in and eat that hay. She may grab a bite and come flying back out, or she may feel uncomfortable going that far. This is all just practice, so you are in absolutely no hurry. In fact, you may want to just get to stage one for a few sessions and move onto the next stage some other day.

The first few times she steps all four feet onto the trailer, you can step up into the trailer with her and help her feel more comfortable. At some point, she is going to go in every time you ask her and walk right up to the hay. *Again, don't rush.* Let her learn to relax in there. This is where people often start to rush ("Okay, she's in, slam the door shut!") and then ruin all their good work, betray the horse, and in many instances create a good wreck in the process. I've heard many sad tales of horses who were rushed into trailers before they were ready, broke the butt chain struggling to get out, and came flying back with enough force to knock themselves over backward, hit their head, and die—as fast as that. Don't be in a hurry. It just isn't worth it. It will end up taking longer.

Shutting Her In

Wait until your horse has proven that she's calm and relaxed standing in the trailer munching some hay. If she starts to back up, you can tap her on the rump with the lead rope or your hand to get her to step back up to the front—no big deal. If she eats hay and props up one back leg to relax, all the better. Gently but efficiently lift the butt bar or close the door. If she raises her head and checks out what's going on behind her but doesn't freak out about it, you've done a good job. A horse who learns about the trailer in this way will make your horse life so much easier. Tie her at the head and be sure to untie her first before opening the back door or butt bar.

Hauling a Horse Trailer

First, make sure your vehicle is powerful enough. Check the owner's manual to see how it rates for towing; don't just slap a hitch on it and go. The vehicle needs an engine strong enough to haul the trailer and its contents up any hill you may come across and should have a transmission cooling system to help the engine alleviate excess heat from the strain of hauling.

When towing a horse trailer, the key is to always drive slower than you think you need to. The horse can easily be tossed around if you have to make any sudden moves.

Good Handling, Good Horse

Good handling results in horses who are simply a joy to be around. Things such as trailer loading, foot work, and deworming go a lot smoother. And if they don't go smoothly, you at least have some tools to fall back on to improve the situation.

Don't rely on gimmicks and quick fixes; take the time to learn good horsemanship and good handling. That knowledge will be with you for the rest of your life.

CHAPTER 12

Types of Horsemanship

A common question asked by people when they find out you have a horse is, "What do you do with your horse?" You may not have an interest in "doing" anything. Riding or caring for your horse gets you outdoors, provides you with some exercise, and that, along with the social environment of other riders, is really what you enjoy in your horse life.

But for thousands of horse owners this is not enough. They either got into horses to be involved in a specific equine activity or they became interested in a specific activity shortly after they became involved with horses. And it's not uncommon to go through more than one type of horsemanship interest during your horse career.

Lots of Possibilities

You may already have an idea of what kind of riding and horsemanship appeal to you. Maybe you have a friend who goes to horse shows every weekend and seems to have a lot of fun. Perhaps you have gone on a few trail rides at rental places on vacation each summer and nothing seems more relaxing to you than strolling through the woods on the back of a horse. Or you might be the kind of person who likes a faster pace, and so fox hunting, barrel racing, or polo seem to be right for you. Whatever your interest or inclination, there is a horse activity and type of horsemanship to match it, including ones that don't involve riding at all!

Most equestrian pursuits break down as either "Western" or "English," meaning that the activity is appropriate for either a Western or an English saddle (see Chapter 13, "Tack, Apparel, and Accessories," for a description of the different kinds of saddles and specific equipment for specific activities). This chapter will introduce you to the many types of activities you can enjoy with your horse.

ESSENTIALS
The Web site for the American Horse Shows Association is *www.ahsa.org*. You'll find information about becoming a member, upcoming competitions, and much more, as well as lots of good links to other horse sites.

Western

Reining

Similar to the evolution of many competitive events, the equine event of reining started as a way to show off the moves your horse could do that were used in a practical way to work cattle. It has since become an end unto itself. Reining involves precise moves; your horse needs to be taught the cues it needs to stop exactly when you ask him to, to spin in a circle moving only its front feet and stopping before overshooting the number of spins that is required of the particular pattern you are following, and to canter calmly in small and large circles without breaking stride. Again, this is a discipline that can require many hours of drill work with your horse and is probably not in the realm of pleasure/recreational riding. But it sure is fun to watch a reining pattern performed by a topnotch horse and rider!

Cow Work

If you are going to do team penning, getting your horse accustomed to cattle is obviously important. But you don't have to ride Western or plan to do team penning for cow work to be valuable to your horse's education and your abilities as a rider. Even in an English saddle, the benefits of giving your horse exposure to a cow, helping her learn how to move her feet precisely at your request, and learning how to make those precise requests are tools you can use anywhere. With a cow in the picture, you will know when you asked too much or too little; you will either lose your cow back to the herd or send it too far and have to start all over! So, no matter what kind of riding you decide to get into, find yourself someone who will lend you a couple cows and head 'em up and move 'em out!

Rodeo

Cowboys invented the rodeo to have fun, but riding in the rodeo circuit is now an intense activity in and of itself. If you want to become a rodeo rider, you will probably need to be in the western part of the United States and Canada, where rodeos abound. For the armchair rodeo rider, you can often find a rodeo as Saturday night fare on the sports channels on television.

Roping

Roping horseback usually involves cattle. If you want to become a skilled roper, you have to practice, practice, practice. You can practice with a fake cow—there are cow heads you can buy to stick into a bale of hay or attach to a sawhorse—and rope the "cow" while it's stationary. And when you are ready to rope a moving cow, you can even buy motorized fake cows on tracks that pivot and turn almost like the real thing (the real thing can be cheaper, but it's harder to come by). Expert ropers are incredible to watch; the minute you pick up a 60-foot lariat yourself and begin to "build a loop," you come to really appreciate how fine an art it is. There are occasional classes in horse shows that involve roping, but "classes" involving this skill are more likely found at the rodeo.

ESSENTIALS

To learn the basics of roping, get yourself a rope (one source is King Ropes, Sheridan, Wyoming 307-672-2702) and the video "There's Roping to Do" with Joe Wolter and friends, a two-hour instructional video that shows the basics of day-to-day roping encountered on a working ranch (available from Real West Records, at *www.realwestrecords.com*).

English
Jumping

There are three basic ways to become involved in jumping:

1. **Show jumping:** Also known as "stadium jumping," this is where the jumps are set up within the confines of a show arena. This can be a class in a show, a show in itself, or one of the three legs of a three-day event. Riders are expected to follow a specific predetermined pattern around the jump course. Your run around the course is timed, and faults are given for any rails knocked over.

2. **Cross-country:** As with stadium jumping, cross-country jumping can be an event in itself or one of the three legs in a three-day event. The jump course is set up in a "cross-country" setting through woods and fields. There is a specific course to follow, judges are stationed at each jump, and your run is timed.

3. **Fox hunting:** Being involved with a "hunt" is another way to get into jumping. The hunt club designs a course that includes jumps. There is usually ample opportunity for novice riders to follow the hunt without jumping or only jumping the smaller jumps.

Dressage

In French, *dressage* basically means "training." In dressage competition, one is basically showing off the level of training of his or her horse. The training is not for battle or to drive a carriage. In fact, it has become an end in itself, and riders now "do dressage" as an equestrian activity. It is taken quite seriously, requiring years and years of discipline and practice.

Dressage competitions are different from the typical "horse show." For one thing, although you are still competing against a group of other riders, you compete in the ring alone. On the one hand, you don't need to worry about other riders around you and can concentrate on your own performance; on the other hand, you are alone out there, and all eyes are on you. Once you gain experience and become comfortable with dressage itself, you will become so focused on your performance that you won't even think about the "all eyes are on you" aspect of your test.

After you register for the show, you are sent a card telling you (sometimes you need to call and ask) your ring time. Get to the show well in advance to get your horse ready, settled, and warmed up. Sometimes the tests prior to yours move along faster than their allotted time, and you may be able to do your test earlier than planned; but you can still stick to your given time if you want to.

QUESTIONS?

What are rails?
Rails are the individual horizontal bars that make up a jump. They can be easily removed or added to make the jump lower or higher.

Beginning dressage riders and their mounts start at training level and progress through the eight levels of dressage, ending in the highest "Grand Prix" level. Once you have graduated beyond one level and have begun working in the next, you and your trainer may decide that your horse is not the right horse in mind and/or body to take you to the next level of competition. It may be like expecting your trusty Saturn sedan to take you from its current job driving along the highway, which it does quite well, to competing in the Indianapolis 500. This is where it gets way beyond pleasure riding, and you will need to make some decisions regarding your goals as an equestrian.

Do you want to spend years and years on this horse, or is it time to trade up? Is it this horse that is the most important to you, or is it dressage competition? Maybe you would love to see your nicely trained second-level horse in the hands of a young competitor. Or maybe it's time to take the same horse and do something different. I'm not suggesting one choice is better or worse than another, but it is probably what you will come up against if you progress through the stages of dressage competition (and to get to any competition's highest levels).

Three-Day Eventing

A three-day event is an English-riding competition that has three components: dressage, cross-country, and stadium jumping. Also known as "combined training," the three-day event was added to the Olympic program in 1912. The intent is to show the physical and mental versatility of you and your horse—that you can go from being cleaned up and collected in the dressage ring one day to flying through the woods and over jumps the next, to jumping over six rails amidst bleachers full of spectators on the last day. The winner is the team with the best combined score over the three days.

FACTS

Olympic equestrians David and Karen O'Connor are in the midst of making three-day eventing a household name. David brought home a gold medal from the Sydney Olympics, the first equestrian gold medal for the United States since 1984. In an interview, the couple pointed out that the equestrian segment is the only Olympic event in which men and women compete as equals. Their Web site, *www.oconnoreventteam.com,* is well worth a visit.

Fox Hunting

Fox hunting is an extremely organized undertaking with a very strictly followed protocol for beginners, who are expected to become familiar with the complex rules and etiquette of the hunt. You might be surprised how many areas of the country currently support a local fox hunting club. Check with hunter/jumper boarding stables or instructors to find one near you.

Most fox hunts these days do not involve real foxes and are what has commonly been called "drag" hunts, which comes from the practice of dragging a fox-scented cloth for the hounds to follow. Fox hunts still involve baying hounds, galloping horses, beautiful countryside, challenging jumps, and many riders. It is a great way to get your horse exposed and accustomed to a lot of excitement.

Trail Riding

The nice thing about trail riding is that all it takes is you, your horse, and a trail through the woods. That's it—you're trail riding. It can also get as complicated as the Cross State Trail Ride (a longtime long-distance ride originating in Vermont) or the Tevis Cup endurance ride, which involves lots of preplanning, conditioning, and preparation. Or you can do both—condition your horse all through the beginning of the riding season (if you live in cold climates) on local trails, then end the season with a competitive, more complicated event. If you plan to go to a competitive event and have any interest in "placing," it will help to have some experience competing in the trail riding venue beforehand.

FACTS

The Tevis Cup is to trail riding what the famous Alaskan Iditarod race is to dog sledding. Its slogan, "100 miles in one day," doesn't reveal the roughness of the 100-mile terrain. It is said to have 19,000 feet of uphill riding and 22,000 feet of downhill riding. The trophy is awarded to the first rider to complete the ride "whose mount is fit to continue."

Team Penning

Team penning is an activity similar to the gaming events. It can be fun, but since it requires cattle, it probably isn't something you will set up in your backyard. You should scout out a local team penning club that has events on a regular basis, offers some practice time, and is open to riders new to the event.

Here is a basic description of team penning: A team of three riders picks a number out of a hat. A herd of as many as thirty young cattle with numbers painted on them are waiting in the arena, and three of the cows (or steer) have the same number on their side as the number the team picked. Two of the team members cut one of the cows with their number out of the herd and work the cow down to a small pen somewhere near the other end of the arena. When they get the cow into the pen—which is no small task, given a cow's desire to remain with the herd—the third rider stays behind to keep the cow there. Two riders head back to the herd, cut out the second cow with their number, and do the same thing until all three cows are in the pen. When the pen door is shut, the stopwatch is stopped, and the team's time is recorded.

After all teams have competed, the team with the best time wins. Since this is a timed activity, horsemanship is not scored, but the better your riding skills and the more in unity you are with your horse, the less time you will waste in getting to the cattle and moving your horse where you need her or holding her position. Being involved with team penning will also expose your horse to cattle, yet another thing for you to support her through and help you gain further trust.

Games

Polo

If you become interested in polo, you don't have to move to England or Argentina. There have been plenty of opportunities to play polo since James Gordon Bennett brought the sport to New York in 1876. Polo's real heyday was in the 1930s, but the last twenty years has seen a resurgence in popularity. Polo is a fast-paced game played on a field 160 yards wide and 300 yards long; it is played in six seven-minute "chukkers" over approximately ninety minutes. To compete, you need access to numerous polo ponies. (Polo ponies are not a breed; they are compact, usually short in height, horses who have been exposed to the idea of having mallet-wielding riders on their backs.) You must be a confident and extremely balanced rider in order to make quick turns and gallop for most of the game.

ESSENTIALS   To find a club near you, learn all the rules of the game, and obtain lots more information about polo, check the United States Polo Association Web site at *www.uspolo.org.*

Polocrosse

Polocrosse is a sister sport to polo that originated in Persia hundreds of years ago. According to the American Polocrosse Association Web site (*www.americanpolocrosse.org*), it became popular in Australia in the first half of the twentieth century and has made its way to the United States, where its popularity is increasing. The game is organized quite like polo but with some key differences. For example, each rider uses only one horse and sits out chukkers to catch his or her breath, and the ball is moved with a racket, not a mallet.

Gymkhana

Gymkhana are competitive games on horseback. They are usually won or lost solely on timing. In barrel racing, for instance, a horse and rider go as fast as possible around a group of barrels at the end of an arena. The team must follow a very specific pattern regarding which side to approach the barrel on and what barrel to go to next. This is a strictly timed event, with time points taken off and elimination for knocking over barrels, going off course, or using some unsanctioned equipment. A similar activity is pole bending, in which the horse and rider need to weave around tall poles following a specific pattern.

An interest in the ancient activity of jousting has cropped up over the past few years. Although not widespread, jousting competitions can be found in pockets around the country and are enjoyed at popular Renaissance festivals. Today's rider aims his or her lance at a ring instead of an opponent. With each round, the ring gets smaller, so accuracy at top speeds is the name of the game.

FACTS

Drill team work consists of riders, in formation, doing things in lines of two, three, four, or more lines. If viewed from above, you would see horses meeting at a point at the exact same time, moving together in the same gait and rhythm, and drifting apart at the same point. Every pairing in the drill team does the pattern in unison and in the same way as every other pairing, at the same point, in the same gait, and so forth.

A great Web site with a lot of information and plenty of interesting links is the Gymkhana Rider Online at *www.gymkhanarider.com*. The site includes Western and English games, catalogs, safety equipment sources, and even an etiquette page.

Showing

Horse showing is probably the most common horse activity. It has something for everyone—beginner and advanced rider, Western and English riding, in hand or under saddle, high speed games or relaxed circuits around the show ring.

You must understand up front that the horse show world is competitive and can be expensive, even at the most local levels. If you think you are interested, you should be sure you are fully prepared for the commitment of time and money that is required to be successful, which means, of course, winning ribbons or placing.

You may be thinking, "Oh, I don't care about winning ribbons. I just like to go to the shows." Don't kid yourself. Horse shows are about competing, and competing successfully means placing above as many of the other horse and human teams as possible. Good or bad, it's as simple as that. Don't get me wrong; that doesn't mean that it doesn't entail good sportsmanship. It certainly should! And it is true that competing in horse shows whether you win ribbons or not can be personally rewarding depending on the goals you set for yourself. Maybe you consider a show successful if your horse gets through one class without getting out of control. Maybe the next show is successful if your horse gets through the entire day calmly and without upset. But at some point, the show competitor expects his or her team to win a ribbon. And to do that, the team needs to be competitive in the circuit in which they are showing.

In order to be relaxed and ready to show, it's important to arrive fully prepared. Here are some things you won't want to be without:

For the horse:

- First aid kit
- Saddle(s) and pad(s)
- Leg wraps
- Bridle(s)
- Grooming equipment and products

- Hay and grain
- Feed and water buckets
- Blanket(s)
- Fly spray

For the rider:

- Clean clothes for almost every class you signed up for
- Helmet
- Hairpins, bands, and barrettes
- Riding boots

- Comfortable shoes for before and after the show
- Rain gear
- Personal items

The average-sized regional horse shows are made up of several classes that might last for fifteen to twenty minutes and have about twenty-five riders. Classes are divided up into three general categories:

1. **Pleasure classes:** Pleasure classes are subjectively judged and are based on the performance of the horse. Both English and Western riding styles have pleasure classes; typically there is a separate class for each and also an open class where both styles and all ages and levels compete together. Pleasure classes are judged on how "pleasurable" to ride the horse appears—to win, your horse needs to be well behaved and to change gaits immediately and only on command. The gaits should be smooth and in keeping with the style of riding you are

presenting with your attire and tack. Although the rider is not judged, it doesn't make a pretty picture if the rider is up there bouncing around and interfering with his or her horse's ability to perform.

2. **Equitation classes:** In equitation classes, the riders are judged for their riding skills. Also, they need to know the current style of riding—for example, Western riders using one hand to hold the reins have to know what the current acceptable position is for the other hand. The rider also needs to be able to give commands smoothly and effectively to his or her horse.

3. **Timed classes:** These classes are, as the name says, based on time. Often they consist of games, such as barrel racing or pole bending. Other classes have a specific objective. For instance, there is the "fun" class called Egg and Spoon, in which the last rider still carrying both the egg and the spoon wins. Jumping classes combine the two types of classes—they often have time limitations and you lose points for knocking down rails.

How to Be Competitive—the Horse

You don't need a specific kind of horse to become part of the show world unless you are interested in breed-specific shows; almost all the breeds have their own breed shows. If you are buying a horse with the intention of showing it, you should pay particular attention to conformation. Conformation flaws won't eliminate you, but it is an advantage to have a mount that is put together well.

Training

How does your horse need to be trained to compete? Whether you agree with the style or not, your horse needs to move the way everyone else is moving. For instance, for several years the appropriate style for Western Pleasure riding for stock-type horses has been to ride with the horse's head and neck tilting toward the ground and at speeds in every gait that are very slow and don't bounce the rider around (i.e., the horse is "pleasurable to ride"). If you don't agree with that way of moving for your horse but you want to show in Western Pleasure classes, you have two choices: you can either go against your beliefs and train your horse to move this way, or you can let her move the way you think is appropriate for a horse but be prepared not to win.

Chances are you want to win some competitions, so teaching your horse the correct style for the class you are in and type of horse you have is crucial. You need to spend as much time as needed in the practice ring to teach your horse what it needs to know; however, you also need to know how to teach your horse in the first place. Chapter 11, "Handling," and Chapter 14, "Riding and Driving," cover this in more depth. But ultimately, training a horse to compete in horse shows is a long process that cannot be learned from a book!

In the show world, there is an appropriate etiquette—how and when to pass a horse who is slower, for example—and your instructor/trainer can help you learn these things. The rules can be different for each kind of show and type of riding. Make sure you know which rules apply to the show you're entering.

Beyond Your Backyard

If you plan to participate in shows more competitive than your local riding club fun shows—either regional or national—then you will probably need to work with a trainer to succeed. The trainer for your discipline will know all the rules, all the current accepted styles, and where all the shows are—and many are well known by the judges. Many riders who get serious about horse showing board their show horse at a trainer's barn, pay the trainer to continue to work with their horse, take regular lessons from the trainer or the barn's instructor, and travel with the trainer and the trainer's other students to the shows. Or they do all this with a horse that is owned by their trainer or instructor. Whatever you decide, make sure your bank account for your horse activities is well padded. It may all be well within your price range, but you need to know that there will be constant costs.

There are also many administrative things to keep track of, such as registering for the show, picking classes, paying for classes, asking for tack change breaks between classes if they are allowed, and bringing health certifications as needed for your horse.

How to Be Competitive—the Rider

In order to be competitive in the show ring, you need to constantly upgrade and refine your riding skills, on your own and with an instructor.

If you are into horse showing for a long time, you may also need to occasionally consider changing horses as your competitive needs change. Some horses are not suited for the pressures of showing—which include long hours in the trailer traveling to an event, a constant changing of environment, long periods of time confined to a stall or tied to the side of the trailer, and going around and around a show ring. This can cause a lot of stress for some horses; even those who used to like showing can suffer "burnout" and need a break or permanent retirement from the show ring.

ESSENTIALS

Attend one or two national shows as a spectator before you decide to compete in one. That way, you can get a feel for the atmosphere and whether you can ever be comfortable competing at that level.

Local Shows

The local riding clubs are lots of fun and are a great way to accumulate some horse friends for people who keep their horses at home and don't get the advantage of the built-in peer group that you get when you board your horse at a stable. Local shows are also good places for beginners to get over some early show jitters (both rider and horse!) before venturing into the more competitive arenas. The shows are smaller, which means that there are fewer horses and smaller classes and, therefore, that you might be able to build your confidence and win some ribbons early on. Fewer people can mean as much comradery as competitiveness. Local shows and clubs also offer the opportunity to widen your circle of horse friends by volunteering in any number of capacities, from club treasurer to ring steward, or simply to tidy up the ring and grounds after a show.

Regional Shows

Regional shows are often sponsored by state components of national organizations. Almost every breed has them—the American Quarter Horse

Association has an affiliated club in almost every state, with some more active than others. Morgans, Arabians, and many other breeds also have similar state groups. They often put on statewide shows, where the competition gets a little tougher—in numbers and in skill level. These types of shows might be a good next step after spending some time showing locally.

National Shows

The shows put on nationally, which are often also affiliated with breed associations, are highly competitive and mostly well attended. It is really not worth the time and money to attend one of these with your horse unless you have spent the energy in thorough preparation, probably gaining experience in the local and regional shows first. It's a good opportunity to talk to some other competitors about their experiences showing at the national shows. And if it all sounds exciting, then by all means go for it! (For a discussion of the different riding classes you will find at horse shows, see Chapter 14, "Riding and Driving.")

Halter Classes

Halter horses typically compete against each other by age group and are judged on conformation. For example, are her legs and feet of a sufficient size compared to her body? Is her neck nicely built without an overall structural flaw such as getting very narrow toward the head? In breed-specific shows, horses are competing against their own breed; in larger nonbreed shows, there will often be different classes for different horses of the predominating breeds.

For showing at halter, your horse must be impeccably groomed, and you should follow the style of the moment. Are horses' hooves being painted black or is *au naturel* in this year? How are manes being groomed? Are they trimmed short or left long and natural? Are they braided? If there is no particular style, you should do whatever shows your horse's best qualities and disguises or covers up her worst. If your horse has a nice neck, clip or braid her mane. If her neck is her worst feature, let her mane cover one side of it. Judges won't be fooled, but the overall picture will look better.

The other thing about horses being shown at halter is that in the big leagues, horses are selectively bred for looks not riding, so the traits that are "in" for a few years when it comes to halter classes may not be the best traits for riding the horse. While this is important to think about, showing at halter can be fun for someone who wants to be involved in horses but doesn't want to ride.

Showmanship Classes

Although not a riding class, showmanship is considered a performance class. Unlike halter classes, where your horse stands there and is looked over, in showmanship, you are required to move your horse through a pattern. That pattern is usually posted at least an hour before the class, so be sure to study it. Types of things you will need your horse to be able to do include leading, backing, and turning around (with either the forehand or the hindquarters staying in one place).

Natural Horsemanship

In the past fifteen to twenty years, an approach to teaching and riding horses has been, for better or worse, tagged Natural Horsemanship. A few horsemen started going around the country holding hands-on educational clinics showing people how to start young horses under saddle using a different approach from the "ride and spur them into submission" methods that predominated for the better part of the nineteenth and twentieth centuries. These clinicians also showed people how to communicate more meaningfully with their older horses who were already under saddle. Teaching the human about how to *educate* their horse through feel, rather than *train* them in a mechanical way, has become a popular activity.

With the novel *The Horse Whisperer* by Nicholas Evans, and the subsequent movie directed by and starring Robert Redford, this approach really has been heavily commercialized by national clinicians. However, the original intent—which is really not new—has been a bit convoluted.

The basic premise of this different way of working with horses is this: Instead of beating their natural instincts out of them and creating a horse that is submissive to humans through fear and intimidation, horses are treated as the thinking, living beings that they are—they are educated, not trained, and that education is accomplished through working with those natural instincts (such as herd dynamics).

FACTS

Churchill Downs, the famous racetrack in Louisville, Kentucky, opened in 1875 and the first Kentucky Derby ran that year. The grounds are spread across 147 acres, with over 1,400 stalls in forty-seven barns. The Churchill Downs Web site (*www.kentuckyderby.com*) includes tips on hosting your own derby party (including a recipe for the traditional mint julep drink), a showing of the hat parade, historical information about women and African-Americans in the Derby, and a primer on betting on the big race.

If you are willing to spend a lot of time at this approach, it can result in a horse that works in a relaxed frame of mind and has learned to be respectful of its handler. When learning new things, the horse can be comfortable searching for the answer without being worried that a wrong answer is going to result in some painful punishment. And horses who respect their rider/handler and come to look to him or her for support are more apt to tuck some of their natural reactions aside and instead trust their handler/rider to help them through new situations.

One of the keys to success in dealing with your horse this way is to perfect your timing and be consistent in your interactions with the horse, especially in his early education. If you give the horse one message one time, and a different one the next, he will become confused and frustrated. If you are totally inconsistent, the horse whose personality is very forgiving will fill in for your inadequacies and get along as best she can (many horses are exactly this way, which is the only reason so many people get along as well as they do with horses). But the horse who is not as forgiving of your lack of timing and consistency—well, let's just say that that horse will be the impetus that drives you to one of these clinics.

This is a simplistic explanation for something that takes a few lifetimes to learn. But if it intrigues you, as it has me, it will provide you with at least one lifetime of learning.

Racing

Horse racing is perhaps the most popular equine event known to the average person. The chances that you will ride a racehorse as a jockey are slim. If you want to be involved, you need to be serious and dedicated, and start spending time at the racing stables now!

Racing isn't just for Thoroughbreds in Kentucky, although they still make up the majority of the races and certainly the most glamorous ones, including the Triple Crown trio—the Kentucky Derby, the Preakness, and the Belmont Stakes. Quarter horses also have an active and prestigious racing circuit, including the famed Ruidoso Downs in New Mexico. Arabians have a racing component in their registry, as do Appaloosas and many other breeds.

Flatracing (think Kentucky Derby) refers to the under-saddle kind of racing that most of us know. Racing on horseback—and the gambling that goes with it—has been around since ancient times, and with the number of racetracks around the United States, it's not going away!

Steeplechasing—which sort of combines flatracing and jumping—is best known by the Grand National event in Liverpool, England, that has taken place since 1839. The event started out with three jumps. Now it includes thirty fences and a field of forty horses, many of whom do not complete the race. The course is run twice for a total of 4.5 miles, sixteen jumps on the first round and fourteen on the second.

In harness racing, the horse pulls the human in a cart. Harness races are popular in more local settings, such as agricultural fairs. Standardbred horses are often the breed used for harness racing.

Don't Forget the Fun!

You certainly won't be able to fit each type of horsemanship into your riding career (and this isn't even an exhaustive list!), even if you were to spend a lifetime. Be sure of your chosen activity before you outfit yourself and your horse with every piece of equipment for that activity. And don't get so serious that you forget to have fun, especially if you originally got involved in horses for recreation.

CHAPTER 13

Tack, Apparel, and Accessories

As with any sport, activity, interest, or hobby, you can easily collect a lot of "stuff" when you are involved with horses. There are zillions of items for you, the rider, as well as for your horse, to choose from. And if you keep your horse at home, there are a zillion more items you can collect to enhance your stable.

Stable supplies and equipment are covered in Chapter 6, "Stabling," and medical supplies for your horse are covered in Chapter 9, "General Health." This chapter covers the items you need, or may want to have, to handle and ride your horse.

Equipment and Accessories for the Horse

Some of these items you just plain need; others simply come in handy. If you are a beginner, realize that over time you will develop your preferences for materials and types of equipment; sometimes it just takes trial and error and no matter how frugally you go about collecting, you may end up with things you find you don't like or don't really need.

ESSENTIALS

If you'd like to get rid of items you no longer need, check out tack shops that sell used equipment, find a pony club or 4-H group that is looking for donations, or set up or attend a tack swap during the nonriding season.

Handling Equipment

Halters

First and foremost, you will need a halter and a lead rope. You will establish your preferences for what these are made of as you become more experienced. Basically, there are three kinds of halters:

- **Leather halters:** If you are going to buy a leather halter, buy one of top quality. The fittings should be brass, and the leather soft and strong. Seams should be double-stitched, not screwed or tacked together.
- **Web halters:** Made of nylon webbing, these halters are the most common and least expensive. They come in a variety of colors. Web halters also come in breakaway models, which have one leather piece that will break in a major struggle.
- **Rope halters:** Rope halters are made of marine or rock-climbing-type ropes and are great for young horses being taught by effective handlers or with pushy horses and less-than-effective handlers. The thinner rope has a bit more "bite" than the web halters, which spread the pressure over a wider area.

Lead Ropes

Lead ropes typically come around 8 to 12 feet long for general use, and can be made of leather, cotton, flat webbing, or poly rope. The important matter is how the lead rope feels in your hand.

ALERT

Stay away from lead ropes with lengths of chain on the end; they are intended to wrap around the horse's nose for better control. However, if you teach your horses to be respectful at the end of the lead, you will not need the chain, which just gets in the way in regular use.

Lunging Equipment

If you plan to exercise your horse on the ground by lunging before riding or instead of riding, you will need approximately 30 feet of line and probably a lunge whip. Lunge lines are readily available for $10 to $15, and it's worth getting a line designed for horse handling. They are strong and often have a "donut" on the end for hanging onto (without having to strap your hand into a loop, which you DO NOT want to do) if your horse happens to bolt while on the lunge line.

Lunge whips are standard tall whips with a long snapper, are inexpensive, and often help you make just the right triangle (horse, line from his head to you, whip from you to his rear) to keep your horse moving forward on the circle. Lunge whips are not intended to use to actually hit the horse.

Driving Reins

Many people who train young horses often use driving reins to teach the horse about the bit and reins before the horse is even started under saddle. Driving reins are attached to a headstall and run through a harness around the girth of the horse, allowing the person to walk behind the horse, driving the horse from the rear as if driving a cart.

Riding Equipment

Saddles

If you are going to ride your horse, you almost definitely need a saddle. Some people ride bareback, but even if you choose to, it's usually for a short time and for fun. If you plan to go on lengthy trail rides or show your horse, a saddle to distribute the weight comfortably on your horse's back and away from her spine is a must.

Your first question to answer is whether you want an English saddle or a Western saddle. Perhaps you have riding experience from the recent past in which you rode in one type of saddle and you're reluctant to try the other. But the decision should be based on what activities you'll be taking part in with your horse.

FACTS

A shopping excursion to a used tack shop can provide the beginner with almost everything she needs to get started. Most horse equipment is made to wear extremely well, so many used items are in extremely good condition. A reputable shop will clean everything up and be honest about any required repairs. The classified ads can require more running around, but you can often find bargains on saddles and other larger items if you know what you are looking for.

Saddle Cost

Cost isn't going to be much of a deciding factor between English and Western. A high-quality custom-made saddle will run you around $3,000, English or Western. You can get a very nice factory-made saddle by well-known companies in either style for around $1,500. And you can go the lower end with a factory-made saddle with low-quality leather for $500, either type. You can find used low-end saddles selling for as little as $200 or $300. A used high-end saddle, on the other hand, will retain a lot of its value, since they are made to wear well and are even better broken in!

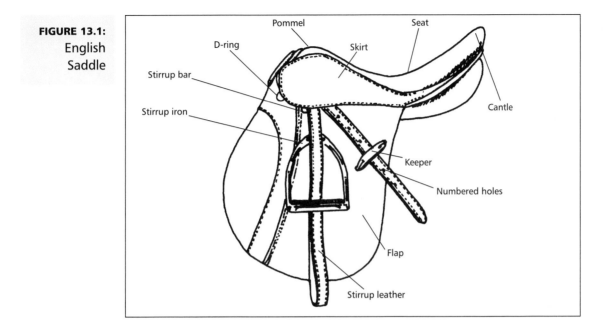

FIGURE 13.1:
English
Saddle

English Saddles

English or "flat" saddles basically come in three types: dressage, hunter/jumper, or all-purpose.

1. **Dressage:** The design of this saddle is intended to keep the rider's legs fairly straight underneath them for the more upright position of dressage riding.

1. **Hunter/jumper:** As the name implies, this is the type of saddle you would choose if you were interested in jumping activities (fox hunting, cross-country riding, stadium jumping). The saddles are designed for a more forward seat and a more bent leg, and they have varying degrees of knee rolls for the bent knee to rest on.

1. **All-purpose:** Intended for the general rider, all-purpose saddles often come with a slant toward hunter/jumper position or dressage position.

There are many measurements you can take to fit saddles. Work with your saddle maker or better tack shop to determine these measurements.

But to decide whether you have saddle fitting problems, in either English or Western, here are some things to look for:

- After a workout, look at the bottom of the saddle pad. Is it unevenly dirty? Are there odd hair patterns, swirling or flattened areas that indicate uneven and misplaced pressure?
- When you groom your horse, does she drop her back away from your hand?
- Are there any sore spots, white hairs, or bumps where the saddle comes in contact with her?
- Does she exhibit agitated behavior when you are about to saddle her?
- Does she move in a constrained manner under saddle but fluidly loose?

These aren't necessarily indications of poor saddle fit, but they definitely could be.

For a copy of Smith-Worthington's saddle fitting brochure, which also includes information on taking measurements and photographs for saddle fit, write to Smith-Worthington Saddle Company, 275 Homestead Avenue, Hartford, Connecticut 06112; or call 860-527-9117.

Western Saddles

Western or "stock" saddles are notoriously heavier and more accessorized than English-style saddles, mostly because the types of activities associated with the Western saddle include the heavy work occupations of ranch life. Saddles used for doctoring cattle or long days on the trail or ranch need a horn for roping, strings for holding things such as rain gear and a bedroll, a rear cinch to keep the back of the saddle in place when the cow comes to the end of the rope that is dallied onto the horn, maybe a pocket for a knife, and a breast collar to keep the saddle better in place over rough terrain.

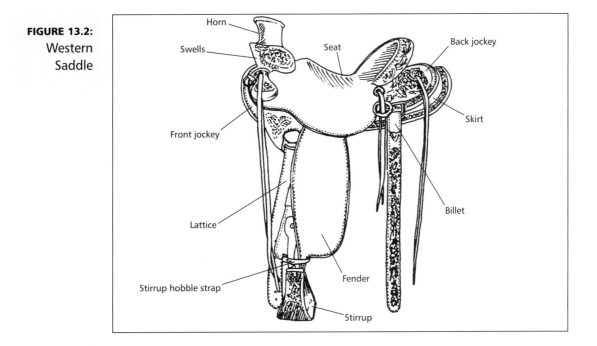

FIGURE 13.2:
Western
Saddle

Horn

Swells

Seat

Back jockey

Skirt

Front jockey

Lattice

Billet

Stirrup hobble strap

Fender

Stirrup

Western saddles break down mainly into working saddles and show saddles. Working saddles are usually extremely ruggedly built for heavy use. Show saddles are laden with as much silver as you would like. Most people reserve their show saddle for the show itself and practice in it only enough to be comfortable at the show, keeping a less ornate saddle for everyday use.

Western-style endurance saddles are sort of a hybrid of English and Western, but look mostly like a regular Western saddle without the horn. They draw on features of cavalry saddles and are well suited for long hours of riding. Mounted police units often use them.

Saddle Construction

All saddles, English or Western, are made around a basic structure called a tree, which can be made of wood or fiberglass and other synthetic (and often lighter weight) materials. The tree of either style saddle can be wider or narrower; Quarter Horses, for example, tend to have a wider back, but Arabians, although typically thought narrower than a Quarter Horse, can have what are referred to as "well sprung" ribs, requiring a saddle width that will accommodate them. The rider's major concern when it comes to the saddle tree is the twist, which is the degree of slant in the sloped area in the front of the saddle tree. The steeper the slant, the narrower the saddle will feel to the rider.

Girths and Cinches

English riders call them girths; Western riders typically refer to them as cinches. Regardless of the name, their purpose is to hold the saddle on.

Girths are typically made of all leather, with buckles on both ends that fasten onto billet straps on both sides of the saddle. Some girths have a section of elastic on one side of the buckles, which can make it easier to snug the saddle up. You can also buy leather girths with coverings of fleece or foam, or you can buy all-cloth girths, which don't have the strength or give of leather.

Western cinches come in many materials, including foam-like neoprene, web material with felt or fleece lining, or wool-blend or mohair string girths, which consist of multiple strings gathered at rings with hooks on either end. Rings with buckles that fit into a hole in the latigo strap tend to be more secure than the empty ring that the latigo ties into. Look for cinches with small rings on either side of the middle of the girth for attaching accessories such as breast collars and belly straps (for rear cinches).

Breast Collar

The breast collar (also referred to as a breast plate) comes in many styles. The saddle you buy, English or Western, will probably have a matching breast collar, which you can choose whether or not to buy. Sometimes a horse's conformation makes a breast collar almost mandatory to keep the saddle from slipping back. Breast collars can also be just one more piece of assurance that the saddle won't slip under the horse (often an important consideration when starting horses under saddle for the first time). Also, they can be used to attach equipment or sometimes simply for decoration.

QUESTIONS?

What is a tree?
A **tree** is the basic structure, usually made of wood or fiberglass, that both English and Western saddles are built upon. They can be narrow or wide, depending on the type of horse and the comfort of the rider.

Saddle Pads

A saddle pad should always be placed between the saddle and the horse's back to protect the horse from chafing. As with everything else, there are many types of saddle pads to choose from. For Western riders, heavy wool-felt pads in varying thicknesses up to 1 inch can be used alone or covered with a thinner wool blanket. Traditional Navajo-weave blankets in many beautiful colors and patterns are a perennial favorite in Western style. Hunter/jumper-type saddle pads follow the shape of the saddle with very little pad exposed and are often made of fleece. Square-quilted cotton pads used more with dressage saddles come in many colors and fabrics and can be customized, like Western pads, with monograms and barn logos in the corners. They have nylon billets and girth straps to fit them to the saddle and keep them in place.

Contemporary materials have brought about the gel-cushion saddle pad and temperature-sensitive foam, which are designed to be therapeutic in nature. Pads, inserts, and risers can be used to adjust saddles that don't fit the horse quite right, but, of course, it is always better to have the saddle fit well without the need for shims. Shims are available for both English- and Western-style saddles.

Keeping saddle pads clean is a necessity for the comfort and health of your horse, but it can be a chore. Some tack shops specialize in cleaning and repairing horse clothing and are worth checking out. Felt pads for use under a Western saddle are relatively cheap, and save wear and tear on the underside of the exposed saddle blanket. And when they are too dirty to use with a saddle, the barn cats love to sleep on them, dirty side down, in the sunny spots in the barn!

One technique to clean saddle pads is to take the pad to the hand car wash and hose the hair and dirt off with the power sprayer. English saddle pads are less bulky and most can be run through the washing machine.

Bridles and Other Tack

The entire headpiece—headstall, bit, chin strap, and reins—is known as the bridle. The bridle's function is mostly to keep the bit in the horse's mouth.

FIGURE 13.3:

Bridle

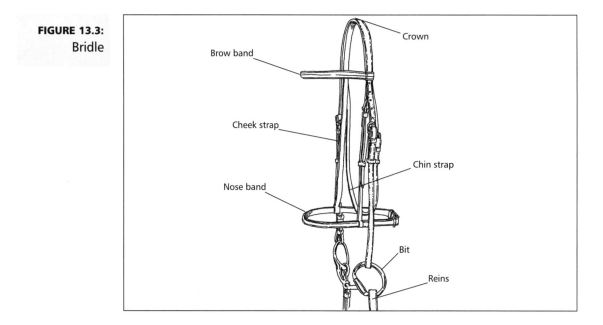

Choosing the right bit is very important. Although it would take a separate book to go into the different bits that are out there, I feel compelled to say up front that a lot of the bits you will see in tack shops and tack catalogs are absolutely abusive, especially in a beginner's hands. Your money is better spent learning better horsemanship than buying bits to increase the leverage you use to put pressure on your horse's mouth.

A snaffle is basically a jointed piece of metal that goes in the horse's mouth and is attached to the reins with either O-shaped rings that can slide loosely around the ends of the bit or D-shaped rings that stay stationary. Snaffle bits are the best educational bit for the horse at any age and for the everyday rider. They are the mildest bit (although any bit can be harsh when in harsh hands) and allow the horse to think about what you are trying to teach her rather than the pain she is experiencing in her mouth. The bit is a communication tool between you and your horse. When you pick up the reins and the bit comes in contact with the corners of the horse's mouth, the horse should be taught to understand that this means something. Although what it means can vary with the type of riding and horsemanship you learn and the level of education of your horse, the most common thing pressure from the bit means to a horse is to slow down or stop. You will eventually learn to communicate this to your horse in other ways—for example, by getting heavier in your seat and having less energy in your body—but the bit will always be one more communication tool.

ALERT

The only bit you will probably ever need, English or Western, is a snaffle bit. If your horse is giving you problems and someone recommends that you get a harsher bit with more leverage (i.e., longer "shanks"), find someone else to get your riding advice from.

You will also see hackamores used in Western style. Forget the awful-looking things you see in tack shops and catalogs known as mechanical hackamores, which look more like the steel jaw traps once used to catch animals for pelts. A real hackamore consists of a headstall or hanger, a mecate (a type of long rein with a built-in lead rope), and the bosal, which is an oval-shaped piece of soft braided leather that serves the same purpose as a bit, only the bosal doesn't go in the horse's mouth but instead rests on the horse's nose.

The chin strap is a strap of leather under the chin of the horse attached to each bit ring; it helps to keep the bit from sliding through the horse's mouth. These do not need to serve any other purpose and should hang loosely at the chin.

You can match your headstall with leather reins, which, in Western style, are usually two separate pieces, called split reins. You can make a fashion statement with bright colors by choosing reins of the same web material as your halter. Vaquero-style mecate reins have become popular for general use and Western showing. They are made of nylon, braided parachute cord, mohair rope, or the traditional horsehair rein and consist of one long piece that runs through leather slobber straps attached to the bit; once a loop is run through for reins, the rest of the long tail serves as a lead rope and can be tied off to the horn or *loosely* tucked into your belt or chaps.

English reins are usually attached in the middle by a buckle. They can be all leather with either flat or braided ends or part leather and part rubber, in the area of the rider's hands.

FACTS

Cleaning your tack regularly allows you a chance to inspect it for wear. Of course, repair or replace anything that is about to break, and keep a close eye on anything overly worn. Good quality horse tack is made to hold up to the job it is made to do, but keeping it clean will help it hold up that much longer.

Cleaning Leather Tack

To clean leather, you will need a good sponge, warm water, your favorite leather cleaning product (commonly called saddle soap), and a bottle of your favorite leather conditioner. Undo any straps, remove the cinch from your saddle, and unbuckle any pieces that buckle on and off so that you can be sure to get to every little nook and cranny where dirt loves to hide and grind at the leather. Wash everything down with warm water and the sponge, opening up the pores of the leather. Use some elbow grease to remove any surface dirt. Rinse off, get some clean warm water, dab some leather cleaner onto the sponge, and lather up your leather. Rinse it off and let it dry some. Before it is completely dry, work in some leather conditioner. Keep in mind that some leather conditioners may darken light leather, so test a hidden area first before doing the entire piece.

Keep your leather tack—saddles, bridles, and leather halters—in a cool, dry place. Dampness will cause mold to form on the leather, and too much heat and sun exposure will dry it out.

Horse Apparel

Leg Protection

Boots on the horse are used for protection either from external injury—usually the horse striking one leg with another foot—or from striking a rail when jumping or rocks and fallen branches on the trail. Learn to put them on snug enough but not so snug as to cut off circulation. There are several different kinds of boots:

- **Shipping boots:** These padded wraps are used for all four legs during trailering. You can purchase one-piece wraps or cotton sheets wrapped in place with stretchy wrapping (also referred to as polo wraps).
- **Bell boots:** Bell boots are basically rubber boots (they also come in synthetic materials such as Cordura) that look like the business end of a toilet plunger and hang from the horse's fetlock joint.
- **Splint boots:** This protection is for the lower front leg area, both from striking it with the other foot or from the concussion of hard or deep, heavy footing. These wrap around the leg between the knee and the fetlock and have Velcro closures.
- **Galloping boots:** Usually made of leather, these boots protect the back of the horse's front legs/feet from overreaching with the back legs at the gallop.
- **Open front boots:** Another boot used in jumping, they are for the front legs and are open in the front.

Blankets

The following are the basic types of blankets available:

- **Fly sheet:** This is a thin mesh sheet that is cool in warm weather but protects the horse's body from biting flies.
- **Anti-sweat sheet:** This is a lightweight sheet used for cooling out a sweaty horse.
- **Cooler:** Traditionally wool, this light blanket traps air while the horse cools off and provides some warmth once the horse has cooled.

- **Rain sheets:** Made of waterproof material, these sheets are also made big enough to cover a saddle while you're waiting for your class.
- **Lightweight sheet:** This provides some warmth and protection from the wind.
- **Turnout rug:** These are traditionally wool lined with a heavy canvas outer shell used to provide protection from the weather.
- **Exercise rug:** Worn while riding, this rug fits under the saddle and covers the rump, keeping the loin area warm during warm-up.

Equipment and Apparel for the Rider

Helmets

Helmets have been much more accepted in the English-riding world than the Western one. The deep bucket of a Western hat offers a limited amount of protection—and is rarely still on when you land. There have been some attempts to make a protective helmet that looks like a Western hat, but the acceptance of these has not been widespread. Typically, when riding recreationally, riders in Western gear simply wear the basic helmets available. Unfortunately, when riding in Western classes in shows, riders wear Western hats, not helmets.

The most important thing about the helmet you pick is its size. The helmet should fit snugly on your head and should be buckled under your chin before you mount up. The helmet should also be certified with the American Society for Testing and Materials (ASTM). This group oversees all safety standards for manufacturing in the United States. Any safety equipment you buy should be certified to meet their standards.

ALERT

Head injuries account for the largest percentage of all serious injuries resulting from horseback riding accidents. Buy a helmet that fits well and always wear it when you ride, whether you're riding English or Western.

Helmets come in all sorts of styles and even a few colors these days. There are different designs that are considered more appropriate than others for different types of riding. The velvet kind with the little button on the top is the style you'll see on the fox hunting grounds. Schooling helmets tend to have a lot of open ventilation, and helmets are even used in dressage competitions. You can accessorize your helmet with decorative helmet covers, rain covers, and even a cool pack to keep your helmeted head extra cool in hot temperatures.

Safety Vests

Not many recreational riders wear safety vests, but if you plan to do a lot of jumping or start a lot of young horses under saddle, a safety vest is a worthwhile investment. Like helmets, vests are available that meet ASTM safety standards. They are very lightweight and have lots of features to make them more comfortable than ever. They run between $100 and $200.

Clothing and Footwear

Pants

Western-style riders tend to go for jeans. If you wear jeans for riding, look for brands that have the wide, double-stitched seam only on the outside of the leg and have a simple seam on the inside.

ESSENTIALS

For help in choosing clothing to accent your horse in the show ring, depending on his color, go to *www.hobbyhorseinc.com*. This Web site includes a catalog of clothing to choose from and has information on what colors and styles are in.

English riders typically wear riding breeches, which are extremely comfortable and come in stretch fabrics that are intended to fit very tightly. Almost all have suede patches inside the knees. You can also get full-seat breeches in which the suede runs from the knee of one leg all the way around the bottom, and back down to the knee of the other leg; not only do they wear better, but the full suede seat helps you to keep your seat in the saddle.

Chaps

One way to save wear and tear on your jeans is to wear chaps. Chaps are very common in Western-style riding apparel and are often used by English riders as well. Western chaps can be leather or suede and may or may not have fringe. They are made to zip on the outside and fit quite snugly to your leg.

Boots

Boots come in both English and Western styles that are traditional and popular. English riders in competition tend to wear knee-high leather boots.

Western-style boots are probably one of the most common icons of the cowboy tradition. They come in various styles as well. Western riders also embrace lace-up boots and ankle-high paddock boots.

Riding boots should have a significant heel to prevent your foot from slipping completely through the stirrup. Avoid rubber-soled boots, which can get slippery; leather is best. Absolutely do not wear sneakers riding or working with horses; they are slippery in the stirrup, and they provide absolutely no protection if you are stepped on.

FACTS

Boots for riding have a completely different purpose than boots for barn work. There's not much distinction between English and Western styles in this area—sturdy boots are a must, and you'll definitely want a waterproof pair around. In winter, you'll also need a pair of warm boots. Manure and urine take a toll on leather and rubber, so expect to have to replace your boots at least every couple of years.

Hats

If boots are the most recognizable cowboy icon, the Stetson hat is a close second. (Find out all about this company, which started in 1865, at their Web site: *www.stetsonhat.com*.) Plan to have a good Western hat if you are showing in Western classes.

Dressage riders can feel comfortable in the wide range of safety helmets available today, but traditional dress includes a derby hat. When mounted, as I mentioned before, the hat on your head should be in the form of an ASTM-certified helmet!

Spurs

Like dressage whips and riding crops, spurs should be considered a means of supporting your leg but used only as incentive, never as punishment. Both English and Western riders often wear spurs, and styles are promoted for each. Large spinning rowels (the part of the spur that connects with the horse) are what commonly comes to mind when imagining a cowboy with spurs on, but the most common spurs worn by most riders have very short shanks.

Find a Style That's Right for You

This is just an overview of the equipment for horse and rider that is needed and is available, but it will get you started. Once you begin to look through catalogs and tack shops, you will get a sense of what styles are right for you. Keep in mind that there is a range of prices that suits every budget. The most important thing is comfort; don't give up comfort for the sake of fashion. And if the price of something—a bit, a device, a piece of equipment—seems too good to be true, it is. Don't waste your money on it. Buy the simplest equipment of the best quality you can afford.

CHAPTER 14
Riding and Driving

Although horse owners take great pleasure in caring for their horses, riding is still typically the ultimate intent. It's fun, challenging, interesting, and good exercise, all wrapped into one.

There's a lot you can learn from reading, but let me say up front that you will not learn how to ride from a book or a video. The real place to learn to ride is on a horse. If that's all you ever did was ride—if you never picked up a book, watched a video, or took a lesson—you could still become a fantastic rider, but you need to learn how to learn from your horse. Having an instructor help you get started is probably a more expedient way to learn to be in the saddle in a way that helps the horse instead of hindering him. But often it boils down to time in the saddle. In this chapter I'll tell you all about riding—and driving—your horse.

Develop Your Awareness

A little common sense and awareness will take you a long way. In order for a horse to be comfortable carrying your extra weight, you need to learn to be balanced in your seat so that you aren't using your horse's mouth for balance, and you need to learn not to flop around in the saddle. If you become aware of how the horse is responding to what you do, you will be able to adjust what you are doing to fit the horse.

Be Particular About Who You Learn From

I get very frustrated watching videos and competitions in which people who are either instructing others or are considered the top competitors in their discipline have horses that are foaming at the mouth (some say that this is an indication of something good, but I don't agree) and kept under control only by an iron grip on the reins. Don't aspire to that. While they are claiming that having every part of their body in the exact right position is best for the horse, their horses are there in living color telling them differently. Pick your teachers carefully.

FACTS

When I got back into horses after a decade of not riding, I realized I'd better take some lessons. But I needed more saddle time than the weekly lesson. A friend offered to let me ride her older mare during the week when she couldn't get to the barn. This helped keep her mare exercised, and gave me riding time on a solid horse.

Do aspire to be a relaxed rider who can instill calmness in your horse. Even if all the technical details aren't perfect and every inch of your body isn't where the "professionals" say it should be, it is much better to be a relaxed horse and rider.

Learning How to Ride

If you've never ridden a horse before, probably the best place to take your first ride is at a reputable riding stable that teaches beginners the fundamentals. Not only will they have horses and instructors, but they will have saddles and helmets for students to use, and you won't have to spend a lot of money before you've even sat on a horse. However, do have a pair of sturdy boots, even if they aren't "riding" boots. For safety, the boots should have at least a half-inch heel, then, in the unfortunate event that you get tossed from your horse, your boot won't go through the stirrup and trap your foot.

How to Find a Good Lesson Barn

Your phone book is a starting place for collecting locations—look under Riding Academies or Riding Stables. You should do some investigating and asking around before signing up for lessons.

Another place to look is on the bulletin board at local tack shops and feed stores for flyers from local stables offering lessons. As you start to investigate, ask the staff at the feed store whether they know anything about the stable.

Once you've collected names, you can start with a phone call. Talk with the stable manager, who may or may not be one of the instructors, about what is offered, asking questions such as these:

- *What kind of riding lessons does the barn offer? Is there a concentration in any one discipline?* If you just want to have a few lessons to get on a horse and start to develop your ability, it may not matter what the stable's focus is at first. But if you end up wanting to continue and the barn you started with doesn't offer what you're interested in, you will have to switch barns. That may not be an issue, but it would be best to find a barn that has at least some range of disciplines. It's hard enough to find a place in which you feel comfortable without having to change not long after you start.
- *Are both private and group lessons available?* Some beginning riders may want to start with private lessons until they develop their seat, and then after a few weeks, when they are more comfortable, they can join a group lesson to learn how to ride with other horses and riders around. Some people prefer just the opposite—to ride with a group for the moral support while learning, then develop and refine their skills with private lessons.

- *What should I bring with me to the lesson?* The stable will most likely provide everything you need, but don't assume anything. Find out whether you need your own helmet. Although even if they do provide one, having your own personal helmet that fits you correctly is best. And if you decide horseback riding isn't for you, a helmet will be easy enough to sell.

FACTS

There are dozens of places to go on riding vacations in the United States, either with your own horse or one belonging to the stable. Here is a sampling:

- Hidden Creek Ranch
  Harrison, Indiana
  800-446-3833
  www.hidden-creek.com

- Pasos del Parador
  Blanchardville, Wisconsin
  608-523-1701

- Vermont Icelandic Horse Farm
  P.O. Box 577
  Waitsfield, Vermont 05673
  802-496-7141
  www.icelandichorses.com

- *Do they have lesson horses available?* Again, any barn that spends a lot of time on giving lessons probably has lesson horses on the premises, but don't take that for granted. And if they do, ask about the horses' backgrounds. Are they ex-show horses? Camp horses? Horses that the stable uses during the off-season of a trail riding outfit?
- *Can I eventually take lessons on my own horse?* Maybe you already own a horse but would like to learn on a lesson horse first, then switch to your own. Find out up front if they are comfortable with this idea.
- *May I come for a visit and watch a lesson?* This may be your most important question of all. My personal view is that if a barn is uncomfortable with you stopping by and watching what takes place there, then maybe you won't be comfortable with what takes place there. Granted, the instructor should always ask the student who is having a lesson if it is okay if a prospective student watches. Otherwise, however, dropping in on a public facility that you'd like to develop a relationship with should not be a big issue.

Finding an Instructor

This is where some self-analysis will come in. People teach and people learn in myriad ways. If an instructor has a drill sergeant approach barking out orders and screaming at you, telling you how stupid you are every time you do something wrong, and you have the tendency to crawl within yourself whenever you get yelled at, this is not the right instructor or approach for you! Some people get a lot out of this "tough love" kind of instruction—the more they are yelled at, the more they are challenged to perfect what they are doing.

Some people need to be constantly reassured and encouraged. This may sound like the ideal approach, but actually this can go too far as well. You want to be praised for your accomplishments, but if you want to become a good and better rider, you also need some constructive criticism.

Somewhere in between is probably best for most people, especially the beginning rider. Praise for what you are doing right while being made aware of where you need to adjust and improve can move you along from the beginner to the advanced beginner stages quickly.

ESSENTIALS

You might enjoy browsing through *www.riderswest.com,* which is in an online magazine format and has articles about riding and show results from around the country.

You can learn something about how an instructor teaches by watching him or her give a lesson. But this can be a bit misleading, since the instructor knows you are watching and evaluating. The best test of an instructor is to take one or two lessons—a good lesson barn will even suggest that. Don't sign up for a series of lessons; just pay for them as you go. If the first one goes well, pay for another. Do this three or four times, and if the relationship continues to go well and there is a financial incentive to buy a few lessons at once or in joining a group lesson of a series of six lessons for a set fee, then you can feel comfortable doing that. If the first couple of lessons do not go well or you just aren't sure, try out other instructors until you find your match.

The Lesson Horse

A riding stable that concentrates on giving lessons will have lesson horses—typically well-trained horses probably in their teens that have had a lot of exposure to the outside world. They tend to be calm and cool about being ridden and also to be very tolerant of riders of different skill levels.

The horses themselves will tell you a lot about the overall quality of the barn and the experience you will have taking lessons there. Do the horses seem content? One of the most obvious things you can judge is how well they are cared for—lesson horses can work pretty hard, which means they should be fit and trim, but not skinny. Are their coats shiny, appropriately long or shed out, depending on the time of year? Are their feet well cared for? Do you see lame horses being ridden for lessons? (Although you do not want to be part of an establishment that makes their lame horses work, keep in mind that some horses do have chronic lamenesses that allow for light work such as giving a beginner riding lesson.)

Lessons on Your Own Horse

If you own your own horse, you may have it in mind to eventually use your horse for your lessons. Depending on your horse, the beginning rider may find it best to take a few lessons on the stable's horses in order to advance his or her skills on horses that know the drill. Once you have perfected the basics, you can switch to your own horse with confidence.

QUESTIONS?

What does truck-in mean?
When you take riding lessons and bring your own horse, you are referred to as a **truck-in.**

The hardest part about taking lessons on your own horse is that you may have a specific way of doing things with your horse and your instructor may do things differently. If that is the case, you need to find a middle ground. And you want your horse's education far enough along that you can concentrate on your lesson, not on trying to control your horse.

Clinics

Over the past ten years, the clinic scene has exploded. These learning environments usually offer the opportunity to be a spectator or bring your horse and participate as a student. And with clinics, the human is the student, and the horse is the project.

As an older rider re-introducing myself to horsemanship, I embraced clinics as a way to learn, especially about handling and working with young horses. Most areas of the country offer clinics somewhere within trailering distance, as clinicians tend to travel all over the country most of the year.

If you are experiencing problems with a horse or want to improve your riding so that you can be more comfortable with your horse, clinics are a great place to spend an intensive amount of time. You and your horse will develop a stronger relationship just by learning together under good instruction. And the clinic environment provides instant comradery and instant access to a teacher.

Getting the Most Out of Attending a Clinic

I have been to literally dozens of clinics given by several different clinicians in many different disciplines over the past decade, some as a spectator, and some as a participant. In my experience, these are the things you need to consider in order to get the most out of your time and money, both of which can be considerable!

- *Check out the clinician before you sign up to participate.* The best way to do this is to be a spectator. Perhaps a clinician is coming to a place near you. Get his or her schedule and see where else he or she is giving a clinic. Maybe you can combine a little vacation with a trip to the clinic in another area. This is a great way to meet horse people in other parts of the country, and you can observe the clinician before signing up for the clinic near you. Many clinicians also offer videos, but the best way to check out their style is to watch them in person.
- *Find out everything you need to have for the clinic for both you and your horse.* Typically, for a general horsemanship clinic, to

participate you need whatever you normally ride in. Horsemanship clinics are sometimes offered in specific disciplines, such as jumping or roping; you will need your usual equipment to perform in that discipline. But beyond that, do you need shavings? Buckets? Muck bucket and manure fork? Sponsors usually send out information sheets along with release forms; if you have any questions that still aren't answered, call and ask. You don't want to lessen your experience by being unprepared.

- *Be willing to try new things.* The clinician will have ideas about exercises and activities that work to teach certain things. You are there to learn, so join in and fully participate.

FACTS

There are currently dozens of clinicians traveling the country giving clinics in horsemanship, colt starting, and handling. Here are five with whom I've ridden or watched several times (many others are listed in any horse publication):

- Buck Brannaman, Houlihan Ranch, 642 U.S. Highway 14, Sheridan, Wyoming 82801
- Joe Wolter, P.O. Box 173, Guthrie, Texas 79236
- Greg Eliel, Eliel Ranch, 70 Ross Road, Ellensburg, Washington 98926
- Bryan Neubert, P.O. Box 726, Alturas, California 96101
- Ray Hunt, Rattlesnake Ranch, HC 87 Box 20, Mountain Home, Idaho 83647

- *Don't spend your time making excuses for your horse or your riding.* If your horse is being a jerk, spend your time learning how to help your horse not act like a jerk. Your riding level isn't an issue—you are there to learn! If the clinic offers a couple of different classes, be sure you sign up for the class that is most appropriate for your level of experience. You have the perfect opportunity to change things under the direction of a very knowledgeable person, so make use of it. A clinic is not a horse show where you are showing off what you and your horse know. It is a learning experience.

- *Watch everything.* Show up early to take care of your horse and be ready for the first class, whether or not you are in it. Some things that are going on may not look like they have anything to do with you and your horse, but you would be surprised how much you can learn from something that seems completely unrelated. Participate fully in the clinic. Even lunch can be a learning experience.
- *Ask questions.* Participation in a clinic can be expensive. Sometimes even spectator fees are substantial. Feel free to ask questions, even if they seem stupid. A good clinician will be happy to answer questions—in fact, they often seem to wish people would ask more questions!

Moving On

The things you learn at a clinic will likely give you the knowledge and comfort level you need to move out into the real world with your horse. Clinics are safe environments in which to try things under controlled circumstances with knowledgeable help at your fingertips.

ESSENTIALS

It can be disconcerting to ride with people who haven't learned to do things the same way you have. But you will begin to appreciate how much you and your horse have learned when you ride outside the clinic environment and your education and the education you are providing your horse all holds together.

Fitness

Both you and your horse need to be physically fit to be comfortable for any length of time in the saddle. The overweight, unfit horse will quickly get winded and sweaty. She will also get saddle sores, girth sores, and other soreness related to carrying around too much weight, as well as be prone to injury and illness. You need to be fit enough to use your body to request your horse to do what you ask—this doesn't at all mean that horseback riders need to be supermodel thin. But riding horses is a physical activity that requires some level of fitness and flexibility no matter what your size.

Fitness of the Horse

Prepare your horse for the level of riding you plan to use him for. If you take him out just on weekends for a trail ride a couple of miles long, he can probably be a little overweight and out of shape and deal with it. But don't expect that same horse to go out one weekend on a 25-mile trail ride. He will be sore, it is likely he will damage something making him unrideable for a few weeks, and it just isn't fair. Condition your horse for the amount of riding you plan to do. And if you want to do that 25-mile ride, plan ahead for it.

If you live in the northern states, where winter is mostly down time, gradually build your horse up for riding season. Bring him to an indoor arena a couple of times a week if you can (arenas often will rent time by the hour) and keep him in some level of shape over the winter. Up your conditioning as spring approaches. Perhaps you live close enough to the ocean that the beach can provide some nice footing in the snow months. Be creative—take your horse for walks along the road if the conditions aren't safe enough to ride her; that will be good exercise for both of you!

Fitness of the Rider

Being around horses will bring you some innate strength training just from day-to-day chores such as lifting water buckets, grain bags, bags of shavings, and so on. But there are some things to add to your overall fitness regimen that can be helpful, specifically for riding.

Stretching is very important. Add some good yoga and stretching books to your library and pick out some exercises. Of course, like any physical activity, you should do some basic stretches before you get on your horse. But also some more in-depth stretching is good, perhaps some yoga poses. You will be able to get on and off your horse easier, your muscles won't be as sore from the stretching they get from simply being astride a horse, and if the horse spooks and stretches your muscles even further, they won't be starting from such a tight place. Your horse will move better and respond to your body better if you are more supple.

And you will be able to move with the horse better and liven up that energy you need to transfer energy to her.

Your lower back absorbs a lot of the shock of the motion of riding. A strong back and corresponding strong abdominal muscles will help keep this shock absorption from making your back hurt. Strong abdominal muscles will also help your posture in the saddle. So the upshot—add stomach crunches to your exercise program!

QUESTIONS?

What are psychocybernetics?
This is the technique for using your subconscious power to achieve the positive results that you desire. In *That Winning Feeling?* Jane Savoie talks about this concept in relation to horses and riding.

How to Ride

Explaining how to ride a horse in a book is a tall order. But there are a few basic things to know that you will run into the first time you climb on board a horse.

The Gaits

The horse has three basic gaits (plus a few others if you ride a "gaited horse" such as a Tennessee Walker) that the beginner will encounter and want to master:

1. **The walk:** The horse walks with three feet on the ground and one foot raised at any one time. Each hoof strikes the ground individually—one, two, three, four.
2. **The trot:** The trot is a two-beat gait; two feet are on the ground and two feet are in the air at any one time. The feet operate on a diagonal pattern, with the left front and right hind either up or down at the same time, and the same with the right front and left hind, with a brief moment when all four feet are off the ground. (In the gait known as the pace, the two feet on the same side move together.) In Western riding parlance, the trot is known as

the jog. In the show world, the jog tends to be a little slower pace than the trot.

3. **The canter:** This is a three-beat gait with a hind leg pushing off, then the other hind and the opposite front, then the other front leg, with a moment of complete suspension of all four legs. Again, in the Western showing world, the canter is called the lope and is typically a little slower gait than the canter of the English riders in the class.

FIGURE 14.1:
Foot Patterns

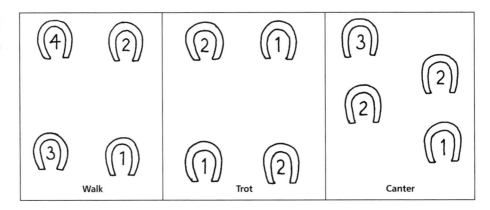

Riding the Three Gaits

- **The walk:** Sit deeply in the saddle and move your body with the movement of the horse. Expect the horse to walk with energy and life, none of this dull slow walking. You should both look like you are enjoying yourself and have somewhere to go! At first, your body movements may be a bit exaggerated, but you will learn to have life in your body without swinging like a monkey up there.

- **The trot:** At some point, you will want to learn to "sit the trot" using your lower back to absorb the shock of the up and down movement, and not flop around like a dying fish in the saddle. However, you will probably also want to post. Posting is a method to rise and fall with the movement of the horse—you rise out of the saddle with the rise of the outside (the one along the fence rail or arena wall) front foot, and you sit back into the saddle as that outside front foot falls to the ground. Posting is easier if the horse is trotting with some speed. And don't fret if you don't get it at first—once you get the posting movement down, it will be like riding a bicycle and will never leave you. This is where a good school horse helps, because they know to keep their trot pace up even though what you may be doing with your body interferes with their ability to move out. Although you won't see Western riders posting to the trot in a class at a show, you can easily post in a Western saddle if it makes you and/or the horse more comfortable.

- **The canter:** Typically the canter is a gait that beginners are very uncomfortable with. This is, I think, mostly because of the additional speed with which the horse is moving. If you can find a smooth reliable horse to learn to canter on from the very beginning, you will save yourself a lot of canter angst and get this gait down very soon in your riding career. This can be truly that proverbial rocking horse feeling. You need to learn to sit up straight to keep your weight balanced and in your stirrups and scoop your seat along with the movement of the saddle/the horse's back. Sometimes a novice rider has trouble getting a horse to canter at all—their anxiety makes their body block the horse from moving out. Like with anything involving horses, the more you canter in a controlled environment, the sooner you will be comfortable with this gait.

ESSENTIALS

To learn a specific discipline, look for an instructor in that discipline. He or she will be able to teach you what kind of tack you will need, how to ride in the proper position, what to wear if you plan to compete, and the etiquette of competition for that discipline.

The most important thing is to start with the basics of riding, the things that are universal no matter what discipline you plan to ride or what type of equipment you plan to use. Here are some of the most important basic things to master in order to ride well:

- *Be calm.* Your calmness will help your horse to be calm. Horses very often take after their owners—a nervous person will make a horse nervous too, and a laid back person will tend to bring out the laid back part of a horse. The more calm you are on top of your horse, the better. If you take lessons, your instructor will probably tell you a million times to breathe. Holding your breath or taking shallow short breaths has an effect not only on you but also on your horse. Keep in mind that the horse can feel a fly land on any part of its body—imagine how much it can feel what you are doing up there!

- *Learn about how your horse perceives things and try to assess a situation from her perspective.* A horse does not think like a human; it's as simple as that. The advantage we humans have is that we can analyze our own behavior and the behavior of others. Use that ability and learn about how the horse thinks. And your horse *does* think, every second of the day! They are not stupid; they just think like horses. This isn't to say you should spend your time second guessing them. But if you come upon a trouble spot with your horse, put yourself in your horse's shoes and think about how she might be perceiving the situation. Lots of research has been done here, so there's plenty of information to read. And there's always the best teacher of all—your horse—to learn from.

- *Sit on your horse like your intention is to be there.* Don't slouch like a sack of potatoes and expect your horse to react positively to what you ask of him. Likewise, don't sit stiff as a board. Move with the horse, and exhibit energy when you want your horse to exhibit energy. Instructors will tell you to hold your shoulders exactly in this position and your legs in exactly that position and to hold your reins this or that way and tilt your wrists at this or that angle, but not too far. Relax! Hold yourself on your horse in a warm, inviting way in a position that is conducive to riding with purpose.

- *Do what you are ready for.* This isn't to say you shouldn't push yourself, but also keep in mind that the only time line you have is self-inflicted. Your horse couldn't care less if the two of you progress beyond a certain level in a sport. Don't step up to the canter out on the trail if you don't think either of you are ready for it. Do what you are ready for and work on preparing to be ready for more.

- *Avoid gimmicks.* If a piece of tack or a training device claims to work miracles, don't buy it. Becoming a good rider that a horse can rely on for moral support is hard work, and you should plan to work hard to become the team you can be proud of. If you don't enjoy hard work, you probably should take up a different hobby.

- *Don't drill your horse.* Yes, you will need to do things enough times that the horse learns it, but don't spend all evening working on one thing. Mix it up for the horse. Give your horse the benefit of being the thinking, reasoning animal she is and give her some variety. Add exterior stimuli to your riding sessions—you'd be amazed how much a few ground rails, barrels, low jumps, tarpaulins, gates to go through, or even a couple of cows can add to your horse's interest level.

It's just not worth risking your safety or that of your horse to attempt something that gives you pause, such as crossing a questionable wooden bridge or riding across that highway instead of getting off and leading your horse across. It is your responsibility to keep your team as safe as possible.

Here are some additional basic riding elements:

- **Transitions upward/downward:** When a horse switches gaits, it is known as a transition. An upward transition is from a slower gait to a faster gait. A downward transition is from a faster gait to a slower gait. You need to help your horse make these transitions smoothly and upon request by learning to ride the changes smoothly yourself and how to best request that the horse change from one gait to the other.
- **Counter canter:** A horse canters on a specific lead when going in a circle. The lead is determined by the back inside leg, which provides balance and support to the inside of the circle. The horse cantering in a circle to the left should be on a "left lead." A counter canter is cantering using the opposite lead from the one that would be appropriate for the direction the horse is going. A counter canter is sometimes used intentionally for conditioning and strengthening.
- **Flexion:** Flexion is the vertical—back to front and up and down— flexibility of the horse.
- **Lateral movement:** These refer to sideways movements of the horse.

- **Working on a line:** As you ride, you will want to have an imaginary line out ahead of you that you aim to stay on. This is most evident in jumping, where before the horse and rider have finished sailing over one jump, the rider is already looking toward the next jump and aiming the horse along the imaginary line he or she has determined to get to the exact position they want to be in when they arrive at the jump.

Some Things You Want from Your Horse

To be safe riding, there are a few things I have learned to expect of my horses. These are things that make me feel safe when riding. Riding a horse is fraught with danger—but if I have these things at my disposal, I feel comfortable about being able to work through most any situation, and I feel more in control. I am always working toward refining the following things.

ALERT

Constantly bumping your legs or tapping with a crop can really make your horse dull. If you need to go to this step, be absolutely sure you get the energy you expect from your horse so that the action will remain effective.

Responsiveness

You want your horse to be responsive when you ask her to do something. If you pick up the reins, you want her to come to attention and come through with whatever you ask her to do. It is up to you to help her understand what you are asking, but you need to expect responsiveness. If you don't expect your horse to be responsive, you teach her that you don't really mean what you ask. And sometimes when you ask for something, it is a matter of safety that your horse be responsive—like stopping to avoid a kick from the horse up ahead or stepping one foot to the left to avoid falling off the edge of a banking.

There are three stages to asking your horse to do something. The first is the "energy in your body" stage. If you bring up the energy by lifting your weight out of your seat and preparing to move with the movement of the horse, your horse will bring up her energy too. That energy will exhibit itself in whatever you are asking of her—if you have contact with the bit blocking forward movement, she will move that energy backward; if you bring up energy without contact, she will move forward.

If your energy means nothing to the horse, you need to go to the next stage, which is the "bump with your legs for forward movement" stage.

If this does nothing, you need to follow through with step three, which is the "whatever it takes" step. Tap the horse with the end of your rein or use a dressage whip or crop to encourage the horse. This is a last resort step, and you should work with your horse in order to avoid it.

Softness

When you pick up the reins, you want your horse to melt into your hands. Picking up those reins is a signal to your horse that you are about to get to work at something. This doesn't mean you have to have contact on the horse's mouth, but you should expect your horse to be alert to what you have in mind for the two of you. Softness means that when you pick up the reins, the horse doesn't resist against you, throwing his head up in the air. If an emergency should come up, you want softness, not resistance, to be your horse's first response to you.

Say you are in a pack of horses riding on the trail and something spooks the group, such as a grouse flying out of the bushes. There's a pretty good chance your horse will spook with the rest—it's only natural. Would you really want your horse to be so dull and sour on life as to not have some reaction to this kind of thing? But what you want then is the horse to turn to you for a message about the situation. If you pick up on the reins and your horse softens, the situation for the two of you will go from explosive to controlled. If the horse's first reaction is to resist your hands and throw his head up in the air, the situation is going to get more frightening.

Step Its Hindquarters Away

When I first ride a young horse, I spend a lot of time asking that horse to bring its head around toward my leg. To do this, I shorten the rein by bringing it back toward my hip on the side I want the horse to bend toward and completely release the rein on the other side to give the horse the room to bend.

Once the horse is readily giving her head, it's time to add on to that by asking with the leg on the same side for the horse to step its hindquarters away. This move takes a lot of work from the ground first (see Chapter 11, "Handling"). It will come in handy in many ways. First, it seems to be very relaxing to the horse, perhaps because it gives the horse something to think about—something relatively easy.

Modified versions of this move can be used for many things, including stepping around an object, opening a gate, and even using up some excess energy on the trail (if your horse is a little too eager, pick up on one rein and use the leg on the same side to get her weaving a serpentine from one side of the trail to the other). You should also guide the front quarters at this point (guide her rear around one leg and her front over with the other).

Backing

Don't satisfy yourself with a pathetic little step backward and think that's backing. Expect your horse to back up as long as you are asking him to and with as much energy as you are asking. When you are first teaching him to back, pick up on the reins, get softness and bending at the poll from your horse, shift your weight back a little, and when he backs even one step, release all pressure—reins, weight, energy. Build on that, asking for more steps as he begins to understand what you want. By the time he really knows how to back, he should back to the next county if you haven't released him yet.

A horse backs up in the same diagonal pattern as the trot—with a hind foot and its opposite front foot off the ground at the same time.

You can put some of these pieces together and back circles. This is a lot more complicated than it sounds! Your horse's head will be a little to the outside of the circle, enough to just see his eye on that side. Ask for your back, and guide your horse's hindquarters with your outside leg to move slightly to the inside and his front quarters with your inside leg to move slightly to the outside as you are backing. If you ask too much with either leg, you won't have a circle at all; your horse will step over behind or across in front in place. If you don't ask for enough energy while backing, you will not get the circle either. It's a great exercise, but it can be frustrating for both of you. Satisfy yourself with perhaps a quarter of a circle for a few times, then half the circle, and build up to the full circle. Your horse's hoof prints in the dirt will show you whether you've made a circle, an oval, or just muddled around!

Falling Off

It happens. For a while when first starting to ride my gelding, and not having been in the saddle for years, I was falling off once or twice each session. Not having ridden for a while, I was particularly unseated; it would take very little in the way of a buck or twist or quick turn to find me sailing through the air. It got old fast! You probably won't repeat my experience, but chances are you will fall off once in a while.

It is important to get back on if you want to continue horseback riding as a pastime, but falling can make you very fearful. Don't just chalk it up to life in the horse lane. Think about why your horse spooked, bucked, reared, or whatever it did to send you flying. Go back to refining those tools mentioned earlier—maybe next time the horse bolts, you can regain control, help him calm down, and settle the scene before he bucks or you lose your balance. A horse occasionally spooking is probably a given—regaining control and defusing the situation as quickly as possible is the key to avoiding the bucks and bolts, and the potential fall. And work on your balance—this can be one of the most important things to help you remain seated.

Driving

Maybe you'd like to try driving your horse. If you plan to get into this intensively, you should find a place to take some lessons and maybe apprentice with someone for a while. One way to find someone is to attend a nearby horse show that includes driving classes.

If you want to drive your horse just for fun, the same approach applies to driving as riding: Don't surprise your horse, but expose her deliberately to things. If you ride your horse, you won't need to expose her to the driving bridle; she will be accustomed to having a bridle on. But here are some things to keep in mind as you begin to harness her:

- Get her accustomed to things dangling around her legs and off her body. You can do this with lots of things in a "sacking out" kind of approach, not just with the harness itself. Start with dangling the lead rope around her legs, use the flag we talked about in the handling chapter, maybe even work up to using a small tarp. Make sure she's okay with all this before hooking all the buckles and straps on the harness and having her freak out.
- Put the harness on one piece at a time. This may mean taking the harness apart a bit more than normal, but it's worth it. When she is fully comfortable with one section of the harness, get her accustomed to the next, until she's got the whole thing on.
- Get help in finding the most appropriate vehicle for your horse. Be sure you feel your horse is thoroughly exposed to the driving reins before strapping a cart behind her. It will pay to have her learn to pull something simple, such as a progression of heavier logs, before hitching her up.

Driving has a wealth of intricacies to learn. Read some of the books in Appendix A, "Resources," and, most importantly, find an experienced person you can learn from.

Riding Experiences Differ

Riding horses is a different experience for everyone. Some people seem to be natural riders with great flexibility and no fear; others have to work very hard to be balanced and at ease on the back of a horse. But once you get the hang of it, you will join the large group of people who have bumper stickers and T-shirts that say "I'd rather be riding."

CHAPTER 15
Youth and Horses

City kids and country kids alike have long been captivated by horses. Unlike what often happens with hamsters, fish, and even puppies, those who have a horse in the barn rarely have to be reminded to tend to the horse and typically want to spend every waking hour with him!

Caring for a horse is a great lesson in responsibility and in the reality that even pleasurable things include a lot of hard work. This chapter discusses how to make kids and horses a winning combination.

Good Responsibility Lesson

Although kids usually don't need to be pushed into the barn to be around their horse, horse care is a big responsibility; kids need to be well supervised in the care of their horse. If a child is a member of a "horsey" family that has a barn full and makes a living at some equine activity or a family in which horses are the main recreational activity, caring for horse comes naturally.

For the kid from a family that has never been around horses, the best thing may be to board the horse, at least for a while. This way the child is automatically surrounded by people who can help her or him learn the intricacies of horse care and give advice when problems arise.

ESSENTIALS

Consider leasing tack or buying good quality used tack for growing children. There are also youth-specific tack items such as adjustable child stirrups, which come as an attachment to a full-sized Western saddle. Most riding apparel and footwear comes in youth sizes. And don't forget to buy a good-fitting helmet!

Many times a horse is only financially feasible because he can be kept in the backyard. If the parents are not horse savvy, then the responsibility is on them to get their child in contact with people who have experience with horses. Maybe there is someone in the neighborhood who has horses that the child can spend time with, preferably before his or her own horse lands in the backyard. Maybe keeping the horse at home frees up a little money to let the child take riding lessons. Maybe there is a barn in the vicinity that will let the child clean stalls or groom horses in exchange for riding lessons. This would be the best of both worlds—learning both riding and general care at the same time! Programs such as 4-H and Pony Club can also provide the novice child with lots of help.

A Word of Warning!

As mentioned earlier, a common scenario is for a horse to end up at a rescue shelter when his undesirable behavior has been left unchecked, making him dangerous. If you see behavior in your child's horse that concerns you—such as aggressiveness during feeding time or turning its rear end to you when you enter the stall—don't let these things continue to the point of being dangerous. Get help from an experienced horse person who you trust and find out what to do to turn these behaviors around before your child gets hurt. If you find someone to help but are uncomfortable with what the person is doing, find someone else. It's easy for things to develop into a pretty nasty situation, since the horse's main concern is self-preservation. If sufficiently threatened (and what constitutes "sufficient" is different for each horse), the horse will take whatever action she feels is necessary to protect herself from what she may perceive as a threat to her existence, even if you know it is not.

The important thing to keep in mind is that a horse in the backyard is a living, breathing domesticated animal with daily needs that can only be met by its human caretakers.

Breed Association Youth Groups

Many breed associations have organized youth groups that allow youths to compete with youth riders of their own age. Breed associations realize that youth riders comprise future adult members of their organization and therefore encourage youths to be interested in their breed.

The Welsh Pony Club Youth Program

The Welsh Pony and Cob Society of America (P.O. Box 2977, Winchester, Virginia 22604) has a special youth program directed toward the many young people who ride Welsh ponies. Their Web site (*www.welshpony.org*) features a youth segment with online articles about pony care and offers tips as well as games, stories, and puzzles.

The American Quarter Horse Youth Association (AQHYA)

The AQHYA is for youths eighteen years and under. The group has 30,000 members and offers scholarships, youth-specific shows and classes in general shows, a leadership conference, and other focused activities such as the Youth Racing Experience. Visit the AQHA Web site at *www.aqha.com* and click on "youth" for complete information about joining and participating in the AQHYA.

The International Arabian Horse Youth Association (IAHYA)

Like other breed-specific groups, this association exists for youths involved with Arabian horses. The IAHYA has over 5,000 members, and its magazine and Web site (*http://iaha.com/youth*) have a special youth section called Generation Equus. The Web site tells about special events especially for youths, such as Youth of the Year and the Youth Nationals Arabian and Half-Arabian Championship Horse Show.

FACTS

There are over 600 Pony Clubs in the United States, with over 12,000 members. The "pony" in the name actually refers to the young rider, not the mount; Pony Club members can ride either ponies or horses. Parental involvement is encouraged and expected, and there is a membership fee. To find a group near you, look on the Pony Club Web site (*www.ponyclub.org*) or contact them at United States Pony Clubs, Inc., 4041 Iron Works Parkway, Lexington, Kentucky 40511; 859-254-7669.

Over-mounted Youths

More than once, I've heard a parent talk about how their child rides a 17-hand horse for his weekly lesson or how their kid gets the runaway horse at the lesson barn because she is not afraid of him or how brave their child was to have been tossed off a horse several times but still get back on. These parents repeat these stories as if they are proud!

Granted, being involved with horses is most likely going to involve falling off once in a while and maybe even managing a runaway horse. But parents should be careful not to set their child up to become afraid of horses. I firmly believe in a child riding a mount of proportional size until he or she is a very experienced rider. This doesn't mean having to always put kids on 11-hand ponies or horses so old you need to check their pulse to see if they are still alive. A 14.2-hand horse is a fine size for many eight- to ten-year-old kids, and although a rule of thumb often considered is that horses under five years old are too young for a novice rider, sometimes even a young horse is fine for a kid—there are many success stories of kids and horses growing up together. But unless the child is exceptionally tall or has ridden since she was two, a 17-hand horse is unnecessarily tall for a young rider!

FACTS

Horse care and horseback riding have long been a topic for 4-H groups. This is an excellent way for kids to learn about horse care. Many 4-H groups focus on a different horse activity, such as showing or trail riding. Contact your county extension agency to find out if there is a 4-H horse group in your area. And if not, you might be a good candidate to lead a new group!

Let the child develop some confidence a little closer to the ground. This means that if/when she falls off, she will have less distance to fall; it also means that when she looks down, things don't look so far away! Her legs should reach a good distance down the horse's sides, and her reins should be a normal length as she learns how to become a well-balanced equestrian.

All this said, many young riders are just awesome to watch ride—their youth often lends balance and flexibility combined with a general lack of fear that allows them to just float with the horse. Once they take the natural ability and create a refined, skilled ability as a rider, then the size of the horse doesn't matter.

In the meantime, don't be one of those parents who takes innocent pride in putting their child in danger on a runaway horse that she "needs to run into a wall" to stop. Think about your child's mount in the same way you would think about what kind of car you want your child with a new driver's license driving.

Fun and Games on the Internet

There are several Web sites that offer games in which participants pretend they are horses. For instance, Galloping Acres (*www.angelfire.com/ut/gallopingacres/*) lets you choose to be either a stallion protecting his territory or a mare protecting her foal. There are rules to follow, and if you disappear for over a week without forewarning the host, you lose your territory. Other equine simulation games include Children of the Moons, Run Away to Freedom, and Wild Souls. Many more can be found under the Kids Stuff links on *www.haynet.net*.

Parents should always supervise children online. Kids need to be warned to never give out their full names, addresses, or any distinguishing features about where they live.

A Natural Combination

Kids and horses are a natural combination. Horses can teach children a lot, and the kids often take on the responsibility of taking care of a horse with pleasure. But parents always need to be involved, helping to keep their kids safe and the horse appropriately cared for. If owning a horse seems to be too much to take on but your son or daughter won't stop talking about horses, don't get too discouraged. With a little creativity, you can find a lot of ways to get your child involved without having to have a horse in the backyard.

CHAPTER 16

Equine Careers

A career involving equines can take many avenues. Some are obvious, such as veterinarian or farrier, but with the current explosion of the horse industry, the career path one can take is pretty much wide open. In this chapter we'll explore some of these career opportunities. If you love horses so much you'd like to make them your life's work, this chapter is for you.

One thing to keep in mind is that no matter what path you might take in making horses the focus of your career, if you plan to open your own business—whether it is a veterinary practice or a tack shop—you will need to fit some business courses in around the equine studies. All businesses, equine or otherwise, have some basic elements that increase the chances for survival.

Equine Veterinarian

An equine veterinarian career can take a couple of paths. You can either have your own practice or join an established practice. You can specialize in large animals or be a general large/small animal veterinarian. Some people like working with a variety of animals, including dogs, cats, goats, sheep, and ferrets, as well as equines; some prefer to stick with just the equines.

As in human medicine, extensive time in school is required to be a veterinarian. As you progress in your education, you may begin to hone in on a specialty that you find yourself attracted to—for example, surgery, therapeutics, or research. Write for catalogs from the veterinary schools (listed in this chapter) to learn more about the level of schooling required and the areas of expertise available to you from veterinary schools around this country.

Pets, including horses, are a vital part of the economy in the United States and developed nations around the world. Veterinarians can make a good living. Most horse veterinarians are on the road a lot doing farm calls, so you need to like to drive, find your way through country towns and roads, and improvise with whatever kind of facility you find at the end of the road. There are equine hospitals, where you might be able to stay put, but they are few and far between.

The following universities are among those that offer equine studies, animal science, and veterinary programs:

- Cornell University
  Department of Animal Science
  Ithaca, New York 14853
  607-255-7191
- Johnson and Wales University
  Equine Studies
  8 Abbott Park Place
  Providence, Rhode Island 02903
  401-598-1000

- University of Findlay
  1000 N. Main Street
  Findlay, Ohio 45840
  800-548-0932
- Washington State University
  College of Veterinary Medicine
  Pullman, Washington 99164
  509-335-9515

- University of Connecticut
  Animal Science Department
  3636 Horseshoe Road Extension U-40
  Storrs, Connecticut 06269
  860-486-2413
- University of New Hampshire
  Department of Animal Sciences
  Kendall Hall
  Durham, New Hampshire 03824
  603-862-1174

- Texas A & M University
  College of Veterinary Medicine
  Suite 101-VMA
  College Station, Texas 77843
  979-845-5051
- University of California-Davis
  School of Veterinary Medicine
  One Shields Avenue
  Davis, California 95612
  530-752-1360

Veterinary Technician

The veterinary technician is a vital part of an animal hospital of any kind. Vet techs in equine practices may find themselves doing anything from cleaning stalls to taking temperatures to regularly checking in-house patients for vital signs, changing bandages, restocking the trucks of the vets on the road, or answering the phones. Some vet techs go on the road with vets and help prepare vaccines, hold horses while care is being administered, and so forth. The academic requirements for a veterinary technician typically involve a two-year vocational program in which the focus is on the vocation itself; few courses outside the topic are required.

Equine Dentist

Veterinarians do not tend to get intensive training in any one area, so the equine dentist is becoming a more common member of the horse care team. Keep in mind that you will spend a lot of time with your hands in a horse's mouth, and unless you can get yourself a few customers who have large facilities with lots of horses, you will also, like a vet, need to travel around the countryside to your customers.

The tools needed for dentistry are minimal, although you can choose from simple hand tools or more expensive power tools that take the strain off of your back and shoulders. This can be tiring but fascinating work, and it is a thriving profession.

Farrier

Let me say up front that farrier work can be hard on the body. If all horses were easy to handle, stood perfectly still for the farrier, and held their own weight up while the farrier worked on a foot, then maybe it would be less of a backbreaking job. But those kinds of horses are more the rarity than the norm.

QUESTIONS?

What's the difference between a farrier and a blacksmith?
A **farrier** is a blacksmith who does horseshoeing but doesn't necessarily do other types of iron work. A **blacksmith** is not a horseshoer but someone who makes things with iron.

The horse's foot is fascinating and its well-being is vital to the overall well-being of the horse. The tools needed for farrier work are fairly simple, the work is varied, and you are your own boss. Like the country vet, you have to travel around the countryside and deal with whatever barn setups you run across. The farrier also often works in conjunction with the veterinarian for foot issues that involve disease and injury.

There are farrier schools around the country that typically offer two- and four-week programs. You should find a farrier you can apprentice with—for which you may or may not be paid. The area of foot care is changing drastically, with new techniques and shoes made of new materials, and the need for people in this area of equine specialty is increasing.

Two horseshoeing schools are:

- Kentucky Horseshoeing School
  Highway 53
  P.O. Box 120
  Mt. Eden, Kentucky 40046
  800-626-5359
  www.kyhorseshoeing.com

- Northeast School of Horseshoeing
  Palermo, Maine
  877-557-5027

Holistic Practitioners

Holistic horse health is of great interest to horse owners these days. If you enjoy the health aspect of the equine industry and like to get your hands on horses, you can become a massage therapist or chiropractor, both of which are in demand, especially in the performance world but also increasingly by the backyard horse owner. Skills in Reiki, acupuncture, and acupressure are all becoming ways to earn money working with horses. (See Chapter 10, "Beyond Conventional Health Care," for more on holistic approaches.)

The following schools offer programs in equine massage:

* Equissage
  Round Hill, Virginia
  800-843-0244
  www.equissage.com

* Geary Whiting's Equine Massage School
  www.gearywhiting.com

Boarding Facility Owner/Manager

In order to own or manage a boarding facility, you will need either years of experience or a degree from an equine management program. And you also need superb people skills! Managing a facility can be the best of both worlds. There are often some perks that go with the deal that need to be considered as part of the salary package. These can be in the form of a stall or two for your own horse(s), a place to live on the premises, and free admission to any events that take place at the facility. You can often feed your own horses cheaply, since you will be buying feed in bulk for the facility, and there are other smaller hidden savings.

Running a boarding facility requires a lot of diversity. You will be arranging for building and equipment repairs, dealing with feed suppliers, dragging the floor of the arena, handling all kinds of horses—the list is endless. It can be challenging and rewarding to run a top-notch facility that is teeming with business—but don't expect much of a private life!

Dick McCoy grew up around horses in Lancaster, Pennsylvania, where his father had a cattle brokerage. He became a partner in the business for 28 years and developed an interest in showing stock horses. He also developed an interest in roping and cutting horses. As the stockyard business changed, Dick found his cattle commission work becoming obsolete.

"I was always trying to figure out how to make a living with horses," he says. When a position with Willow Brook Farm in Catasaqua, Pennsylvania, came up in 1991, he signed on with a one-year deal of managing the horse and cattle part of the farm, including developing a grazing program.

ALERT

If you choose to build, own, and manage a boarding facility, keep in mind that if you decide you don't like this type of work, it could be a bit difficult to get out of. While equine facilities are valuable, they are specialized real estate, and it can take a while before just the right buyer comes along.

Ten years later, McCoy is still there, but things have changed over the years. The cattle aspect was cut back dramatically with the building of an eighteen-hole golf course on 500 acres of the farm. His time is now mostly spent setting up and marketing horse-related functions at the facility, which houses two indoor arenas, a large outdoor arena, and 128 stalls. When he first started at Willow Brook, the so-called "natural horsemanship" movement was just making headway. Dick embraced the idea in both his own horsemanship as well as in wanting to get this idea out to other people. Willow Brook now hosts numerous clinics each year with the highest quality clinicians. And reining and roping is still a big part of the facility.

To enjoy this kind of job, McCoy says, you need to enjoy constant communication with different kinds of people. Throughout the day, you need to shift your mindset according to the type of person you happen to be talking with, nonhorse people and horse people alike.

Equine Lawyer

Our proverbial "litigious society" is quick to extend that tendency to the horse world. If law interests you and you are thinking of law school, you can begin to tailor an expertise in equine law from your personal horse experience. People have sued over unbelievable equine-related things—you will never lack for variety!

When James Clark-Dawe of New Hampshire began practicing law in 1990, he had no idea he would eventually specialize in horses. He had been involved with horses as a youth but didn't own a horse until well into adulthood.

"The business base for a lawyer," Clark-Dawe says, "is either geographical or a niche specialty. I began to analyze my practice and decided I wanted to specialize in something that didn't restrict me geographically. Equine law seemed like a possibility."

With that in mind, he started marketing his practice to the equine community. Now, horse-related cases represent over half of his business. In order to represent equine cases, says Clark-Dawe, you need to be able to teach the basics about horses to judges and juries who probably know little if anything about horses. He has also taken his equine legal expertise into the equine industry through things like his current role as president of the New Hampshire Horse Council.

Clinician

Horse clinics have become a thriving industry within the horse world. In order to conduct these educational sessions as a business, you need to prove yourself knowledgeable in a certain area. Your clinics may consist of hands-on work with people's horses or simply instructing people about their own horses. You should be organized, able to communicate, and willing to publicize yourself and your clinics in order to fill them. Unless you have your own facility and plan to conduct all your clinics there—which limits your customer base dramatically—you need to travel around the country and find places to rent or sponsors for your clinics. It is a hard job, but it can be extremely rewarding to help people have a more safe and better experience with horses.

Riding Instructor

If you have become an expert in a particular discipline, a career as a riding instructor may be just right for you. Good riders are always trying to better their skills. And you don't have to have competed in the Olympics to help people be better riders (although you may get more publicity and more customers that way!).

You will need to have a place to offer classes, whether at your own facility or by renting someone else's. If you are in a part of the country where winters make outdoor footing impossible to ride on, you need to have access to an indoor arena in order to keep your business going through the winter. (You also need to be willing to stand out in the cold all day.) Or you need to find something else to do over the winter months.

FACTS

Your instruction program can be set up in numerous ways. Many people figure out how much time per week they can spend teaching riding and fill in the slots as customers come along. Typically, you will make more per hour with group lessons. However, most people taking lessons, especially beginners, expect to ride school horses. Therefore, if you give group lessons, you need to have enough horses to go around. That certainly adds to the expense of this kind of business.

Horse Trainer

Perhaps you like working with young horses and would like to make a living at starting horses under saddle. This is perhaps one of the hardest—and one of the most rewarding—ways to make a living with horses. If you become very good, your services will be in great demand.

A so-called professional horse trainer (usually self-proclaimed, since there is no license or any official certification required to hang out a horse trainer shingle) trains other people's horses for a fee. The traditional scenario for years went like this: If you bought a young horse who had never been started under saddle, you sent him away to a horse trainer who specialized in the discipline you were interested in—for example, showing, reining, trail riding, dressage. Three months later, with perhaps a couple of visits in between, your trainer called you to tell you that your horse was ready and you could pick him up. You picked your horse up and rode off into the sunset, occasionally maybe sending him back to the trainer for a tune-up.

ESSENTIALS Like other equine professions in which you work directly with the horse, you will need an appropriate place to work with horses as a trainer, either by building and owning a place, leasing a place, or renting time at a facility. Be sure to factor in this expense.

This scenario is not the only one anymore. If you wish to be a horse trainer, you should be prepared for customers who want to be involved in their horse's training. They are not willing to just disappear for three months and not care what you are doing with their horse as long as the horse comes back rideable. Owners these days tend to not only care but also want to learn to work with their own horse and be able to understand the process of educating a horse to riding.

This is one reason why the national clinic scene has become extremely popular. When clinics started offering sessions on how to start your own horse under saddle, established trainers became concerned that they were losing their future customers and perhaps worried that their trade secrets would be revealed to all. What really happened is that the astute trainers got more business—those were the ones who became interested in learning what was being taught at the clinics and applying it to their training program. And the people who attended the clinic had someone to go to for help when the clinician left town. The key difference, however, is that professional trainers now often work with people just as much as they do with horses.

Breeder

Involvement in horse breeding can be approached in two ways: You can be a veterinarian who specializes in reproduction or you can learn a lot about genetics and breed, raise, and sell your own horses.

QUESTIONS?

What does LFG stand for?

LFG means "live foal guaranteed" and is what you should expect to have to offer if you offer stallion services. Mares are receptive to a stallion for limited periods of time. If the mare aborts the foal, the mare owner will expect to rebreed at no additional stud fee.

Breeding and selling horses can be a complex undertaking. Typically, you would choose a breed, maybe two, to specialize in. You will want to learn a lot about equine genetics in order to be able to choose the best pairings of stallions and mares. Color tends to sell in the horse world, and there are some very specific genetic patterns that make it more likely that you will get palominos, buckskins, paints, or whatever color you are interested in. However, luck of the draw always figures in prominently.

To have a breeding program, you will probably keep a stallion on the premises. Learn how to handle a stallion and perfect your handling abilities accordingly! You can also carry out your breeding program with a complement of mares who get artificially inseminated.

Equine Arts and Antiques

The options in hand crafting equine products are endless. After years of perfecting a craft, you can charge good prices for high-quality handmade products, from saddles and other leather tack to saddle pads to equine jewelry, art, and riding apparel and horse clothing.

After twenty-eight years in the radio business, frustrated by all the changes, Fredericka Olson decided that it was time to find something else to do. She had already done some equine antique collecting, especially items related to driving horses. She didn't know anyone else who had a business that concentrated specifically on equine antiques. "I thought I'd give it a try," she says, and Equine Antiques was born. Four years later, Olson has loads of horse paraphernalia filling a 1,550-square-foot first-floor space and spilling out into other areas of the barn of the family farm.

"Horses pop up in anything," Olson says as she points to a stainless steel condiment tray with a riding boot salt shaker and buggy-whip spoon. "Horses played a major part in everyone's lives for hundreds of years. Everyone appreciates their beauty."

Her customers are very creative with their purchases. Some buy snaffle bits to use as curtain tiebacks. One customer is redecorating her kitchen and plans to use antique metal stall guards from which to hang pots and pans.

To succeed in a business like this, Olson advises, you need to be a good communicator, contacting customers when items come in that they may like. She loves meeting the people, who are interesting and from whom, she says, she always learns something new.

ESSENTIALS   Equine Antiques is located at 365 Meaderboro Road, Farmington, New Hampshire 03835. You can also call 603-330-0944 or visit the Web site at *www.equineantiques.com*.

Don't Stop Here

If nothing mentioned so far interests you, put on your thinking cap and come up with other ideas for making a living involving equines. You can be a researcher, an archaeologist researching horse history, a supplier of herbs for horses, a show or trail ride judge—the list is only as limited as your imagination!

APPENDIX A

Resources

Books and Magazines

General

Boone, J. Allen. *Kinship with All Life.* 1978: Harper San Francisco.

Brannaman, Buck. *Groundwork: The First Impression.* 1997: Rancho Deluxe Design.

Dorrance, Bill, and Leslie Desmond. *True Horsemanship Through Feel.* 1999: Diamond Lu Productions.

Dorrance, Tom. *True Unity: Willing Communication Between Horse and Human.* 1994: Word Dancer Press.

Herrigel, Eugen. *Zen in the Art of Archery.* 1999: Random House.

Hunt, Ray. *Think Harmony with Horses: An In-Depth Study of Horse/Man Relationship.* 1991: Quill Driver Books.

References

Beckett, Oliver, Ed. *Horses and Movement.* 1988: J. A. Allen.

Benedik, Linda, and Veronica Wirth. *Yoga for Equestrians.* 2000: Trafalgar Square.

Blake, R. L. V. *Dressage for Beginners: U. S. Edition.* 1976: Houghton Mifflin.

Budiansky, Stephen. *The Nature of Horses.* 1997: Free Press.

Budiansky, Stephen. *The World According to Horses.* 2000: Henry Holt.

Burns, Deborah, Ed. *Storey's Horse-Lovers Encyclopedia.* 2001: Storey Communications.

Ganton, Doris. *Breaking & Training the Driving Horse.* 1984: Wilshire.

Grandin, Temple. *Thinking in Pictures.* 1995: Doubleday.

Green, Ben K. *Horse Conformation as to Soundness and Performance.* 1969: Northland.

Griffin, James M., M.D., and Tom Gore, D.V.M. *Horse Owner's Veterinary Handbook.* 1998: Howell House.

Harris, Sarah. *Factfinder Guide: Horses.* 1999: PRC Publishing Ltd.

Jackson, Jamie. *The Natural Horse.* 1992: Northland.

Kamen, Daniel. *The Well Adjusted Horse.* 1999: Brookline.

Kowalski, Gary. *The Souls of Animals.* 1991: Stillpoint.

Lyons, John, with Sinclair Browning. *Lyons on Horses.* 1991: Bantam.

Maltz, Maxwell. *Psycho-Cybernetics.* 1960: Wilshire.

May, Chris. *The Horse Care Manual.* 1987: Quarto.

May, Jan. *Equus Caballus.* 1995: J. A. Allen.

McCall, Jim. *Influencing Horse Behavior.* 1998: Alpine Publications.

Mettler, John J., DVM. *Horse Sense.* 1989: Storey.

Norback, Craig and Peter. *The Horseman's Catalog.* 1979: McGraw Hill.

Podhajsky, Alois. *My Horses, My Teachers.* 1997: Trafalgar Square.

Price, Steven D. *The Whole Horse Catalog.* 1998: Fireside.

Rees, Lucy. *The Fundamentals of Riding.* 1991: Roxby Paintbox Co.

Roberts, Peter, Ed. *The Complete Book of the Horse.* 1985: Gallery.

Savoie, Jane. *Cross-Train Your Horse.* 1998: Trafalgar Square.

Steffen, Randy. *The Revised Horseman's Scrapbook.* 1986: Western Horseman.

Stoneridge, M. A. *Great Horses of Our Time.* 1972: Doubleday.

Swift, Sally. *Centered Riding.* 1985: Trafalgar Square.

Thomas, Heather Smith. *Storey's Guide to Raising Horses.* 2001: Storey Communications.

Twelveponies, Mary. *Everyday Training.* 1980: Breakthrough Publications.

Visual Dictionary of the Horse. 1994: Dorling Kindersley.

For Kids

The Saddle Club (Sky Lark Books) has titles that include *Sidesaddle, Horse Crazy, Saddle Sore,* and *Horse Fever.*

Thoroughbred series (Harper Entertainment) has titles that include *Melanie's Last Ride, The Horse of Her Dreams, Ashleigh's Farewell,* and *Wonder's Yearling.*

Pony Pals series (Little Apple) has titles that include *The Pony and the Missing Dog, The Newborn Pony, Lost and Found Pony,* and *Western Pony.*

Pine Hollow series (Bantam), including *The Long Ride,* takes on high school age horse lovers, confronting issues like how to make time for friends, boyfriends, jobs, and horses.

Alternative Therapies

Brennan, Mary, D.V.M. *Complete Holistic Care and Healing for Horses.* 2001: Trafalgar Square.

Cameron, Carrie, and Doris Halstead. *Release the Potential: Myofascial Release for Horse and Rider.* 2000: Half Halt Press.

De Bairacli Levy, Juliette. *Complete Herbal Handbook for Farm and Stable.* 1991: Faber & Faber.

Hourdebaight, Jean-Pierre. *Equine Massage.* 1997: Hungry Minds, Inc.

Mariani, Gael, and Martin Scott. *Bach Flower Remedies for Horses and Riders.* 2000: Half Halt Press.

Self, Hilary Page. *A Modern Horse Herbal.* 1996: Half Halt Press.

Snow, Amy, and Nancy A. Zidonis. *Equine Acupressure: A Working Manual.* 1999: Equine Acupressure Inc.

Tellington-Jones, Linda. *Improve Your Horse's Well-Being.* 1999: Trafalgar Square.

Wanless, Mary. *For the Good of the Horse.* 1997: Trafalgar Square.

Wilde, Clare. *Hands-On Energy Therapy: for Horses and Riders.* 2000: Trafalgar Square.

Equine Fiction

Dimmick, Barbara. *In the Presence of Horses.* 1999: Picador USA.

Esstman, Barbara. *Night Ride Home.* 1997: Harcourt Brace.

Evans, Nicholas. *The Horse Whisperer.* 1995: Delacorte Press.

Kuban, Karla. *Marchlands.* 1998: Scribner.

Maristed, Kai. *Belong to Me.* 1998: Random House.

McCarthy, Cormac. *All the Pretty Horses* (book one of *The Border Trilogy*). 1993: Vintage Books.

McCarthy, Cormac. *The Crossing* (book two of a *The Border Trilogy*). 1995: Vintage Books.

McCarthy, Cormac. *Cities of the Plain* (book three of *The Border Trilogy*). 1999: Vintage Books.

Rosenthal, C. P. *Elena of the Stars.* 1996: Saint Martin's Press.

Veterinary Manuals

Giffin, James M. *The Horse Owner's Veterinary Handbook* 1998: Hungry Minds, Inc.

Hawcroft, Tim. *A–Z of Horse Diseases & Health Problems.* 1990: Hungry Minds, Inc.

Kellon, El, et. al. *Dr. Kellon's Guide to First Aid for Horses.* 1992: Breakthrough Pub.

Pavord, Marcy and Tony. *Complete Equine Veterinary Manual.* 1998: David & Charles.

Essays

Brannaman, Buck, with William Reynolds. *The Faraway Horses: The Adventures and Wisdom of a Real-Life Horse Whisperer.* 2001: Lyons Press.

McGuane, Thomas. *Some Horses.* 1999: Lyons Press.

Pierson, Melissa Holbrook. *Dark Horses and Black Beauties: Animals, Women, and a Passion.* 2001: W. W. Norton.

Proulx, Annie. *Close Range: Wyoming Stories.* 1999: Scribner.

Smith, Lindy, and Verlyn Klinkenborg. *Straight West.* 2000: Lyons Press.

Breed Associations

American Buckskin Registry
    Association, Inc.
P.O. Box 3850
Redding, CA 96049
530-223-1420
www.americanbuckskin.org

American Connemara Pony Society
2360 Hunting Ridge Road
Winchester, VA 22603

American Haflinger Registry
4078 Broadview Road
Richfield, OH 44286
330-659-2940
www.haflinger.com

American Icelandics
P.O. Box 453
Buellton, CA 93427
805-688-3891
www.americanicelandics.com

American Paint Horse Association
P.O. Box 961023
Fort Worth, TX 76161-0023
817-834-2742
www.apha.com

The American Quarter Horse
    Association
1600 Quarter Horse Drive
Amarillo, TX 79104
806-376-4811
www.aqha.org

The American Shetland Pony Club
81B E. Queenwood
Morton, IL 61550
309-263-4044
www.shetlandminiature.com

American Shire Horse Association
P.O. Box 739
New Castle, CO 81647
970-876-5980
www.shirehorse.org

American Saddlebred Horse
    Association
4093 Iron Works Parkway
Lexington, KY 40511
859-259-2742
www.asha.net

Appaloosa Horse Club
2720 W. Pullman Road
Moscow, ID 83843
208-882-5578
www.appaloosa.com

The Arabian Horse Registry
    of America, Inc.
12000 Zuni Street
Westminster, CO 80234
303-450-4748
www.theregistry.org

Arabian Jockey Club
12000 Zuni Street
Westminster, CO 80234
303-450-4714
www.arabianracing.org

Belgian Draft Horse Corporation
    of America
P.O. Box 335
Wabash, IN 46992
219-563-3205
www.belgiancorp.com

The Cleveland Bay Horse Society
    of North America
P.O. Box 221
South Windham, CT 06266

The Fell Pony Conservancy of
    North America
129 Edwards Farm Lane
Dobson, NC 27017
www.fellpony.org

The International Arabian Horse
    Association
10805 E. Bethany Drive
Aurora, CO 80014
303-696-4599
www.iaha.com

The Jockey Club (Thoroughbred
    registry)
821 Corporate Drive
Lexington, KY 40503
859-224-2700

National Museum of the Morgan Horse
P.O. Box 700
Shelburne, VT 05482

Norwegian Fjord Horse Registry
1203 Appian Drive
Webster, NY 14580
716-872-4114

Palomino Breeders of America
15253 E. Skelly Drive
Tulsa, OK 74116-2637
918-438-1234
yellahrses@aol.com

The Tennessee Walking Horse
    Breeders' and Exhibitors'
    Association
250 N. Ellington
Lewisburg, TN 37091
800-359-1574
www.twhbea.com

The Welsh Pony and Cob Society
    of America
P.O. Box 2977
Winchester, VA 22604
540-667-6195
www.welshpony.org

Videos

"Acupuncture Points of the Equine" (Shoemaker)
"Riding with TTEAM" (Tellington-Jones)
"From the Ground Up" (Brannaman)

Web Sites

Information on Alternative Treatment and Practitioners

www.acadvethom.org
www.altvetmed.com (alternative, complementary and holistic medicine)
www.animalacupressure.com (Tallgrass Publishers LLC)
www.animalanimal.com
www.bachcentre.com (Bach Flowers)
www.brassringhorsemassage.com
www.chinahealthways.com (China Healthways Institute)
www.dianathompson.com
Home.earthlink.net/~fourwinds
www.equisonicqgm.com
www.halfhaltpress.com
www.haynet.net/Veterinary_Resources/Alternative_ Therapies
www.hiltonherbs.com; e-mail: *helpline@hiltonherbs.com*
www.holistichorse.com

www.horseandriderbooks.com (Trafalgar Square Publishing)
www.IAATH.com (International Alliance for Animal Therapy and Healing)
www.naturalholistic.com
www.rainbowcrystal.com (flower remedies)
www.tellingtontouch.com
www.TheNaturalHorseVet.net

Suppliers of Alternative Treatments

www.biomagnetic.com
www.chamisaridge.com
www.dropinbucket.com
www.equisonicqgm.com
www.equilite.com (offers seeds)
www.hiltonherbs.com
www.Kyolic.com (Kyolic garlic)
www.morrills.com (Morrill's New Directions)
www.norfields.com (magnetic products)
www.nutramaxlabs.com/index.cfm
www.respondsystems.com
www.springtimeinc.com
www.uckele.com
www.vitaminshoppe.com

APPENDIX B
Glossary

Alternative medicine: Refers to diagnostic and treatment systems (modalities) not commonly taught in medical/veterinary schools such as nutrition, herbal medicine, homeopathy, chiropractic, and acutherapies.

Amino acids: The group of organic compounds that form the structure of proteins. Hay from alfalfa and clover is rich in amino acids and gives horses extra energy.

Azoturia: Also known as "tying up" or "Monday morning disease," azoturia refers to the cramping of a horse's large muscles.

Backyard horse: A horse that lives at the home of its owner. People can have more than one backyard horse depending on the size of their backyard. The term has been used to indicate horses of lesser quality, but that, of course, is in the eye of the beholder!

Blacksmith: A blacksmith is not a horseshoer but someone who makes things with iron.

Breeding stock: A mare or stallion that meets the eligibility requirements (e.g., through lineage) to be registered in the paint breed but does not exhibit the color trait of a paint. With careful breeding, these horses can be bred to consistently produce color offspring.

Conditioned response: A training approach in which a horse (or any thinking animal, including humans) is conditioned to respond to the same stimulus the same way every time she confronts that stimulus.

Conformation: The overall structure of the horse is known as its conformation. Few horses, if any, have perfect conformation. What is considered good conformation depends a great deal on what you plan to do with the horse.

Esophagal choke: A condition that is often caused when horses gulp down pelleted feeds too rapidly. To deter this, place a couple of stones or half a salt block in the feed bucket—having to eat around them makes the horse slow down.

Farrier: A farrier is a blacksmith who does horseshoeing but doesn't necessarily do other types of iron work.

Flehman response: A term that refers to the curling of the upper lip by a male horse in response to the scent of a female.

Groundwork: The practice of teaching your horse at the end of a lead rope. Many of the things you teach him in groundwork are transferable to the saddle.

Hand: In tack room terms, a hand is the unit used to measure horse height. One hand equals four inches; thus, a horse that stands 15 hands tall is 60 inches tall, or five feet.

Herbivore: An animal that subsists totally on plant life. Horses are herbivores. This distinction makes the horse a prey animal (with those that hunt them considered predators), a category that contributes greatly to the overall behavior of the species.

Hogging: Hogging, also known as roaching, refers to a mane that has been completely shaved.

LFG: Stands for "live foal guaranteed"—what you should expect to have to offer if you offer stallion services. Mares are receptive to a stallion for limited periods of time. If the mare aborts the foal, the mare owner will expect to rebreed at no additional stud fee.

Proud flesh: A wound that won't heal produces scar tissue that protrudes from the wound area. This scar tissue is commonly referred to as "proud flesh."

Psychocybernetics: The technique for using your subconscious power to achieve the positive results that you desire.

Rails: The individual horizontal bars that make up a jump. They can be easily removed or added to make the jump lower or higher.

Sound: If the horse is perfectly healthy, it is said to be "sound."

Tree: The basic structure, usually made of wood or fiberglass, that both English and Western saddles are built upon. They can be narrow or wide, depending on the type of horse and the comfort of the rider.

Truck-in: When you take riding lessons and bring your own horse, you are referred to as a truck-in.

Turnout: The period when your horse is out of the confinement of her stall and loose in a larger area—either outside in a corral or pasture, or in an indoor arena if the weather is bad.

Unsound: If the horse is temporarily lame or has some problems eating, it is considered "unsound." Anything that adversely affects a horse's health is considered an "unsoundness." If the horse's problem is chronic, the horse is "permanently unsound."

Index

We Have EVERYTHING!

Everything® **After College Book**
$12.95, 1-55850-847-3

Everything® **American History Book**
$12.95, 1-58062-531-2

Everything® **Angels Book**
$12.95, 1-58062-398-0

Everything® **Anti-Aging Book**
$12.95, 1-58062-565-7

Everything® **Astrology Book**
$12.95, 1-58062-062-0

Everything® **Baby Names Book**
$12.95, 1-55850-655-1

Everything® **Baby Shower Book**
$12.95, 1-58062-305-0

Everything® **Baby's First Food Book**
$12.95, 1-58062-512-6

Everything® **Baby's First Year Book**
$12.95, 1-58062-581-9

Everything® **Barbeque Cookbook**
$12.95, 1-58062-316-6

Everything® **Bartender's Book**
$9.95, 1-55850-536-9

Everything® **Bedtime Story Book**
$12.95, 1-58062-147-3

Everything® **Bicycle Book**
$12.00, 1-55850-706-X

Everything® **Breastfeeding Book**
$12.95, 1-58062-582-7

Everything® **Build Your Own Home Page**
$12.95, 1-58062-339-5

Everything® **Business Planning Book**
$12.95, 1-58062-491-X

Everything® **Candlemaking Book**
$12.95, 1-58062-623-8

Everything® **Casino Gambling Book**
$12.95, 1-55850-762-0

Everything® **Cat Book**
$12.95, 1-55850-710-8

Everything® **Chocolate Cookbook**
$12.95, 1-58062-405-7

Everything® **Christmas Book**
$15.00, 1-55850-697-7

Everything® **Civil War Book**
$12.95, 1-58062-366-2

Everything® **Classical Mythology Book**
$12.95, 1-58062-653-X

Everything® **Collectibles Book**
$12.95, 1-58062-645-9

Everything® **College Survival Book**
$12.95, 1-55850-720-5

Everything® **Computer Book**
$12.95, 1-58062-401-4

Everything® **Cookbook**
$14.95, 1-58062-400-6

Everything® **Cover Letter Book**
$12.95, 1-58062-312-3

Everything® **Creative Writing Book**
$12.95, 1-58062-647-5

Everything® **Crossword and Puzzle Book**
$12.95, 1-55850-764-7

Everything® **Dating Book**
$12.95, 1-58062-185-6

Everything® **Dessert Book**
$12.95, 1-55850-717-5

Everything® **Digital Photography Book**
$12.95, 1-58062-574-6

Everything® **Dog Book**
$12.95, 1-58062-144-9

Everything® **Dreams Book**
$12.95, 1-55850-806-6

Everything® **Etiquette Book**
$12.95, 1-55850-807-4

Everything® **Fairy Tales Book**
$12.95, 1-58062-546-0

Everything® **Family Tree Book**
$12.95, 1-55850-763-9

Everything® **Feng Shui Book**
$12.95, 1-58062-587-8

Everything® **Fly-Fishing Book**
$12.95, 1-58062-148-1

Everything® **Games Book**
$12.95, 1-55850-643-8

Everything® **Get-A-Job Book**
$12.95, 1-58062-223-2

Everything® **Get Out of Debt Book**
$12.95, 1-58062-588-6

Everything® **Get Published Book**
$12.95, 1-58062-315-8

Everything® **Get Ready for Baby Book**
$12.95, 1-55850-844-9

Everything® **Get Rich Book**
$12.95, 1-58062-670-X

Everything® **Ghost Book**
$12.95, 1-58062-533-9

Everything® **Golf Book**
$12.95, 1-55850-814-7

Everything® **Grammar and Style Book**
$12.95, 1-58062-573-8

Everything® **Guide to Las Vegas**
$12.95, 1-58062-438-3

Everything® **Guide to New England**
$12.95, 1-58062-589-4

Everything® **Guide to New York City**
$12.95, 1-58062-314-X

Everything® **Guide to Walt Disney World®, Universal Studios®, and Greater Orlando, 2nd Edition**
$12.95, 1-58062-404-9

Everything® **Guide to Washington D.C.**
$12.95, 1-58062-313-1

Everything® **Guitar Book**
$12.95, 1-58062-555-X

Everything® **Herbal Remedies Book**
$12.95, 1-58062-331-X

Available wherever books are sold!
To order, call **800-872-5627**, or visit **everything.com**
Adams Media Corporation, 57 Littlefield Street, Avon, MA 02322. U.S.A.

Everything® **Home-Based Business Book**
$12.95, 1-58062-364-6

Everything® **Homebuying Book**
$12.95, 1-58062-074-4

Everything® **Homeselling Book**
$12.95, 1-58062-304-2

Everything® **Horse Book**
$12.95, 1-58062-564-9

Everything® **Hot Careers Book**
$12.95, 1-58062-486-3

Everything® **Internet Book**
$12.95, 1-58062-073-6

Everything® **Investing Book**
$12.95, 1-58062-149-X

Everything® **Jewish Wedding Book**
$12.95, 1-55850-801-5

Everything® **Job Interview Book**
$12.95, 1-58062-493-6

Everything® **Lawn Care Book**
$12.95, 1-58062-487-1

Everything® **Leadership Book**
$12.95, 1-58062-513-4

Everything® **Learning French Book**
$12.95, 1-58062-649-1

Everything® **Learning Spanish Book**
$12.95, 1-58062-575-4

Everything® **Low-Fat High-Flavor Cookbook**
$12.95, 1-55850-802-3

Everything® **Magic Book**
$12.95, 1-58062-418-9

Everything® **Managing People Book**
$12.95, 1-58062-577-0

Everything® **Microsoft® Word 2000 Book**
$12.95, 1-58062-306-9

Everything® **Money Book**
$12.95, 1-58062-145-7

Everything® **Mother Goose Book**
$12.95, 1-58062-490-1

Everything® **Motorcycle Book**
$12.95, 1-58062-554-1

Everything® **Mutual Funds Book**
$12.95, 1-58062-419-7

Everything® **One-Pot Cookbook**
$12.95, 1-58062-186-4

Everything® **Online Business Book**
$12.95, 1-58062-320-4

Everything® **Online Genealogy Book**
$12.95, 1-58062-402-2

Everything® **Online Investing Book**
$12.95, 1-58062-338-7

Everything® **Online Job Search Book**
$12.95, 1-58062-365-4

Everything® **Organize Your Home Book**
$12.95, 1-58062-617-3

Everything® **Pasta Book**
$12.95, 1-55850-719-1

Everything® **Philosophy Book**
$12.95, 1-58062-644-0

Everything® **Playing Piano and Keyboards Book**
$12.95, 1-58062-651-3

Everything® **Pregnancy Book**
$12.95, 1-58062-146-5

Everything® **Pregnancy Organizer**
$15.00, 1-58062-336-0

Everything® **Project Management Book**
$12.95, 1-58062-583-5

Everything® **Puppy Book**
$12.95, 1-58062-576-2

Everything® **Quick Meals Cookbook**
$12.95, 1-58062-488-X

Everything® **Resume Book**
$12.95, 1-58062-311-5

Everything® **Romance Book**
$12.95, 1-58062-566-5

Everything® **Running Book**
$12.95, 1-58062-618-1

Everything® **Sailing Book, 2nd Edition**
$12.95, 1-58062-671-8

Everything® **Saints Book**
$12.95, 1-58062-534-7

Everything® **Selling Book**
$12.95, 1-58062-319-0

Everything® **Shakespeare Book**
$12.95, 1-58062-591-6

Everything® **Spells and Charms Book**
$12.95, 1-58062-532-0

Everything® **Start Your Own Business Book**
$12.95, 1-58062-650-5

Everything® **Stress Management Book**
$12.95, 1-58062-578-9

Everything® **Study Book**
$12.95, 1-55850-615-2

Everything® **Tai Chi and QiGong Book**
$12.95, 1-58062-646-7

Everything® **Tall Tales, Legends, and Outrageous Lies Book**
$12.95, 1-58062-514-2

Everything® **Tarot Book**
$12.95, 1-58062-191-0

Everything® **Time Management Book**
$12.95, 1-58062-492-8

Everything® **Toasts Book**
$12.95, 1-58062-189-9

Everything® **Toddler Book**
$12.95, 1-58062-592-4

Everything® **Total Fitness Book**
$12.95, 1-58062-318-2

Everything® **Trivia Book**
$12.95, 1-58062-143-0

Everything® **Tropical Fish Book**
$12.95, 1-58062-343-3

Everything® **Vegetarian Cookbook**
$12.95, 1-58062-640-8

Everything® **Vitamins, Minerals, and Nutritional Supplements Book**
$12.95, 1-58062-496-0

Everything® **Wedding Book, 2nd Edition**
$12.95, 1-58062-190-2

Everything® **Wedding Checklist**
$7.95, 1-58062-456-1

Everything® **Wedding Etiquette Book**
$7.95, 1-58062-454-5

Everything® **Wedding Organizer**
$15.00, 1-55850-828-7

Everything® **Wedding Shower Book**
$7.95, 1-58062-188-0

Everything® **Wedding Vows Book**
$7.95, 1-58062-455-3

Everything® **Weight Training Book**
$12.95, 1-58062-593-2

Everything® **Wine Book**
$12.95, 1-55850-808-2

Everything® **World War II Book**
$12.95, 1-58062-572-X

Everything® **World's Religions Book**
$12.95, 1-58062-648-3

Everything® **Yoga Book**
$12.95, 1-58062-594-0

Visit us at everything.com

Everything® is a registered trademark of Adams Media Corporation.

We Have

EVERYTHING KIDS'!

Everything® Kids' Baseball Book, 2nd Edition
$6.95, 1-58062-688-2

Everything® Kids' Joke Book
$6.95, 1-58062-686-6

Everything® Kids' Mazes Book
$6.95, 1-58062-558-4

Everything® Kids' Money Book
$6.95, 1-58062-685-8

Everything® Kids' Nature Book
$6.95, 1-58062-684-X

Everything® Kids' Puzzle Book
$6.95, 1-58062-687-4

Everything® Kids' Science Experiments Book
$6.95, 1-58062-557-6

Everything® Kids' Soccer Book
$6.95, 1-58062-642-4

Everything® Kids' Travel Activity Book
$6.95, 1-58062-641-6

Available wherever books are sold!

For more information, or to order,
call 800-872-5627 or visit everything.com

Adams Media Corporation, 57 Littlefield Street, Avon, MA 02322. U.S.A.

Everything® is a registered trademark of Adams Media Corporation.